Managing Career Transitions

YOUR CAREER AS A WORK IN PROGRESS

SECOND EDITION

Kit Harrington Hayes
NORTHEASTERN UNIVERSITY

Prentice Hall
Upper Saddle River, New Jersey 07458

Library of Congress Cataloging-in-Publication Data

Hayes, Kit Harrington.
    Managing career transitions: your career as a work in progress /
Kit Harrington Hayes. — 2nd ed.
        p.   cm.
    Includes bibliographical references and index.
    ISBN 0-13-924051-9
    1. Career changes. 2. Continuing education. 3. Career
development.
    HF5384.H384   2000
    650.14—dc21   99–18145
                                                                    CIP

Publisher: *Carol Carter*
Acquisitions Editor: *Sande Johnson*
Managing Editor: *Mary Carnis*
In-House Liaison: *Denise Brown*
Production: *Holcomb Hathaway, Inc.*
Director of Manufacturing and Production: *Bruce Johnson*
Manufacturing Buyer: *Marc Bove*
Editorial Assistant: *Michelle M. Williams*
Marketing Manager: *Jeff McIlroy*
Marketing Assistant: *Barbara Rosenberg*
Illustrations on pages 105 and 142 by *Jefferey H. Hayes*

© 2000, 1996 by Prentice-Hall, Inc.
Upper Saddle River, New Jersey 07458

Printed in the United States of America

10 9 8 7 6 5 4 3 2

ISBN 0-13-924051-9

Prentice-Hall International (UK) Limited, *London*
Prentice-Hall of Australia Pty. Limited, *Sydney*
Prentice-Hall Canada Inc., *Toronto*
Prentice-Hall Hispanoamericana, S.A., *Mexico*
Prentice-Hall of India Private Limited, *New Delhi*
Prentice-Hall of Japan, Inc., *Tokyo*
Pearson Education Asia Pte. Ltd., *Singapore*
Editora Prentice-Hall do Brasil, Ltda., *Rio de Janeiro*
Prentice-Hall, Upper Saddle River, *New Jersey*

BRIEF CONTENTS

For the complete Table of Contents, see page v.

CONTENTS

v

ELEVEN   Presenting Your Candidacy   193

TWELVE   Making a Contribution   217

THIRTEEN Starting Your Own Business   229

DO YOU HAVE WHAT IT TAKES?   230

Do You Have a Great Idea? ■ *Are You Willing to Give Your All?* ■ *Do You Believe in Yourself?* ■ *Are You a Risk Taker?* ■ *Should You Start a Family Business?*

CHOOSING A FORM OF BUSINESS   232

Sole Proprietorship ■ *Partnership* ■ *Corporation*

WRITING A BUSINESS PLAN   233

Executive Summary ■ *Nature of the Business* ■ *Analysis of the Competition* ■ *Organizational Plan* ■ *Financial Projections*

DEVELOPING A MARKETING PLAN   234

ESTABLISHING A PRIVATE PRACTICE   235

Valerie Goes into Private Practice   235

BUYING A FRANCHISE   236

Craig and Gretchen Buy a Franchise   236

WORKING AS AN INDEPENDENT CONTRACTOR   237

Greg Becomes an Independent Contractor   237

CREATING A PORTFOLIO CAREER   238

Deb Pursues a Portfolio Career   238

ADDITIONAL TOOLS FOR YOUR CAREER   240

Additional Resources for Entrepreneurship and Small Business ■ *Journals*

FOURTEEN Managing Your Career   243

LISTEN TO CAREER CHANGERS WHO HAVE GONE BEFORE YOU   245

PREFACE

M*anaging Career Transitions* addresses the career concerns of adults. As we enter the new millennium, increasing numbers of adults are returning to the classroom to gain new skills and direction for their work lives. All kinds of political, social, economic, ecological, and technological factors have converged to bring about this phenomenon. Adults facing a career transition often experience feelings of upheaval, confusion, anxiety, and frustration as they try to develop plans that will lead to satisfying new careers. In order to survive—and hopefully thrive—in this changing world, adults need new skills: skills for employability and skills to self-manage.

This book walks readers through the career transition maze, providing information, skills, and support as they navigate the rapidly changing workplace. Chapter One discusses the typical circumstances that have led adult students back to the classroom and offers suggestions for moving forward. Chapter Two provides the theoretical underpinnings for a discussion of career development and introduces both a step-by-step model for career development and a cyclical model for career transitions over the life span.

Chapters Three, Four, and Five lead the reader through the self-assessment process, step one of the career development model. Chapters Six and Seven guide career exploration, step two of the model. Chapter Seven specifically discusses current trends, such as globalization and reengineering, as well as changing work patterns, such as outsourcing and contracting. Decision making and goal setting, steps three and four of the model, are discussed in Chapters Eight and Nine. It is here that students integrate what they have learned about themselves with the realities of the marketplace, make career decisions, and develop an action plan for implementing their decisions.

In Chapter Ten, readers learn how to write winning resumes and cover letters. This chapter also discusses research and networking skills as indispensable for competing in today's job market. Chapter Eleven thoroughly covers the interview process, from preparing for an interview to negotiating a salary or handling rejection. Chapter Twelve offers advice for a surefooted start in a new position, and Chapter Thirteen examines the alternative of starting a small business. Finally, Chapter Fourteen reminds readers to anticipate going through the career change process again, perhaps several times, during their work lives.

Each chapter includes several "Work in Progress" exercises that give readers an opportunity to analyze their current situation and apply material covered in the book. In some cases, the exercises are integrated into the chapters so that students read and immediately apply material before proceeding to a new topic. Instructors can assign their favorite exercises, and students will likely complete additional exercises that they find relevant to them.

Another "Work in Progress" feature briefly recounts true success stories taken from the lives of individuals who were at various stages of managing a career change. These personal profiles help readers see the broad range of experiences that lead individuals to new careers.

Changing careers is a challenging process, but it can also be an exciting one, filled with self-discovery and hope. *Managing Career Transitions* will help readers take full responsibility for their career decisions. By anticipating and preparing for change, readers can look forward to creating satisfying careers and meaningful lives for themselves.

ACKNOWLEDGMENTS

Inspiration for this, my lifework, came from my dad, who in different times earned a gold watch from Veeder Root, Inc.; from my mom, who, ahead of her time, reentered the workforce in the 1950s; and from my son, who is managing his career by the new rules that emerged in the turbulent 1990s.

During my eighteen years with Northeastern University, I have had the privilege of working with hundreds of adult students and alumni. In generously sharing their career journeys, they have taught me as much as I've taught them. They have my utmost respect and appreciation.

I wish to thank the many other people who contributed to development of this book. At Northeastern University, they include Vice President Jane Scarborough, Dean Carol Lyons, Catherine Jessup, Craig Bettinson, Julie Jersyk, Paul Karofsky, James Molloy Jr., Luciano Messori, and Dr. Barbara Okun. The six-step model presented in Chapter Two is based on a model developed by Northeastern University's Department of Career Services.

My sincere thanks to the following people, who read all or part of the manuscript and provided valuable suggestions and feedback: Bruce Bloom, DeVry Institute of Technology; Kris Sullivan, Simmons Graduate School of Management; Sue Ekberg, Webster University; Melissa Everett, author; Hank Sunderland, Marist College; Carol Eastin, Antelope Valley College; Katy Kemeny, Lansing Community College; Valerie Nelson, Cabrillo College; and Terry Rafter, Valencia Community College. Thanks also to Deborah Sosin, who provided editorial expertise on early drafts.

CHAPTER ONE

RETOOLING FOR TRANSITION

RETURNING TO THE CLASSROOM

Adults from all walks of life are returning to the classroom or taking courses through distance learning in order to gain new skills for today's demanding workplace. Political, economic, social, environmental, and technological circumstances all contribute to this phenomenon. The increase in the pace of change in our lives is probably the single greatest contributor. People used to acquire an education and then work for 30 or 40 years. Now we can expect to return to school at several points to retool ourselves and reinvent our careers.

Some of you are college-educated professionals who have been laid off by your employer. Companies large and small continue to downsize in order to remain profitable, indeed viable, with increasing global competition. You may have found that your skills are obsolete and have returned to school to acquire new expertise that will lead to reemployment. This is an extremely common phenomenon today that cuts across many fields. Some of you will pursue graduate degrees while others will earn certificates in "hot" demand areas such as technology.

We can expect to return to school several times to reinvent our careers

Others of you left high school with little or no interest in continuing your education. You may have gone into the military or worked in secretarial or clerical positions, manufacturing or retail jobs, or service positions at hotels and restaurants. You may also have found yourself "dead–ended," that is, without opportunity for advancement into better-paying and more satisfying positions. You tried to make it without a college degree, and now you're responding to the current market demand for a more highly educated workforce.

Some of you might be returning to the classroom to prepare for reentering the workforce after an elective period of time away from it. Perhaps you chose to spend that period raising children and managing your household, dealing with personal or family matters, volunteering in a religious or community organization, or pursuing personally enriching activities such as travel.

Perhaps some of you are returning to school simply because you're ready to make a change. You may have survived layoffs only to find yourselves in work environments that demand more hours and higher productivity, yet fail to provide returns that satisfy your financial, professional, or personal needs. You would like to reclaim ideals like job satisfaction, commitment to an organization, and job security. You may even be worried about future layoffs. These situations can create a great deal of stress. You may be looking for a better quality of life, and for work that provides personal satisfaction and meaning, and have therefore returned to the classroom to arm yourselves with skills and courage for career transitions.

Returning to school means new directions, new opportunities

While these scenarios do not depict *every* returning adult student, they identify common patterns. For some of you, the return to school is motivated by the desire for new directions, new opportunities. For others, the motivation is survival in a society and a marketplace that have become increasingly competitive, demanding, and unpredictable. If you find the marketplace confounding, be assured that you are not alone. It is difficult to fathom, let alone keep pace with, many of the changes occurring today.

ASK HARD QUESTIONS

As adults fill the classrooms of community colleges, evening programs, and graduate schools at universities, they raise important questions about what to pursue in the way of academic studies. No clear signals indicate the areas of our economy guaranteed to grow in the next 10 or 20 years or longer. The global economy is increasingly competitive. What impact will this have on you as you plan for work in the 21st century? Where will computer and telecommunications technology take us? Where will advances in biotechnology lead? Education reform? Deregulation? Ecommerce? A crystal ball would be a handy tool!

Major changes are also taking place within U.S. companies and other work settings. As mentioned earlier, companies have downsized or "right sized." Many companies have changed their organizational structures. For example, large bureaucratic organizations with traditional management styles and vertical reporting structures have transformed into horizontally configured organizations emphasizing collaborative teams of workers. More of the work being done is considered "white collar," but responsibilities may be broad, ranging from negotiating in meetings to interacting with customers to rolling up your sleeves and getting down on the floor to troubleshoot an equipment failure.

Organizations are also using large numbers of contract workers—people hired temporarily for specific projects—in place of permanent, full-time employees. Charles Handy, a British economist, predicted that by the year 2000, 70 percent of the U.S. workforce could be composed of temporary workers (1990). While this projection will not come to pass, it is clear that the workplace is restructuring.

Changes such as these will fundamentally alter how we define *career*, what we mean by *employment*, and what kinds of opportunities and options will be available to us in the future. As returning students, you have many legitimate questions about what's ahead: Where will the jobs be in the coming years? How can you prepare for the future marketplace? What skills and knowledge will be in demand? If Handy is correct that the majority of workers in the future will be independent contractors, how will you cope with marketing yourself every six months or even every two years?

The answers to these questions are not easy to predict, but important clues can be found. In this book, we will look at existing signs and evolving trends. It is important for you to understand that *no one* has definitive answers about the future. Our country and the world, for that matter, are in a period of transition that makes it particularly difficult for you to find answers to burning questions about the future in general and your own personal future in particular.

ACCEPT YOUR PRESENT SITUATION

As a returning student, you may have a tendency to be hard on yourself. Try to avoid expending energy looking back and judging past decisions: "If only I'd gone to college right after high school"; "If only I'd taken the other job"; "If only I hadn't dropped out"; "If only I'd taken advantage of training opportunities at work"; "If only I hadn't put all my energy into the family." We all have regrets.

We can't let feelings about past decisions and missed opportunities dominate our thoughts or inhibit our present efforts. For whatever reasons, you made the choices you made. You did your best at that time. Now you are facing a new horizon, ready to make new choices and move in new directions. Accept and forgive your past. Embrace your future. And live in the present, enjoying new challenges, absorbing new learning, creating new opportunities, and making your life what you want it to be. You are ready.

If external circumstances have forced you into a career transition, you may have many powerful emotions stirring inside of you. Anger, fear, grief, and loss are normal responses to events such as being laid off or fired, or suffering a disabling injury. These feelings are also a natural response to having been passed over for a promotion or having a proposal rejected. All of these are painful experiences. Before you can move on to new solutions, you will have to resolve feelings that could impede your growth. This will be discussed in more detail in Chapter Two.

Forgive your past, embrace your future, but live in the present

TAKE CHARGE OF YOUR LIFE

Personal transitions, whether by choice or chance, are difficult to undertake because they expose our innate fear of the unknown. See the personal transitions in the profiles in Figure 1.1. Attempting a transition when so much of the world is in flux is extraordinarily challenging. It is also exciting! There are no well-worn paths to follow, no boxes to fit into. The possibilities are limitless. How we work, where we work, and how our lives in general will look in the future are like paintings that we have the opportunity to create. Our only guarantee is that change will continue to occur.

The rest of your life is a painting to be created... by you

This book is intended to serve as a guide for your transition. You will have the opportunity to look at yourself and your circumstances in new ways. You will also be guided in exploring the work world. You'll have the opportunity to develop or perfect many skills that will help you to make sound decisions, define personal success, plan a satisfying career or series of careers, and navigate a highly competitive and specialized marketplace. It's your canvas. Get out the brushes and start your masterwork.

FIGURE 1.1   People profiles.

LOGGER ➤ ➤ ➤ ➤ ➤ ➤ ➤ ➤ NURSE

Jim was a logger in Oregon. Government legislation stopped the cutting of trees to protect the habitat of the spotted owl, and Jim found himself unemployed. After months of lobbying to change government policy, Jim decided he'd better face reality: he had a wife and three young children to support. When he explored the regional job market, Jim learned there was a shortage of nurses. He opted to return to school and become a nurse. His wife, Laura, took a waitressing job to help meet expenses while Jim was retraining.

HARDWARE   SOFTWARE
ENGINEER ➤ ➤ ➤ ➤ ➤ PROGRAMMER

Heather was a hardware engineer for a high-tech company in Massachusetts. After 16 years, she was laid off when her company downsized. Heather had seen the layoffs coming and started taking courses in software design. She got a new job as a software programmer when she finished her certificate just a few months after the layoff occurred.

SECURITY OFFICER ➤ ➤ PERSONAL TRAINER

Tony was a security officer at a defense installation in southern California. He worked there for five years, mostly on the second shift, which he liked because he could work out at the gym in the morning when it wasn't crowded. Sitting in the guardhouse gave Tony a lot of time to think, When he thought about his future, he couldn't see himself sitting in that booth every night. He wanted more. The wife of one of Tony's buddies worked at a local university, and she suggested he take a career development class there. As a result of taking the course, Tony has begun studying health and fitness and hopes to become a personal trainer.

BOOKKEEPER ➤ ➤ ➤ ➤ ACCOUNTANT

Catherine was a part-time bookkeeper and divorced mother with two boys, ages 7 and 10. Her goal was to become an accountant. Taking one course at a time, Catherine chipped away at the associate's degree requirements. It took her seven years in all to complete her degree. "So who's counting?" asks Catherine, who is continuing on toward a bachelor's degree. Meanwhile, she has accepted a position as an accounting assistant with a small manufacturing company near her home.

TELEPHONE   SALES
REPAIRER ➤ ➤ ➤ ➤ REPRESENTATIVE

Gary worked for the telephone company for 13 years, following in the footsteps of his dad. He often thought about doing something else but didn't think he could match his income outside the company. Then came divestiture. After surviving a couple of layoffs and internal reorganizations, Gary lost his job permanently. He was actually relieved when the notice finally arrived, ending the continued uncertainty. He took advantage of a retraining opportunity provided by federal funding and learned the welding trade. However, Gary was not happy in this work and continued to explore other possibilities. Eventually he moved into sales within the telecommunications industry and began to experience genuine excitement in his work. His job uses both his technical experience and his communication skills.

UNEMPLOYED   HUMAN
WELFARE RECIPIENT ➤ ➤ SERVICES WORKER

Marceta was 19 and receiving public assistance for her two children, ages 9 months and 3 years. She was also participating in YouthBuild, a drug rehabilitation program for teens. In the program, Marceta met a counselor who saw her strength and potential and referred her to an advisor at the neighborhood community college. With the help of financial aid, Marceta returned to school to prepare for work in the human services field. She has a co-op employer lined up in her own inner-city neighborhood where she will train as a home health aide.

INDUSTRIAL ➤ ➤ ➤ ➤ ➤ PART-TIME
ENGINEER   INSTRUCTOR

Harold had been an industrial engineer in the Midwest for 30 years when his company offered an attractive retirement incentive. After much soul-searching and extensive market research, Harold became a part-time faculty member at a college in his area. He also developed a small consulting practice. These changes required a major economic downshifting in his family's lifestyle, one that he and his family agreed was acceptable.

OFFICE MANAGER ➤ ➤ ➤ ➤ ➤ ➤ ➤ ?

Barbara managed a busy doctor's office. She scheduled patients' appointments, completed insurance claim forms, handled payroll, ordered supplies, and kept the office running smoothly. The office was so busy it was hard to find a moment to think about herself from one day (or year) to the next. After 10 years of this, Barbara started to feel frustrated. Despite the office's conversion to computers and many other labor-saving changes, there was always more work instead of less. Barbara began to hunger for something else, something new. What will motivate Barbara to move out of her safety zone?

Back to the Classroom

Purpose: The intent of this exercise is to get you thinking about why you have returned to school and how you feel about being here.

Directions: In the space provided, write your answer to the following questions.

Welcome back to the classroom! For some of you, it's been awhile. How are you feeling about returning to school?

....
....
....

What are your concerns? Fears?

....
....
....

In what ways are you "older and wiser" than when you were last a student?

....
....
....

In the space below, write a paragraph about what circumstances led you to return to school.

....
....
....
....
....
....

Reflections: If you feel comfortable doing so, share your feelings with your classmates, either during class or afterwards. Many life circumstances have brought each of you back to school. For some of you, this is an exciting next step; for others, it may be a difficult or scary one. By sharing your feelings, you have an opportunity to support one another.

Expectations

Purpose: Although you're just getting started, you probably have some ideas about what you hope to get from reading this book and taking this course. This exercise will help you describe those expectations and think about your part in seeing that they are met.

Directions: Reflect on your hopes for this course. What would you like to get from this experience? List your expectations below.

....
....

Reflections: You can contribute to having your expectations for the course met. First, share them with your instructor and the class so that you can gain a mutual understanding. Second, make a commitment to yourself to get what you want. You will get from the course what you put into it in terms of effort and reflective thought. It is, after all, your life and your career that you will be addressing.

Hotline

Purpose: This activity will help you get connected with your classmates. You have an opportunity to develop a new support system through this class.

Directions: In the space provided, list the names and telephone numbers of your instructor and your fellow students.

....

....

....

....

....

....

....

Reflections: You probably haven't gotten to know your classmates yet, so having their phone numbers may seem unnecessary. Notice as the course goes on if you bond with people and reach out to them. You can both give and receive support within this group.

Introduction to Goals

Purpose: You will probably spend several weeks or even months in this course. Many things can happen in that length of time. Goal setting will not be covered in detail until later, but this exercise will introduce you to the practice now. This assignment will be read only by you, since you will be making a contract with yourself.

Directions: On a separate piece of paper, write a list of goals that you hope to accomplish by the last day of class. These goals can relate to things you hope to achieve in the class as well as things you want to strive for at home, at work, and so forth. When you have a list you are happy with, seal it in an envelope. Address the envelope to yourself and give it to your instructor for safekeeping. Your instructor will return it to you on the last day of class so you can evaluate how you did in achieving your goals.

Reflections: How do you feel about the goals you set for yourself? Are you excited? Doubtful? Scared? Noncommittal? Do you think you will reach your goals? How committed are you to achieving them?

CHAPTER TWO

UNDERSTANDING THE CAREER DEVELOPMENT PROCESS

What determines someone's choice of career? What makes people feel a sense of fulfillment and satisfaction in their work? How do they navigate the complicated world of work in order to find their niche? Is there a better way? This chapter will examine theories of career and adult development and the process of transition and present a model for moving through the career development process during times of transition.

CAREER THEORIES GIVE US CLUES

Many career development theorists have attempted to explain the whys and wherefores of occupational choice and satisfaction during the past century. Their research and analysis contribute to our understanding of career development. Early theorists were sociologists, and, as might be expected, the subjects of their studies were boys and men. These theorists determined that the occupational choice of an individual's father and the social class of his family were primary determinants of career choice. In the early 1900s, psychologists began developing theories that focused on specific traits of individuals, such as intelligence and abilities, personality and interests. They generally believed that if they could accurately test or measure the traits they thought key to people's career choice and satisfaction, they could guide them to suitable occupations.

    The next wave of theorists, beginning in the 1950s, took a more interdisciplinary approach. They identified stages of career maturity and saw them as related to environmental factors, educational level, emotional factors, and personal values. Thus, the science of understanding career choice and satisfaction was becoming more complex. Finally, we have the life cycle theorists, who

How do we find our niche?

believe the process involves all the factors identified by earlier theorists and continues to evolve throughout adult life (Sonnenfeld & Kotter, 1982).

Later in this book, we will discuss individual career theorists and provide activities based on their work. These activities will provide "pieces of the puzzle" as you learn more about yourself and select the direction of your personal journey.

ADULT DEVELOPMENT PROVIDES THE CONTEXT

When you were growing up, adulthood probably looked good to you. You may have been eager to acquire certain privileges, make independent choices, and assume responsibilities not available to young people. From the vantage point of youth, adulthood typically appears to be a clearly defined, static state, where people live "happily ever after." Even developmental psychologists, who until recently focused exclusively on childhood and adolescent development, viewed adulthood as "a stable plateau preceding decline and death" (Okun, 1984, p. 4).

Adulthood is a continuous becoming

Beginning about 40 years ago, psychologists began to study adult life; since then, the field of life-span developmental psychology has blossomed (Smolak, 1993). Researchers have elaborated many theories about the patterns and stages of adult development, recognizing that people don't merely arrive at adulthood; rather, adulthood is "a continuous 'becoming' in itself" (Okun, 1984, p. 22). Adult life evolves through a number of stages and cycles, each characterized by predictable tasks and concerns. On the other hand, adult life is also full of surprises, unpredictable events that may indelibly alter the course of the evolving life.

Okun's Theory

Three domains of adult development: individual, family, and career

Dr. Barbara Okun, university professor and family systems therapist, developed an integrative model for individual, family, and career development of adults. According to her theory, development in all three domains progresses simultaneously and interdependently. Each domain has its own developmental tasks. The tasks listed in Figure 2.1 are only her career-related developmental tasks. To fully appreciate the developmental process of an adult, you would have to consider the tasks concerned with individual development and family development along with the career development tasks. These additional tasks are listed in the Appendix. As you consider the career-related tasks, notice that there are many transition points. Okun provides valuable detail about the functions of choosing, entering, maintaining, and changing careers over the life span.

The increasing complexity of adult life and the related increase in the pace of change are reflected in the developmental tasks presented here. Okun's model makes clear the difference between having a job and pursuing a career. A career in 2000 and beyond demands constant monitoring, fine-tuning, and redirecting. It is a lifelong pursuit involving several jobs. Additionally, individuals may pursue multiple careers. While the list of developmental tasks may appear daunting, it realistically reflects the complexity of our journeys. Can you find your present situation reflected in Okun's model? For many, the midcareer reassessment may have come earlier or more frequently than expected. Keep in mind that we have presented only Okun's career-related developmental tasks and that adults also carry out tasks related to their individual and family development.

EARLY ADULTHOOD

Initial choice

- Make provisional career, living, and education decisions
- Develop a dream
- Decide on an initial career choice
- Develop a plan
- Take steps to implement the plan

Workforce entry

- Begin a job in the field of choice
- Acquire occupational skills, values, credentials
- Accept a subordinate position
- Get along with colleagues and boss
- Find a mentor
- Negotiate boundaries between job demands and outside relationships and interests
- Assess on-the-job feedback
- Reassess and redirect when necessary
- Deal with disappointments, frustrations, successes, and failures

  [Author's note: A transition could occur here if market conditions or other factors warranted. Further education may be necessary.]

Establishment

- Choose special contributions to make in order to become a valued member of the occupational workplace
- Project a competent image
- Work more independently
- Internalize organizational or occupational values
- Plan your next career steps
- Assume higher-level and broader responsibilities

  [Author's note: A transition could occur here if market conditions or other factors warranted. Further education may be necessary.]

Consolidation

- Take on full membership in an occupation
- Consolidate knowledge and experiences about self, competencies, occupation
- Plan goals and strategies for the next decade
- Renegotiate boundaries among self, work, and family
- Appraise risks

MIDDLE ADULTHOOD

Midcareer reassessment

- Reassess your career: self-assessment regarding on-the-job functioning, skills, needs, interests, aptitudes; aspiration–achievement gaps; recognition of career anchors; values reassessment; occupation assessment; world-of-work assessment
- Finalize commitment to career or prepare for midcareer change
- Reassess personal/family and career boundaries

Maintenance

- Implement your midcareer reassessment decision: reality assessment; power and responsibility acceptance; stress management   *(continued)*

FIGURE 2.1

Career-related developmental tasks (Okun, 1984).

FIGURE 2.1

Continued.

- Become your own person in world of work
- Continue education and training
- Rebalance personal resources and energies
- Accept changing influences and challenges

The late-career stage
- Decelerate: find alternative ways of determining self-identity; find new sources of satisfaction; transfer competencies; gradually distance work priorities
- Make preretirement plans: appraise the meaning of retirement; plan your budget; consider all options

LATE ADULTHOOD
- Retire
- Reformulate identity: new roles, let go of old roles
- Make financial plans: current budget, projected budget
- Plan and arrange for health care
- Plan lifestyle: leisure; volunteerism; alternative career; lifelong learning; family; restructure energy, time, resources

From *Working with Adults: Individual, Family, and Career Development* by B. F. Okun. Copyright © 1984 Brooks/Cole Publishing Company, a division of International Thomson Publishing, Inc., Pacific Grove, CA 93950. Adapted by permission of the publisher.

TRANSITIONS HAVE IMPACT

Transitions impact every aspect of your life

As people move through their lives, certain events have major impact, perhaps even changing the course of their lives. You may have experienced such events. Perhaps you've started or ended an important relationship, changed jobs unexpectedly, become a parent or had children leave home, or lost a close relative or dear friend. These occurrences can serve as triggering events, propelling you into life transitions.

Transitions differ from ordinary changes because of the extent of their impact on all aspects of your life and because of the process necessary to arrive at resolution. Let's look first at a straightforward job change.

WORK IN PROGRESS

Gabrielle

Gabrielle was happily employed as a sales associate for a department store in a nearby shopping mall. One Sunday, she spotted an advertisement in the newspaper placed by a more prestigious chain that was opening a store in a new mall on the other side of town. This company was well-known for its training programs and its excellent customer service. Thinking she had nothing to lose, she applied for the position and was called in to interview. The opportunity turned out to be a good match, and Gabrielle changed jobs. Entry into the new job went smoothly; the training program was exciting, and Gabrielle made new friends easily.

As you can see, Gabrielle made this job change quite easily. Other than taking on a longer commute, her life hardly skipped a beat. Now let's look at a situation that turned into a major transition.

Manuel was happily employed as a field service supervisor for a company that manufactured computers. One day, he was called into the field office by his manager and told that he was out of a job. The company was downsizing its workforce by several thousand people nationwide, and every division of the company would be hit. Even though the field office was busy, it had to reduce staff.

Manuel started making calls right away, and within several weeks he started a new job. While all looked rosy during the interview process, Manuel found himself in the "hot seat" after moving into the new position. He discovered that Randy, who now reports to Manuel, had competed for the position. Randy is furious with Manuel and determined to see him fail. Manuel has to work extra hours to stay on top of the political battle unfolding. To make matters worse, Manuel realized, after being hired, that the new company doesn't offer educational benefits, leaving him financially worse off than he was in his last position. Somehow he had forgotten to ask all the right questions during the hiring process. The trouble at work spilled over to his home life and caused stress in his family. Manuel was unhappy and unsure about what to do. He feared that changing jobs again after only three months would reflect badly on him. Besides, the job market had taken a dive recently.

Manuel's predicament evolved into a major life transition. He passed through three stages as he worked through his transition. The first involved getting closure on the past, followed by a neutral period for regrouping, after which Manuel moved forward to new beginnings (Bridges, 1980). Take a closer look at the stages through which Manuel moved.

*Get closure,
regroup, and
move on*

Dealing with Endings

Manuel felt angry with himself for not researching the new job more thoroughly. He also questioned his competence; it wasn't like him to make mistakes. He felt he didn't belong in the new company, which stimulated feelings of loss for his old job and his good friends there. In his haste to find reemployment, Manuel had not grieved the loss of his last job. He had also denied any anger toward his last employer. Those feelings surfaced in the midst of his new crisis, creating tension at home. He and his wife were constantly bickering. "How did my life get so screwed up?" he wanted to know.

To repair the situation that emerged, Manuel needed to spend time with his feelings about what had happened and bring closure to the past before he could deal with rectifying the current situation. He remembered, for example, that his last job wasn't perfect. People had been anticipating layoffs for over a year, and that had created a tense environment. A couple of moves by management had irritated him, too. It wasn't the perfect job after all. He called his good friend Norman at the old company, and they met one night after work. Norman said things were really bad now, and he figured he'd go in the next round of cuts. Manuel began to understand there was no going back.

Cooling Your Heels

The second phase of the transition is a time-out, a neutral period during which internal feelings and beliefs become realigned at a subconscious as well as a conscious level. The internal work requires time alone, time with yourself, time to *be*, not *do*. This is difficult for many of us. Our action-oriented society will demand that we move on, do *something*. Manuel had to accept the chaos that he had inadvertently created in his life when he took the wrong new job. He had to simply sit with his problem. Out of desperation, he went off by himself one weekend to camp and fish and wallow in his misery. While it was hard for him to let go, hope did emerge out of the emptiness. Only then was he ready to move on to the next phase of his transition, new beginnings. He didn't have answers at this point, but he had accepted his situation and was ready to seek answers.

Beginning Again

The third phase, then, is making a beginning. Internally, you move out of neutral and engage first gear. You start to feel energized and renewed, in touch with a new vision of what you want, and highly motivated to get it. Your engine may stall and buck a bit at first, but the forward movement will be discernible. Interestingly, opportunities and resources often present themselves at this time. About two weeks after his fishing trip, Manuel decided he was truly unhappy in his new job and had to look for another one. Having dealt with his many feelings about the situation, he was now able to think more clearly and identify what needed to be done. He began contacting people he knew in other companies and checking job listings in the newspaper. He also called the school where he had earned his certificate to ask about placement assistance. Eventually Manuel identified a new opportunity and went through the interviewing process more aware of his needs.

DEAL WITH EMOTIONS TRIGGERED BY CAREER CRISIS

Anger, sadness, and fear are all acceptable reactions—but deal with them

If external circumstances have propelled you into career transition, you may be feeling intense rage. No one appreciates being forced to make life changes. Sometimes a physical injury forces you to change careers. A divorce may propel you into the job market. A personality conflict with a supervisor may trigger a job change. A layoff may also force you to change. It is appropriate to feel extremely angry in these circumstances. Until you deal with your anger, it will be difficult to look ahead and consider new possibilities.

Acknowledging your anger is an important first step. Denying anger and trying to contain it are usually counterproductive. Many people find it helpful to identify safe ways to expel anger. Vigorous exercise, like running, swimming, or playing tennis or racquetball, is an excellent means of discharging your anger safely. Writing and then tearing up letters in which you express your anger can also be useful.

When you ignore your anger, you end up seething. Unresolved anger can spill out in a job interview. A hostile remark about a former boss may result in your being seen as someone with a chip on your shoulder. Angry people are not likely to be hired.

If your anger is causing you to harm yourself or other people, please seek help right away. These are not appropriate ways of dealing with anger.

Feelings of grief and loss are also common in a career crisis. When you have been laid off from a job you performed for a long time, you may experience a loss of your identity. For many people, their jobs define who they are. Without their jobs, they feel empty, purposeless. The feelings are similar to those experienced when a loved one dies. You may also feel extremely sad about losing your daily contact with friends and colleagues. The losses have to be mourned. You may find that you cry often, especially at first; this is the healthiest thing you can do. Crying releases the feelings of grief and loss. People who do not express these feelings risk going into depression. Talking about your feelings is also helpful. Eventually, reconnect with the friends you worked with; there is no need to permanently lose those cherished relationships. Bring these people back into your life by seeing them socially or talking on the telephone. If they have also lost their jobs, form a support group and meet regularly until you are all reemployed.

Fear is another emotion that has the potential to paralyze you when you are in crisis. You may be afraid that you will never be able to find another job or that you will lose your home or your spouse. These are frightening thoughts. You need to develop some perspective on your situation. People change jobs all the time; it is not the end of the world. What makes it feel so awful is that you didn't get to control the situation. Losing your job is a jarring experience. If you find the fear is blocking you from moving on, seek professional help. You need not cope with it alone.

Dealing with all of these intense feelings sounds like an enormous undertaking. The important thing is that you accept the feelings, allow them to be with you. Avoid denying the feelings or stuffing them down inside. Find healthy ways to deal with them. Eventually, you will be able to accept and let go of your past. Only then will you be able to create the space for a new chapter in your work life.

UNDERSTAND THE CAREER DEVELOPMENT PROCESS

Again, careers are one aspect of the complex lives of adults. Career development evolves over your life span as you engage in the process of careering and re-careering. When you experience a transition in your career, you move from a period of relative stability to a period of turmoil or crisis. As we have seen, this shift can be triggered by external factors such as layoffs, reorganizations, the retirement of your boss, the promotion of your rival, or the introduction of new technology. The shift can also be triggered by internal factors such as acknowledging your boredom, frustration, or disappointments. You may feel that life is passing you by and that there must be more to life than this job.

When events coalesce and are elevated to the level of a career crisis, you will likely find yourself reevaluating all of your previous career decisions, questioning your choice of a career field, and recalling missed opportunities throughout your work life. You may experience considerable anguish about the past. This review is the natural way of dealing with endings in a transition. When you have cleared the decks and come face-to-face with the void that letting go creates, you are in the neutral space you need to be in. Be with yourself. Don't try to control things. Allow the nothingness. Acceptance will emerge. Hope will follow. Finally, solutions will appear.

When you are ready to begin again, there are specific steps you can take to resolve your career crisis and return to career stability and satisfaction. A six-step model outlining the process is presented in Figure 2.2. Each step will be examined in detail in subsequent chapters.

In order to use the six-step model successfully, you will need to be in the third phase of transition, beginning again. That means you will have to let go of the past and make space inside yourself for change. The model offers helpful steps you can take to begin to move forward. These steps can be useful when you are preparing to enter a first career, to change careers, or to change jobs at any point in your life. The model serves as a guide through what might otherwise seem like a frightening, confusing, and frustrating process.

You can resolve your career crisis

FIGURE 2.2

Career development
model.

SIX STEPS TO CAREER SUCCESS

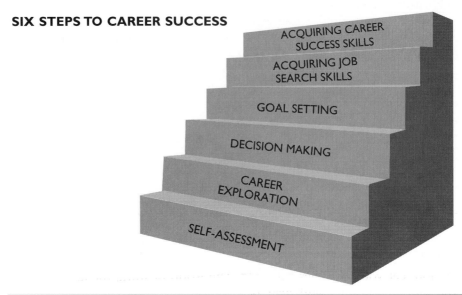

Self-Assessment

Self-assessment
equals
self-awareness

The first step in the career development process is *self-assessment*. At this important stage, you will get to know yourself very well. In particular, you will crystallize your identity and look at your skills, values, interests, and personality preferences. A number of exercises are provided in this book to help you clarify specific areas of self-assessment. Your instructor may also provide standardized tests and instruments to complete and review.

Self-assessment helps you identify what you do well, what motivates you, what brings you pleasure and satisfaction, and what challenges you. It also helps you clarify what bores you, what frustrates you, and what leaves you cold. Your new awareness will lead you to potentially satisfying occupations and away from career paths that may be unsatisfying.

**WORK IN
PROGRESS**

Rick

Rick graduated from a nationally recognized technical institute with a bachelor of science in electrical engineering. His grade point average was mediocre, in part because he never did his homework. He crammed for exams and then quickly forgot what he had learned. In truth, Rick hated engineering. He had majored in it because his father was an engineer, and engineering was the only discipline his father respected.

In his first year out of school, Rick worked for a social service agency caring for handicapped children. The pay was abysmal, but Rick found the work personally rewarding. Then he got a sales position in a record store. The pay was still awful, but the job was more fun. He also returned to school part-time, taking courses in a variety of subjects that interested him, courses he hadn't had time for in his highly structured engineering program—music theory, composition, creative writing, and life/career planning.

In the life/career planning class, Rick began to hone in on what he liked and where his talents lay. He became excited about the prospect of his work being a positive part of his life for the first time. As he got to know and appreciate himself more, he even developed the confidence to talk with his father about his true interests and his dislike for the field of engineering.

Rick's story is all too common. The sad part is that his self-discovery process did not begin until two years after he graduated from college. He spent four years and many thousands of dollars going in the wrong direction. Sometimes people spend even more time and money on careers that fail to tap their strengths and enthusiasm. Other people pursue a career for five or ten years and then hit a wall. They too need to assess themselves. What's important *now*? What skills can I salvage and repackage? The self-assessment process helps you recognize your own uniqueness. With that awareness, you will be able to make better choices about your career direction.

Career Exploration

The second step in the career development process is *career exploration*. This is the time to open up possibilities, and that means letting go of stereotypes. It may also mean considering occupations you have never before encountered. You will be introduced to a variety of resources containing occupational information. Let your fantasies run wild. The world of work, the labor market, and the global economy will also be explored. You may become aware of changes in the workplace that challenge your assumptions about work. These are exciting times.

Let go of stereotypes

Decision Making

The third step in the career development process is *decision making*. Having learned more about yourself, the world of work, and the market, it will be time to synthesize that information and look for the compatibilities between your values, interests, personality, and skills and the needs of the marketplace. Which positions are likely to meet your needs? Which career paths would best utilize your talents and gifts? What career alternatives offer the promise of opportunity well into the next century?

Making decisions is not always easy. How do you make important decisions? Do you gather information and apply logical analysis, or do you make decisions intuitively? Do you allow others to decide for you? Our decision-making model provides a useful structure for making a major life decision.

Synthesize your information, then make a decision

Goal Setting

The fourth step in the career development process is *goal setting*. This step logically follows decision making because once you have made decisions, you need to set specific goals and develop an action plan for implementing those goals. Goal setting is a tool you can use throughout your life. Setting goals regularly, reviewing them frequently, and renegotiating them when necessary will keep you moving forward. Without forward momentum, you are likely to become stuck or even slide backward.

Setting goals keeps you moving forward

Your own action plan could take several months or years to complete. For example, it might include completing a college degree or certificate program to acquire credentials for a new career. You might decide to stay with your current employer in the interim to minimize upheaval. When you are ready to move from planning and preparing for your career transition to actually beginning your search for a new job, you will move to the next step in the career development model.

Ann was a 29-year-old married woman who came to the career center one September for help in finding an accounting job. She had attended night school for the previous five years and expected to graduate the following June.

Ann was not career-oriented when she left high school. She went to a business school for a year and then worked in a series of unsatisfying jobs. During that time, she discovered that she was smarter than most of the people she worked with, and her bosses also recognized her abilities. Eventually, she decided to pursue a bachelor's degree. Her exposure to business settings confirmed her interest in accounting.

Once she'd identified her goal, Ann wanted to move quickly. She decided, therefore, to hold what she called a "mindless" job making keys for a department store. She was able to take a full course load because she could often do homework while on the job. Although she wasn't gaining many marketable skills in this position, she was able to maintain a 4.0 grade point average, which she knew would be an attractive selling point to large accounting firms.

Three years into her studies, Ann and her husband bought a condominium. Ann joined the board of trustees and managed the books for the large complex, gaining many skills that would be transferable to her career. When Ann met with on-campus recruiters in her senior year, she received offers from two of the "big six" accounting firms. Her goal setting and action planning had paid off.

Acquiring Job Search Skills

Good job search skills open up exciting career possibilities

The fifth step in the model is *acquiring job search skills.* At this stage, you are preparing to market yourself to companies or organizations. You will write a resume that recasts your previous experience, emphasizes newly acquired skills, and leads to promising job interviews. Most importantly, you will learn about developing a network of professional contacts who will be valuable throughout your career.

Targeting organizations for your search and strategizing an effective approach are also necessary job search skills. Finally, developing or refining your interviewing skills and ability to negotiate salary and fringe benefits is an important part of this step.

Acquiring Career Success Skills

*Career develop-
ment continues
on the job*

The last step in the career development process involves *acquiring career success skills.* These are the skills that help you fit into a new organization. You will find out how to present a positive professional image, develop a good relationship with your supervisor, add value to your organization, build a support network, take on new responsibilities, and plan your career advancement or enrichment. Learn about ongoing career management and what it takes to become a valued and influential employee, and consider the option of becoming your own boss through self-employment.

BE FLEXIBLE IN APPLYING THE MODEL

The model you have just reviewed is a sequential model. In the chapters that follow, you will move through the model methodically, completing tasks in each of the six steps. By following each step, one by one, you will address the issues that need to be considered in a career transition. The model implies that there is an end to this process. It also implies that the steps are clearly defined, and that when you move on to the next step, you have completed the one before. Oh, that life were so simple! In fact, as you have no doubt discovered, life does not play out in a linear fashion; it is much more complex than that.

Sometimes the pace of the course may necessitate your moving on to the next step before you feel ready. You will be able to learn about the steps and then go back to complete them at a pace that is comfortable for you. For instance, you may make career decisions that require months or years of schooling before you implement your plan. You can still move through the model and learn the skills for job search and career success. Later on when you are ready to change positions, you can review those steps again.

Career transitions require deep soul-searching work and careful planning. Some people change jobs every few years without greatly altering their lives; others stay with a company for decades. Still others make major career transitions from time to time. It is rare in today's rapidly changing workplace for someone to work for extended periods of time without experiencing some changes: changes in technology or methods of operating, changes in organizational structure, changes in company ownership, or changes in the culture of the organization. Downsizing may lead to layoffs or expanded responsibilities, and advances in technology typically lead to the creation of new positions. All of these changes have a direct impact on workers and their jobs; thus they may trigger transitions.

Career transitions take deep soul-searching work

ADD A DEVELOPMENTAL PERSPECTIVE

The six-step model presented here provides a structure for handling transition periods throughout your work life. Adults will likely cycle back through the steps several times. Figure 2.3 depicts a developmental view of career transitions over the life span. The career development model appears at a pivotal point in each transition.

The illustration shows periods of relative career stability alternating with periods of transition. Transitional periods will occur with different frequency for each individual. Statistics indicate that adults entering the workforce today can expect to change careers at least five times. As you move through each career transition, the steps involved in establishing a new career will become easier. The model provides a structure and encourages the development of skills that can be used again and again as needed when negotiating future job changes and career transitions.

Finally, as mentioned earlier, our lives are complex. We do not exist in the world solely as careerists. Our roles may also include being spouses or partners, parents, students, children, members, neighbors, friends, and relatives. Each role is demanding and requires attention. Your career issues may be intertwined with issues emanating from the other sectors of your life. The model is intended to help you sort out and focus on the career issues. The next chapter begins with a closer look at step one of the career development model.

Sort out career issues from other aspects of your life

FIGURE 2.3

Career transitions: Each of us will likely revisit the six-step model several times during our lives.

THE EVER-CHANGING WORLD

Individuals move through periods of stability, crisis, and transition throughout their careers. Career is just one part of their complex lives. Individual and family roles further complicate their lives.

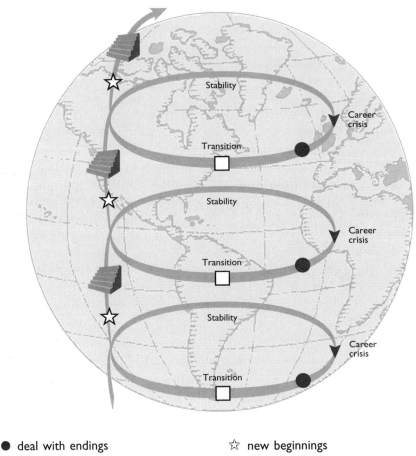

● deal with endings   ☆ new beginnings

□ regroup   six-step model

WORK IN PROGRESS

Your Job Timeline

(We'll use a similar timeline for several exercises.)

Purpose: This exercise will help you recall and quickly review your experiences of working.

Directions: In the space below, let the line represent your whole life. At the far left end of your line, mark a dot to represent your birth and label it with your date of birth. Next, mark a dot on the line to represent today's date and label that.

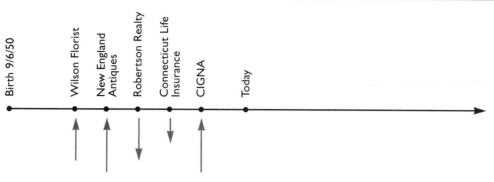

FIGURE 2.4

Job timeline.

Now add dots to your line, between your birth and today's date, to represent every job you've held. Label each dot with a name or short phrase that reminds you of the job. See Figure 2.4 for a sample timeline. When you have finished, draw arrows pointing upward below the jobs that you remember as positive experiences, and arrows pointing downward below the dots of jobs you disliked. Vary the length of the arrows to show the strength of your feeling about each position. Don't worry about whether you've held only one or two jobs or many jobs. Simply be honest in assessing those jobs you have held. And don't forget to include "home manager" if that was your primary occupation at some point during your life.

Reflections: What does this timeline tell you about your work life so far? Looking beyond today, where do you think the next dot will fall? In other words, when do you think you will make your next job change? Do you have any idea what that next job may be? Will its arrow point up or down?

....

....

....

....

....

Transitions Timeline

Purpose: This activity provides a format for looking at turning points in your life. By plotting these points on your life timeline, you will be able to see how events have shaped your life.

Directions: Draw another line to represent your life. Put a dot at the left end to represent your birth and label it. Place a second dot on the line to represent today. Thinking back over your life, place dots on the line to identify any major turning points. Include changes in your work life, family life, and personal life. Label these points on your timeline and write a brief statement about each.

Reflections: Review the timeline you have drawn. At the turning points, did you make a change in your life, or did you go through a transition? What triggered each change or transition? Ultimately, were these periods of growth for you? Why or why not? How do you feel about your life so far?

....

....

....

....

....

Identifying with the Six-Step Model

Purpose: This exercise helps you become more familiar with the model presented in Figure 2.2. By applying the model, you will see that you have already functioned on most of its steps, even if you were unaware of the process the model defines.

Directions: Review the six-step model of the career development process on page 14. Think about your own experiences in making career decisions, searching for jobs, and starting in new positions. Pick two steps from the model that at some time in your career you completed memorably—the experiences may have been good or bad. For example, perhaps during one job change you did a lot of exploring of different options (part of step 2). Write a brief paragraph about the research you did. And maybe in another search, you had some negative interviewing experiences (part of step 5). Write about those in a second paragraph.

....

....

....

....

....

....

....

....

Reflections: Can you see the logic of the career development model? How can it help you? What parts of the model are you most comfortable with? What parts are less familiar to you?

....

....

....

....

....

....

....

Scoping Out the Business Press

Purpose: This activity will raise your awareness of resources available to help you better understand the workplace and many of the changes taking place there.

Directions: Make a trip to the public or school library, and browse through recent issues of publications like *Business Week, Fortune,* and the *Wall Street Journal.* There are several publications of this type to choose from. Alternatively, you may access current issues of these publications using the Internet. Find an article about the economy, employment, global competition, or a related topic of your choice. Read the article carefully, make some notes in the space below, and prepare to tell the class about it. Through this assignment, you and your classmates can pool your efforts to understand the changing workplace. Hold an "economic summit" in class to share your information and discuss what you have learned.

....
....
....
....
....
....
....
....

Reflections: Write a brief paragraph discussing how you have been personally affected by global, national, or local economic conditions.

....
....
....
....
....
....
....
....

CHAPTER THREE

APPRECIATING YOUR UNIQUENESS

In this chapter and the two that follow, you will be looking closely at yourself and assessing many aspects of who you are. This process of self-assessment allows you to focus on your identity, family and cultural influences, values, skills, interests, and personality preferences. You will develop a deeper understanding of who you are and what makes you tick. By undergoing this self-study, you will have an opportunity to design a life for yourself that is personally meaningful and satisfying. You will find exercises both within and at the end of the chapters; for best results, complete the exercises as you come to them in your reading. Enjoy your journey of self-discovery!

A journey of self-discovery

YOUR IDENTITY

Think about how you would describe yourself to someone who has never met you. What could you say about yourself that would capture the essence of who you are?

"Tell Me a Little About Yourself"

Purpose: This short exercise is intended to get you thinking about how you see yourself and how you present yourself to other people.

PART ONE

Directions: Imagine yourself in a job interview with the hiring manager of a company that genuinely interests you. You know nothing about the person

WORK IN PROGRESS

interviewing you. What will you share about yourself when she says, "Tell me a little about yourself"? List four or five major points and then write a scripted response in the space provided.

....

....

....

....

....

PART TWO

Directions: Imagine yourself on an airplane to a distant location. A friendly and attentive person sits down next to you, introduces himself, and asks you about yourself. What would you share with this person? List four or five items and then write a scripted response in the space provided.

....

....

....

....

....

Reflections: When you have finished writing, look over what you have written. What does it tell you about who you are and how you see yourself? Do your responses provide a fairly complete thumbnail sketch of you? Is anything important missing? Do you have a well-developed sense of who you are? How does your response in an interview situation differ from that in a social situation?

When describing yourself in a social situation to someone who has never met you, you might tell that person about your family, where you come from and where you went to school, what you do for work, how you have fun, or what your political views or religious beliefs are. In a job interview, however, you will describe your "career self," focusing on experiences you've had and skills you've developed that relate directly to the position. The emphasis is on your professional identity.

In starting the process of self-assessment, begin by examining your self-concept, your image of who you are. Look behind the masks. We all have personas that we present to the outside world. Find the real you and get to know and appreciate that unique and special individual.

WORK IN PROGRESS

The Me Everyone Knows

Purpose: This exercise explores the issue of identity a little more deeply. The perspectives of individuals who know you well can help you further clarify and integrate your personal identity.

Directions: Interview a family member, a friend, and a work colleague who genuinely appreciate you. Ask each one to describe you, using probing questions such as: What kind of person am I? How am I perceived by others? What are my strengths? My talents? My gifts? If you don't know why they are saying certain things, ask them to give specific examples. Otherwise, let them talk freely while you record their comments. When you have completed your interviews, write a personal description based on their comments and observations.

Reflections: In this activity you have been learning about how others see you. What have you learned from this exercise? Are you surprised by the insights and observations of others? How can you apply this experience in your life?

Our identities are extremely complex. These exercises introduced you to an understanding of personal identity. Now we will look at the sources of personal identity.

Early Messages

Our identities are formed at an early age and contain a compilation of messages that we have internalized from significant people in our lives. If your caregivers told you that you were loved unconditionally and treated you in a way that reinforced that love, then you grew up believing that you were lovable. On the other hand, if you were told (either through words or actions) that you were not valued, very likely that was the message you internalized. Clearly, each of us grew up receiving thousands of messages, often conflicting, about our worth, our lovability, our capabilities, and so on. These messages came from parents or other primary caregivers as well as from brothers and sisters, other relatives, teachers, neighbors, friends, and rivals. They also came from society at large.

A lifetime of messages creates our self-image

If you were told as a kid by older siblings that you were stupid, and later some cranky teacher said you weren't college material, you may be sitting in this class feeling like an impostor waiting to be found out. You may be convinced that you will fail the course. You can replace your negative self-image and low expectations with positive self-esteem and high expectations. It will take some effort on your part to reprogram your self-concept, but it can be done.

Messages

Purpose: This exercise will get you thinking about messages that have been influencing you throughout your life. Once you have identified them, you can evaluate them, choosing to keep those that support you and to discard those that are harmful.

Directions: Make a list of key family members and others who have been influential in your life. Include parents or guardians, brothers and sisters, aunts and uncles, grandparents, in-laws, teachers, employers, coworkers, and so forth. Write down any messages you recall getting from them, either directly or indirectly, about your behavior, your value or worth, and your future. When you have listed your recollections, note messages they gave you about the world at large, and the work world in particular. Samples are given to help you get started. Be sure to include important and influential people from all aspects of your life.

WORK IN PROGRESS

3.3

Mom

Messages about me: You're impossible, stubborn, too sensitive. Do something with your hair. You look tired. You try to do too much. You can't do it all. Play hard to get.

Messages about the world/work: Money doesn't grow on trees. You can't trust people. Take a civil service test and get a secure job with the government.

Dad

Messages about me: I'm proud of you. You have good ideas. You're an intelligent girl.

Messages about the world/work: It's horrible out there. You need a good education. You need to have a profession to fall back on. Of course men make more than women—they have families to support. (1950s!)

Aunt Edith

Messages about me: You're beautiful. You're great. You're smart. You can have and do anything you want.

Messages about the world/work: Get a college degree. Work hard and you can get an exciting job like your cousin Sarah. Then you'll marry a wealthy naval officer and live happily ever after.

Peter Feinberg (employer)

Messages about me: You've done a good job. You've learned the basics of the position quickly. You are well liked by our customers and staff.

Messages about the world/work: Be patient. Keep generating good ideas. Rome wasn't built in a day.

Margaret Gilbert (employer)

Messages about me: Your strengths are your strong command of the technology and your intuitive sense of customers' needs. You have demonstrated strong leadership potential. Broaden your experience base; don't focus too narrowly.

Messages about the world/work: No one ever said life was fair. Politics exist in every organization.

Reflections: What patterns do you see from the messages you received? Which messages have you bought into? Which have you rejected? Have any messages been influencing you without your being aware of them? Are there messages you now want to reject, having identified and thought about them?

All of the messages we receive during our lives are stored, complete and unabridged, in our subconscious. They are not edited or evaluated in any way. Some messages are supportive of us while others are undermining. The transcribed messages shape our sense of self. When you have lived a relatively normal, healthy life, you move into adulthood with a fairly true picture of who you are and what your talents, skills, and abilities are.

However, if you come from a turbulent environment, you may not have an accurate assessment of who you are. Look carefully at the messages you received. If this work is painful for you, you may wish to get help and support from a therapist. If you avoid or postpone introspection, you may make choices in your life based on negative early-life messages and thus limit your options. Until you identify, evaluate, and discard negative messages, they may influence your decisions and interfere with the development of positive self-esteem.

Positive self-esteem is the primary source within you that will drive your efforts, whether they are educational pursuits, career development, or personal relationships. You achieve in life to the extent you believe you are able to achieve, and you receive rewards to the extent you believe yourself worthy. Positive self-esteem gives you energy and hope, and with these ingredients you will be willing to grow, to learn, to recognize opportunity, to take risks, and ultimately to be happy and successful.

Family Influences

As we've seen, your family impacted your personal identity and self-esteem. In addition, it may well have influenced your attitudes toward school, work, and relationships. Remember Rick, whose father respected only engineers? Many children grow up in families who expect them to pursue certain careers, whether those careers are medicine, teaching, or farming. It can be difficult for everyone involved if the children are not interested in following the family's "script."

You achieve to the extent you think you can; you earn rewards to the extent you think you're worthy of them

Even if you make a conscious decision to live your life separately from your family, you are still influenced by them. For instance, connections your family has in the community may help determine which doors in the world open to you. This might include colleges, corporations, and social organizations. Taking advantage of family connections and resources can make sense, especially when those resources are compatible with your personal goals.

In one family, it may be expected that boys will go into a trade such as electrician or plumber. Since unions are strong in these trades, family members often sponsor their offspring for membership. Another family may urge children into high-paying, prestigious professions and have little appreciation for careers in the arts or human services.

Still another family may have a business with two or three generations working together. Lord help the son or daughter who has no interest in the distribution of industrial pumps!

Sometimes it's threatening to a family when a member of the younger generation wants to strike out into new territory. The parents may fear the unknown. While their attitudes can feel incredibly limiting, you can appreciate that these family members ultimately want you to be successful and, because of their own experience, feel most confident of your success if you move in the directions they are familiar with. Some of you may have already spent many years pursuing your family's dream for you. Others may be unaware of how influential your families have been.

Cultural Heritage

Beyond your immediate family is the culture in which your family functions. Rich cultural traditions are passed down from generation to generation. This country's mix of ethnic backgrounds is unique in the world. In the past, the United States has been described as a melting pot where immigrants from all

over the world have tried to blend into the dominant culture brought by set-
tlers from Great Britain. More recently, ethnic groups have been interested in
[...] lt, the U.S. culture is evolving into a mul-
[...] x of workers, the variety of foods sold in
[...] ic restaurants, the different religions prac-
[...] ken.

[...]? You may be a Native American who is
[...] and customs. Or you may be an African
[...] this country against their will and with-
[...] the Middle East, Ireland, Cuba, Vietnam,
[...] talian Catholics on one side of your fami-
[...] r side and have experienced a fascinating
[...] and practices.

Family and [...] heritaᵍ expecᵗ [...] values, behavior, and role expectations
[...] have distinctly different expectations of
[...] e you been influenced by cultural pat-
[...] o stereotype, you can understand a great
[...] bout your cultural heritage. All of these
[...] nd they may influence your lifestyle and
career choice.

Handwritten note:
Ian 11/14/02
1 partner/spouse
2 good health
3 career
4 phys ex
5 fin security
6 pleasant home
7 leisure time
8 stim chall
9 frends
   amily
11 educ
12 comm
13 status/ prestige
14 spiritur

Ian 1992
same
except
partner/
spouse
last

Learning about the cultural traditions of your classmates and coworkers
will help you to appreciate the diversity that is enriching our nation. Sharing
information about your different backgrounds builds understanding and
trust. Employers consider the ability to get along with and work collaboratively with a variety of people to be an important attribute.

VALUES

Values clarify what is important to you and help you determine priorities.
They influence how you treat yourself and others, how you spend time and
energy, and how you deal with money. One individual's values might include
family, security, intellectual stimulation, and good health. Another may value
excitement, challenge, adventure, and freedom. These values are only relevant
when your basic survival needs have been met; if your safety is threatened, it
becomes your priority.

Looking beyond survival, perhaps you value your health above most other things. If that is true, it is likely that you are conscientious about your diet
and you exercise regularly. You may also balance work, school, and family
responsibilities to ensure that you get plenty of rest.

*Your values
influence the
choices you make*   If, on the other hand, your dominant value is the well-being of your family, you may have made career choices that allowed you to be home when
children got out of school. Or you may have turned down a promotion that
would have required a move out of state and away from your aging parents.
You can see how values affect your choice of career and lifestyle.

We all hold many values simultaneously. The combining of our values
creates our value system. No doubt your life has become complex, with
many demands competing for your time and attention. The choices you
make reflect what is important to you *at the time you make them*. Since it is
impossible to have everything at once, you make trade-offs, and in doing so,
you clarify your values. Over time, your values will change along with
changes in your work life, family needs, and personal desires. Priorities today
may not be priorities five years from now.

Personal Priorities

Purpose: Life tends to be filled with competing demands for our time and attention. In this exercise, you will have an opportunity to evaluate what is most important to you at this time.

Directions: To start, write each of the words or phrases listed below on a separate slip of paper:

leisure time	spiritual life
good health	education
physical exercise	pleasant home
career	financial security
friends	community
family	other: ....
partner/spouse	other: ....

Turn all the papers upside down and mix them up. Now turn over and read the top two slips. Decide which of the two items is more important to you. Place the two items in front of you with the most important item on top. Now take a third item from the stack and prioritize this item against the other two. When you have the three items in order of importance to you, take the fourth item, and continue until all items are in order of importance to you. When you are satisfied with your prioritized list, copy it in the space below and indicate today's date.

1. Spouse
2. Family
3. Financial Security
4. Good Health
5. Physical Exercise
6. Stimulating Challenges
7. Spiritual Life
8. Education
9. Friends
10. Pleasant Home
11. Career
12. Leisure Time
13. Community
14. Status / Prestige

Today's date 10/31/02

Reflections: How would your list have been different 5 or 10 years ago? How might it look 5 years from now? 10 or 20 years from now? Are your priorities supporting you in getting what you want from your life? Are there changes you want to make? How can you make them? Write your conclusions below.

1. If I value Good Health, it follows that I need to make Physical Exercise a top priority as well.
2. When making a difficult decision or when juggling multiple tasks, I can refer back to this value list to guide me through.

In addition to knowing what is important to you in your life in general, it is useful to identify what you need from your work life in order to feel a sense of satisfaction. This information can help you to see specifically what is most fulfilling as well as what may be lacking in your present situation. It will also help you to identify what you need and want. Once you know what you need from your career, you can seek opportunities that are likely to satisfy those needs.

WORK IN
PROGRESS

Work Values

PART ONE RATING SATISFACTIONS FROM WORK

Purpose: This exercise, originating with Howard Figler, will help you to clarify what is important to you in your work.

Directions: The following list describes a wide variety of satisfactions that people obtain from their jobs. Look at the definitions of these various satisfactions and rate the degree of importance that you would assign to each for yourself, using the scale below:

1 = Not important at all
2 = Not very important
3 = Reasonably important
4 = Very important in my choice of career

(11) 3 .... *Help Society:* Do something to contribute to the betterment of the world I live in.

(12) 1 .... *Help Others:* Be involved in helping other people in a direct way, either individually or in small groups.

(7) 1 .... *Public Contact:* Have a lot of day-to-day contact with people.

(21) 3 .... *Work with Others:* Have close working relationships with a group; work as a team toward common goals.

(1) 1 .... *Affiliation:* Be recognized as a member of a particular organization.

(8) 1 .... *Friendships:* Develop close personal relationships with people as a result of my work activities.

(10) 1 .... *Competition:* Engage in activities that pit my abilities against others where there are clear win–lose outcomes.

(13) 3 .... *Make Decisions:* Have the power to decide courses of action, policies, etc.

(2) 1 .... *Work Under Pressure:* Work in situations where time pressure is prevalent and/or the quality of my work is judged critically by supervisors, customers, or others.

(3) 1 .... *Power and Authority:* Control the work activities or (partially) the destinies of other people.

(14) 2 .... *Influence People:* Be in a position to change attitudes or opinions of other people.

(23) 3 .... *Work Alone:* Do projects by myself, without any significant amount of contact with others.

(24) 4 .... *Knowledge:* Engage myself in the pursuit of knowledge, truth, and understanding.

(25) 4 .... *Intellectual Status:* Be regarded as a person of high intellectual prowess or as one who is an acknowledged "expert" in a given field.

(15) 3 .... *Artistic Creativity:* Engage in creative work in any of several art forms.

[4] *Creativity (General):* Create new ideas, programs, organizational structures, or anything else not following a format previously developed by others.

(16) 2 *Aesthetics:* Be involved in studying or appreciating the beauty of things, ideas, etc.

(4) 1 *Supervision:* Have a job in which I am directly responsible for the work done by others.

(22) 4 *Change and Variety:* Have work responsibilities that frequently change in their content and setting.

(17) 3 *Precision Work:* Work in situations where there is very little tolerance for error.

(18) 4 *Stability:* Have work routine and job duties that are largely predictable and not likely to change over a long period of time.

(28) 4 *Security:* Be assured of keeping my job and a reasonable financial reward.

(19) 3 *Fast Pace:* Work in circumstances where there is a high pace of activity, and where work must be done rapidly.

[4] *Recognition:* Be recognized for the quality of my work in some visible or public way.

[4] *Excitement:* Experience high degree of (or frequent) excitement in the course of my work.

(5) 1 *Adventure:* Have work duties that involve frequent risk taking.

[4] *Profit, Gain:* Have a strong likelihood of accumulating large amounts of money or other material gain.

[3] *Independence:* Be able to determine the nature of my work without significant direction from others; not have to do what others tell me to.

(26) 4 *Moral Fulfillment:* Feel that my work is contributing significantly to a set of moral standards that I feel are very important.

(20) 4 *Location:* Find a place to live (town, geographic area) that is conducive to my lifestyle and affords me the opportunity to do the things I enjoy most.

(9) 1 *Community:* Live in a town or city where I can get involved in community affairs.

(6) 1 *Physical Challenge:* Have a job that makes physical demands that I would find rewarding.

(27) 4 *Time Freedom:* Have work responsibilities that I can work at according to my own time schedule; no specific working hours required.

PART TWO PRIORITIZING SATISFACTIONS FROM WORK

Purpose: So far, you have been rating each work value separately, and there has been no pressure on you to make choices. That part comes with the second half of this exercise. By now, most of you have learned that life involves compromise. We don't usually get everything we want. It probably doesn't come as a shock that your present job may not satisfy all of the values you rated highly. The next step is deciding what values are critically important to you. It will be these values that you seek in your next career move.

Directions: To find out which values are most important to you, go back through the list of 33 work values in part 1 and cross out 10 that you would be willing to give up if you could have the remaining items. As you consider the items, notice the conversation taking place in your mind. This "chatter" is important because it is the process by which you are clarifying your values. Do the crossing out now. Do not read on until you have eliminated 10 items.

When you have eliminated 10 items, consider the following scenario: You have been looking for a job for three months. You've searched the Internet, answered ads, made phone calls, and have not been invited to interview for even one job. The job market is worse than you could have imagined, but you still want to make a change and are willing to be a little more flexible.

Eliminate another 10 items from the work values listed above. As you review the values, again note the conversations taking place in your mind. They are important to your values clarification process. Do the second round of eliminating now. Do not read on.

When you have completed the second cut, consider another scenario: You have now been looking for a new job for more than six months with no promising results. To make matters worse, you have lost your current job because of a company reorganization. Although you are eligible to collect unemployment compensation, you feel very anxious about finding another position as soon as possible.

Return to your list of values and eliminate eight more items. This will leave you with five values that you will never give up . . . that you would fight for! Again, as you work through the items, make note of the internal bargaining and debating. When you have identified your final five most cherished work values, record them below and fill in today's date:

1. Creativity (General)
2. Recognition
3. Excitement
4. Profit/Gain
5. Independence   Today's date 10/31/02

Reflections: When you are clear about your values, you have important building blocks that help you make appropriate career choices. This work needs to be redone throughout your work life, each time you are considering a change. How do you feel about the values you've selected today? Did you know what your most cherished work values were before doing the exercise? Looking at the five values you have chosen, are they being satisfied in your current work? How can you satisfy these work values?

It can be helpful to look at a potential real-life situation to see how work values influence our choices. Visualize yourself 5 to 10 years from now and in a career transition. After an exhaustive search, you find yourself considering three job offers:

- One offer is with a local company. The position involves doing the work you want to do at this point in your career, but the salary offered is 10 percent below that of your last job.

- The second offer is for a job with the mix of functions you prefer and a salary comparable to your last position, but the job is located 800 miles from where you and your family currently reside.

- A third offer is for a position containing job functions you're familiar with and an opportunity to considerably increase your range of skills. While the salary offered is 20 percent below that of your last job, there is opportunity for profit sharing in this young, start-up company.

There is no single right choice; each of us has a different right choice, depending on what is important to us. A careful review of your values can help you to make the best choice at that time. Decisions are also influenced by other personal considerations. If your spouse or partner is employed or you have school-age children, relocation may be difficult. On the other hand, salary may be less important if your partner is employed.

Changing Social Values

Values are personal and individual, but they are also reflective of society. Following World War II, values in the U.S. workplace remained fairly consistent for the next 15 to 20 years. Workers valued security; they were loyal to their employer and expected to advance as a result of years of dedicated service. These workers respected management, which made all of the important decisions. Meanwhile, management often maintained its power by holding on to information, relaying to workers only what they needed to know to do their jobs.

Several culture-altering events occurred in the United States in the 1960s and 1970s, however, including the assassinations of several cherished leaders, the war in Vietnam, and the Watergate political scandal. As a result, a different set of values emerged in our society in the 1980s. These, too, were reflected in the workplace. Enticed by the rapid economic growth that occurred during the Reagan presidency, workers came to expect sizable pay raises and rapid advancement, based on their ability to perform rather than on their years of experience. If rewards were less than anticipated, workers moved to companies that rewarded performance. They shifted their loyalty from the company to themselves and their careers. Also characteristic of the post-Vietnam and post-Watergate period was the erosion of the public's trust and confidence in people in positions of authority, including bosses. At the same time, the information explosion resulting from computerization left managers in less powerful positions as information became accessible to most workers.

Values are personal, but they also reflect society

Although economic downturns had occurred in the 1970s and 1980s, none caused the dramatic shift in social order that characterized the recession of the late 1980s and early 1990s. Driven by the flagging economy, employers laid off thousands of workers across industries. The unwritten contract between employee and employer was breached. No longer would companies offer lifetime employment. Now, in prosperous times as well, each of us has to learn to manage our own work lives. Behaviors associated previously with highly motivated fast-trackers have become survival strategies for all workers.

These shifts in values and circumstances have been particularly troubling to midlife career changers who were raised with the values of the post–World War II era and have seen those values disappear in the post-Vietnam era.

While they were once respected for staying with the same company for many years, they now find themselves disadvantaged by this choice. The rules have changed. It has meant a difficult adjustment for them.

It is not unusual to experience values conflicts in your work life. A values conflict occurs, for instance, when you highly value honesty and integrity and your boss wants you to lie to a customer. Another values conflict occurs when you value the high quality of your work and an employer is more concerned about volume; this could apply to quantity of parts produced or number of people served. When you experience these conflicts in work situations, you can try to resolve them. While individual incidents may be tolerable, basic differences about what is important and how to perform professionally are difficult to live with for extended periods of time. Ultimately, if these conflicts cannot be resolved, you may have to change jobs in order to feel good about your work and yourself.

LIFESTYLE ALTERNATIVES

Lifestyle—choice or chance?

A common definition of *lifestyle* is a way of life that reflects your attitudes and values. Some people consciously choose a lifestyle, but most probably find their lifestyle evolving out of their work and the income it produces, their family, and their relationships.

How would you describe your lifestyle? Do you live a quiet life in a suburban town, working in a technical job in an office park, sending your children to public schools, and enjoying family vacations at the beach? Perhaps you are single and live in a big city, where you own a condominium, commute to and from work on public transportation, enjoy the theater, and occasionally escape to the mountains to relax and reenergize. Or maybe you run your own business in a small town where everyone knows your name, where no one is in a hurry, and where business is transacted on the golf course or in the bowling alley as often as in your shop.

Your lifestyle is determined in large part by financial realities. The greater your income and resources, the more options are open to you. Your lifestyle may also be defined by your primary relationship and the career choices made jointly with your partner. In traditional relationships, the husband typically pursued a career while the wife stayed home and managed the household and cared for children. In many contemporary relationships, both partners work outside the home. Two patterns have emerged among working couples. Dual-career couples are those in which both partners are pursuing full-time careers; if there are children, they are cared for by someone else, either in the home or at a day-care center. In the remaining dual-earning couples, one partner is usually pursuing a career, and the other has a full- or part-time job but is giving first priority to the family. Many people are struggling with the issue of balancing work and other areas of their lives. Resolving these issues is part of establishing a lifestyle.

Meanwhile, the number of single-parent households has grown rapidly in our country. Most of these are headed by women, and most fall below the poverty line. Even women with college degrees and solid work experience have trouble making ends meet after a divorce.

In this chapter, we have looked at your personal and family history to identify many influences that have shaped who you are and what you value. The next chapter focuses on other areas of the self-assessment process, an understanding of your personality and interests. As you study each facet of yourself, you will have new insights to apply in planning your future.

Affirmations: Reprogramming for Positive Self-Esteem

Purpose: The purpose of this exercise is to give you an opportunity to replace a negative message or belief you've been carrying with positive, affirming self-talk. Once you have learned the skill of reprogramming your "tapes," you can begin to eliminate other self-defeating messages.

Directions: Identify a negative message from your past that haunts you. Try to focus on one that plays frequently in your mind, one that prevents you from being fully who you are. You may need to jot down several negative messages before you select one that seems to regularly get in your way. Maybe the message is, "You'll never really amount to much," or "You'll never finish school," or "You are inadequate," or "You're not worthy of a good job, a good relationship . . ."

Once you've identified the message that holds you back, the next step is to create a new, positive, supportive message to replace the negative one. The new message should specifically counter the original demotivating message. "You'll never really amount to much" could be countered with "I am experiencing (or creating) success in my life." "You'll never finish school" could become "I am gradually, course by course, working toward completion of my certificate," and "You are inadequate" can be replaced with "I am a talented human being with valuable skills and ideas." The last slam can be reprogrammed as "I am worthy of a great job, a satisfying relationship . . ." These affirming messages specifically counter the negative messages mentioned earlier.

Notice that the original messages were in second person, you, while the positive self-talk that replaces the negative messages is in first person, I. The negative messages were often imposed on you by others; the new messages are being generated by you, and about yourself. Once you have the right new message, expand it into a positive, affirming message that you repeat frequently in your mind. This type of message is called an affirmation. Here are examples:

"I, Linda, am a creative and talented educator. I am worthy of a satisfying and enriching career in my field."

"I, Curtis, am a hardworking and dedicated employee. I am prepared to accept additional responsibilities in my job."

"I, Rafael, have many skills, abilities, and experiences to bring to a new career. I have prepared myself well for the change."

Create an affirmation for yourself and write it 10 times in the space provided below. Then repeat it in your mind at least 20 times a day for a week. Be sure to say it several times when you hear your old negative message playing. That message is an old habit, and it will take awhile to break. You will ultimately break it by replacing it with your new message. Another way to keep the affirmation prominently before you is to write it on pieces of paper that you tape to your bathroom mirror, computer screen, car visor, or other personal space.

....

Reflections: Finding the right affirmation may take some time. How is your affirmation working for you? Does it seem to be providing you with the positive message you need to counter old negative tapes?

Mentors

Purpose: We have been focusing on identifying and replacing negative messages. You also received plenty of positive input. This activity zeroes in on people who have had a positive impact on your life.

Directions: Along your life journey, you have no doubt met individuals you've admired—perhaps a teacher or boss, a coach, a fellow worker or volunteer, or a community leader. List the names of those who have made a positive impression on you. Next to each name, identify what it was that earned your admiration. Which of these traits have you adopted into your own personal characteristics? Circle the traits you have incorporated into your own behavior.

→ Mr McLead — french teacher
→ Aliza's friend
→ my dad — reliable, kind, integrity, rock solid & commnty
→ Uncle phil — all round competence and easy, gr

Reflections: Have you had positive role models in your life? How have they contributed to you? Have any of these people had a major impact on you over an extended period of time? If so, they may have served as mentors ("wise or trusted counselors or teachers," according to the dictionary). Do you have positive role models in your life now? If not, how can you find them?

→ Auntie 'Reen — calm + competent
    + unerring in follow through
    (the right amount, not
    too much, not too little)
→ Mark
→ my dad
→

CHAPTER FOUR

DISCOVERING YOUR PERSONALITY TYPE AND INTERESTS

In this chapter, we will examine two additional aspects of self-assessment: personality preferences and interests. Both of these areas provide useful insights into the way we prefer to behave in the world, the types of people we enjoy, and the environments to which we are drawn. This information can be used to identify careers that are likely to suit us and bring us satisfaction.

DETERMINE YOUR PERSONALITY PREFERENCES

Personality encompasses your distinctive traits of behavior and your individual thought processes. It is through looking at your personality that you come to appreciate your distinguishing personal character. While looking at your skills, interests, and values can provide information about what career you might pursue, an understanding of your personality reveals why a particular alternative may be right for you.

Your distinctive behaviors and ways of thinking contribute to your personality

Do you see yourself as highly energetic or easygoing? Driven or laid back? Optimistic or pessimistic? Outgoing or reserved? Organized and controlling or spontaneous and flexible? When you have problems to solve, do you approach them logically or emotionally? These questions are intended to help you see patterns in your behavior.

Understanding your personality can be enlightening. When you know your preferences, you may also find that you need or want to develop behaviors that will help you to be more effective in relation to others and more successful in your work. Preferring to be relaxed and laid back may simply be unacceptable in certain work settings, while it may be highly desirable in others.

Swiss psychoanalyst Carl Jung, who devoted his life to the study of human behavior, believed that individuals possess a "predisposition toward certain types of attitudes and consequently of behaviors stemming from those attitudes" (Singer, 1994, p. 324). He observed, for example, that people exhibited preferential attitudes for *extroversion* or *introversion*. Extroverts prefer to direct their attention to the outer world and to concern for others while introverts focus on their own inner world of thoughts and ideas. Jung also found patterns when he observed how people functioned, particularly when they became aware of people and things and then processed observations to come to conclusions. In other words, he looked at how they *perceived* and how they *judged*. Jung found that people relied on either their *senses* or their *intuition* when taking in information and demonstrated either *thinking* or *feeling* behaviors when making decisions.

Our personality predisposes us to certain attitudes and resulting behaviors

In later research into Jung's typology, Katharine Briggs identified an additional attitudinal pattern that adds considerably to the work of Jung. She observed that people demonstrate a preference for either *judging* or *perceiving*. Those who prefer judging approach life with the aim of ordering events and controlling others. Those who prefer perceiving approach life with the aim of experiencing and enjoying their lives by adapting to circumstances (Myers, 1986).

Before we discuss these personality patterns in more detail, it will be helpful if you complete the following exercise, which will shed light on your preferred attitudes and behaviors.

WORK IN PROGRESS

Your Personality Preferences

Purpose: This exercise explores your attitudes and preferred-behavior patterns and will provide you with insight into your personality. Understanding your personality can help you to identify careers that appeal to you and will likely be satisfying for you.

Directions: There are several pairs of sentences for each indicator. For each pair, place a check in front of the sentence that is more true of you. Select the choice that comes closest to your preference when you are relaxed at home. Try to avoid choosing how you wish you behaved or how you may be forced to behave in work situations. When you have made your selections for each indicator, total the checks and record your personality preference.

Indicator I: Do you focus your energy and attention on the outer world of people and things or the inner world of thoughts and ideas?

EXTROVERSION

.... I am primarily concerned with the well-being of others.

.... After a hard day's work, I like to spend time with family and friends.

✓ When someone asks me a question, I'll usually have an answer for them.

.... I enjoy it when the phone rings or coworkers stop by to chat.

✓ I tend to think out loud.

INTROVERSION

✓ I am primarily concerned with developing my own potential.

✓ After a hard day's work, I like to spend time alone.

.... I usually need to mull over a question in my mind before answering.

✓ I like to concentrate on my work; I don't appreciate interruptions.

.... I tend to do my thinking internally, privately.

(continued)

EXTROVERSION

.... At parties, I enjoy meeting new people.

✓ Looking back, I've pursued a lot of interests.

.... I really like to talk.

.... I have quite a few friends.

✓ I value the recognition I get from others.

Number of checks for Extroversion (E) __4__
Preference __I__

INTROVERSION

✓ At parties, I enjoy spending my time with a friend I know well.

.... Looking back, I've pursued a couple of strong interests in depth.

✓ I really like to ponder.

✓ I have a couple of close friends.

.... I am the best judge of my achievements.

Number of checks for Introversion (I) __6__

Indicator II: In new situations, how do you perceive what's going on? How do you take in information?

SENSING

✓ I tend to focus on facts and details.

✓ I take a practical and realistic approach to solving problems.

✓ I take things apart to figure out the whole.

✓ I prefer clear instructions.

✓ I like set procedures and established routines.

✓ I have great respect for hard work and perspiration.

.... I enjoy life in the present moment.

.... I have a passion for gadgets.

Number of checks for Sensing (S) __6__
Preference __N__

INTUITING

✓ I tend to see the "big picture."

✓ I look for imaginative solutions to problems.

✓ I observe trends and speculate about the future.

✓ I prefer to go with my hunches.

✓ I like change and variety and the chance to be inventive.

✓ I have great respect for ideas and inspirations.

✓ I live in a state of anticipation.

✓ I have a passion for possibilities.

Number of checks for Intuiting (N) __8__

Indicator III: How do you prefer to make decisions?

THINKING

✓ I tend to approach decisions logically and objectively.

.... I try to treat everyone equally.

✓ I analyze situations thoroughly.

✓ I rely on principles and standards.

✓ I have a tendency to "bottle" my emotions.

.... I remain cool, calm, and impersonal in tense situations.

.... I consider the criteria.

FEELING

.... I tend to approach decisions personally.

✓ I try to consider everyone involved.

.... I relate to others' feelings and concerns.

.... I depend on my personal values.

✓ I usually am able to express my feelings and convictions.

✓ I tend to get personally immersed.

✓ I consider extenuating circumstances.

(continued)

✓ It is important that I understand my feelings.

_____ I don't analyze my feelings; I simply experience them.

Number of checks for Thinking (T) __5__

Number of checks for Feeling (F) __3__

Preference __T__

Indicator IV: How do you approach your life and your dealings with other people?

JUDGING

✓ I usually wake up knowing what my day will be.

✓ I am driven to finalize a decision.

✓ In meetings, I tend to keep people on task.

_____ I'm a list maker and a list follower.

✓ I work incrementally toward dead-lines.

✓ I like to get plans scheduled on the calendar.

✓ I don't like to change my plans.

✓ I like to "run" things; then I know they're being run right.

✓ I enjoy finishing things.

Number of checks for Judging (J) __8__

Preference __J__

PERCEIVING

_____ In approaching the day, I welcome the unexpected.

_____ I gather information and consult with others as my decisions evolve.

_____ In meetings, I encourage open dis-cussion.

✓ When I make lists, I revise them fre-quently as my priorities change.

_____ I work best when under the pressure of a tight deadline.

_____ I like to keep my options open.

_____ I'm always willing to be flexible.

_____ I adapt easily to new situations and enjoy what comes along.

_____ I enjoy starting new projects.

Number of checks for Perceiving (P) __/__

You now have a four-letter score, with the letters representing your preferences among the indicators. Record your results here:

__E__ __N__ __F__ __J__

Explanation of the Indicators

Extroversion vs. Introversion

The first indicator looks at where you prefer to focus your energy and atten-tion: on the outer world of people and things or the inner world of thoughts and ideas. People who prefer the outer world, or _extroverts_, are typically out-going and sociable. They may be more concerned about the interests and well-being of others than of themselves. They tend to speak and act sponta-neously and, only later, reflect on what they've said and done. They often have a wide variety of interests and a large circle of friends. Extroverts are quite ver-bal, spontaneously sharing their thoughts and ideas aloud. Because of their external focus, they rely on the feedback of others when evaluating how they are doing. Typically, they prefer jobs in which they interact with other people.

People who prefer the inner world of thoughts and ideas, or _introverts_, are often reflective and value their privacy. They are more interested in knowing themselves and developing their individual potential than in excelling in the public domain. They set their own standards and assess themselves internally. Their interests tend to be highly focused, such that they may become expert in a defined area of specialization. While others may see them as quiet or reserved, they typically have lifelong, deep relationships with one or two close friends. They usually prefer work situations that allow them to concentrate on the task at hand.

Extroverts are usually energized by their interaction with other people, while introverts may be drained of energy in interaction. That is why you'll see introverts leaving parties an hour after they've arrived, while extroverts may outlast the host! If you need to spend time alone in order to recharge your batteries, you may be an introvert.

Sensing vs. Intuiting

The second indicator looks at how you become aware, how you take in information. The opposites in this case are *sensors*, who take in information through their five senses, focusing on details and facts, and *intuitors*, who take information in through their "sixth sense," looking for patterns and relationships.

Interaction with others typically energizes extroverts and exhausts introverts

Sensors are typically detail-oriented, practical individuals who are interested in observing the "precise nature of things." They "take apart things, data, and ideas, to see what makes them tick" (Singer, 1994, p. 330). By fitting together the parts, they will come to see the whole. Sensors tend to live in the present moment, they prefer set procedures and established routines, they derive satisfaction from seeing the tangible results of their labor, and they have an uncanny ability to retain facts.

Sensors carefully examine each tree; intuitors ponder the future of the forest

Intuitors see things whole and focus on their possibilities. They see trends, patterns, meanings, and relationships in the information they gather, but they pay little attention to the details and facts. In work settings, they are more interested in the big picture and its implications than in the day-to-day operations. They tend to be imaginative when it comes to solving problems. They prefer to follow their hunches rather than a set of directions. Intuitors live in a state of anticipation, speculating about the future. As a result, they often miss the present moment. They prefer change and variety and like opportunities for being inventive.

Thinking vs. Feeling

The third indicator assesses how you process information, make decisions, and determine a course of action: as a *thinker* who uses a step-by-step logical process or as a *feeler* who responds to personal values. Thinkers prefer to live in their heads; they are objective, logical, and analytical. In making decisions, they weigh the pros and cons, apply their own principles and standards, establish their objectives, and work toward the desired results. They are concerned about justice and fairness and tend to be critical. Typically, they enjoy a good argument. In a managerial role, they can appear impersonal and policy-driven. Thinkers do have feelings; however, it is important to them that they understand their feelings, which is an intellectual process.

For thinkers, emotions are understood in the mind; for feelers, emotions are experienced in the heart

Feelers live in their hearts; they tend to be emotional, empathic, and appreciative. They base their decisions on their own subjective values and personal convictions. These include "their sense of what is right or wrong, appropriate or inappropriate, [and] urgent or not urgent" (Singer, 1994, p. 331). Feeling decisions tend to be spontaneous responses, rather than responses derived from a reasoned process. As managers, feelers try to find solutions to problems that create harmony among differing viewpoints. They are concerned about how their decisions will impact on others. Feelers have a tendency to overextend themselves meeting the needs of others.

Judging vs. Perceiving

The fourth indicator looks at how you deal with the world around you, as a *judger* who decides to come to a conclusion or as a *perceiver* who continues to gather information and delays judgment. Since we don't seem to be able to judge and perceive at the same time, we tend to develop a preference for either the judging or perceiving function.

Judgers prefer orderliness and may be perceived as inflexible, while perceivers prefer adaptability and may be perceived as disorganized

Those who prefer to be judgers often try to control situations and other people. They prefer to handle life in a decisive, planned, orderly way. Once they've decided to do something, judgers can be dogged in their determination. They can also be opinionated. They tend to be well organized and usually prefer structured work environments. Often they will push for decisions and closure in meetings at work. They are results-oriented and plan projects well in advance to meet deadlines.

Perceivers deal with life in a spontaneous, flexible way, aiming to understand and experience life and adapt to situations as they come along. They can be difficult to pin down because they prefer to keep their options open. They tend to be open-minded, tolerant, and curious. They like loosely structured work environments, and in them they are process-oriented. For example, they pay attention to issues like how decisions are made and how people are treated. They often meet deadlines by last-minute, superhuman effort.

Understanding your personality preferences can give you valuable insights that you can apply to career options. You have reviewed the four preference indicators and identified your preferred-behavior patterns. The preferences can be combined into 16 possible personality types. Individuals of any personality type can pursue any career; those who choose careers compatible with their personality type, however, are likely to feel more satisfied in their choice because the functions they perform in their work will be behaviors they prefer and enjoy.

Personality preferences influence job satisfaction, not job success or failure

A simple example will help you see the connection between the preferences and job-related responsibilities. Receptionists greet visitors, answer telephones, give out information and directions, and generally promote the services of an establishment. As the first point of interface between the organization and the public, they set the tone for the communications that follow. Both extroverts and introverts can be receptionists, but extroverts will more naturally reach out to visitors and callers because they prefer interaction. Introverts prefer not to be interrupted, so they will have to overcome a subtle resistance to interacting each time someone walks in the door or calls on the phone. Introverted receptionists will be especially worn down by the end of the day because they are continually performing nonpreferred functions.

Try to imagine an accountant, a nurse, or a computer programmer who doesn't like details. Conversely, imagine a senior business executive, therapist, or politician who is consumed by details. The chart in Figure 4.1 suggests occupational fields that are compatible with specific personality preferences. These suggestions offer you a starting place for your exploration of career options. Later, you can also apply the information about your preferred behaviors when assessing occupations that appeal to you based on your interests or skills. Interests suggest what you like, skills suggest what you are good at, and personality preferences suggest *why* you may like and be good at certain things.

The lists of occupations that follow are organized according to personality preferences. The occupations have been chosen because the *functions performed in the occupations* tend to be activities that an individual of that personality type would enjoy and feel comfortable doing. People of different personality types are able to perform the same job; however, they may perform the duties differently because of their personality preferences. They may also experience more or less satisfaction because of their personality preferences.

These lists do not consider other indicators of career choice and satisfaction, such as level of education. Personality is one piece of the puzzle; skills, interests, and values are other important factors.

FIGURE 4.1

Occupations suggested by personality type.

ISTJ
Accountant
Administrator
Bank Examiner
Computer
   Programmer
Electrician
Financial Manager
IRS Agent
Librarian
Mechanical Engineer
Medicine
Paralegal
Pharmacist
Teacher
Technical Writer
Technician

ISTP
Athlete
Chiropractor
Computer
   Programmer
Construction Worker
Dental Hygienist
Economist
Electrical Engineer
Machine Operator
Market Analyst
Marketing/Sales
   Forecaster
Medical Technician
Product Designer
Purchasing Agent
Securities Analyst
Statistician
Surgeon

ESTP
Coach
Entrepreneur
Executive Architect
Land Developer
Personal Financial
   Planner
Pilot
Professional Athlete
Retail Sales
Stockbroker

Travel/Tour
   Operator
Wholesaler

ESTJ
Computer Analyst
Computer
   Technician
Dentist
General Contractor
Insurance Agent
Office Manager
Physician, General
   Medicine
Probation Officer
Real Estate Broker
Teacher, Trades
Technical Sales

ISFJ
Guidance Counselor
Health Care
   Administrator
Human Resources
   Manager
Medical Equipment
   Sales
Minister
Physical Therapist
Service Occupations
Social Worker
Teacher

ISFP
Artisan/Craftsperson
Artist
Chef
Construction
   Worker
Dancer
Fiction Writer
Forester
Health Service
   Worker
Musician
Visiting Nurse

ESFP
Artisan/Craftsperson

Caterer
Consultant
Musician
Politician
Public Relations
   Specialist
Salesperson
Small Business
   Owner
Special Events
   Planner

ESFJ
Child-Care Worker
Customer Service
   Representative
Fund-Raiser
Helping Professional
Nurse
Secretary
Service Occupations
Speech Pathologist

INFJ
Clergy
Counselor
Creative Writer
Human Resources
   Manager
Organization
   Development
   Consultant
Psychologist
Social Scientist

INFP
Architect
Artist
Biological Scientist
College Professor,
   Humanities
Counselor
Journalist
Linguist
Minister
Physician
Social Worker
Teacher
Therapist

ENFP
Advertising
   Specialist
Counselor
Employment
   Developer
Entrepreneur
   Human Services
Fund-Raiser
Human Resources
   Consultant
Politician
Public Relations
Sales Representative
Teacher, Liberal Arts

ENFJ
Advertising Account
   Executive
Arts Administrator
Career Counselor
Executive/Director
Manager, Nonprofit
   Organization
Psychiatrist
Psychologist
Sales Manager
Writer

INTJ
Academic Curri-
   culum Designer
Administrator
Biomedical Engineer
Electrical/Electronic
   Technician
Financial Consultant
Manager
Psychologist
Research Forecaster
Scientific Consultant
Scientist
Systems Designer

INTP
Academician
Analyst
Archaeologist
Architect

Attorney
Computer Software
   Designer
Economist
Engineer
Financial Analyst
Mathematician
Plastic Surgeon
Psychoanalyst
Research and
   Development
Scientist
Strategic Planner
Teacher

ENTP
Advertising Specialist
Business,
   Government, or
   Organizational
   Leader
Entrepreneur
Investment Banker
Journalist
Literary Agent
Management
   Consultant
Publisher
Venture Capitalist

ENTJ
Attorney
Business,
   Government, or
   Military Leader
Education or
   Hospital
   Administrator
Employment
   Development
   Specialist
Judge
Labor Relations
   Specialist
Marketer
Politician
Project Manager
Public Speaker
Social Scientist

Sources include Briggs Myers, Isabel. *Introduction to Type,* 5th ed., Palo Alto, CA: Consulting Psychologists Press, 1994; Tieger, Paul, and Barbara Barron-Tieger. *Do What You Are,* Boston: Little Brown, 1992; Tieger, Paul, and Barbara Barron-Tieger. *The Career/Life Planning Profiles,* self-published; and in-house material from various outplacement companies.

We have been making broad generalizations about preferred-behavior patterns, but it is important to remember that even within these patterns, individuals' personalities differ tremendously. Variation in the strength of individuals' preferences on the four indicators, as well as the 16 possible combinations of those preferences, accounts for the wide variety in personalities. It is our intention to help you appreciate patterns in behavior, not simply to label people.

If you would like to know more about your personality type, ask your instructor about taking the Myers-Briggs Type Indicator (MBTI). This standardized instrument, developed by Katharine C. Briggs and Isabel Briggs Myers, is based on the theory of Carl Jung. An excellent tool, it is widely used in career planning. Once you have taken the MBTI and received a thorough interpretation of the results, you may want to read more about personality types. At the end of the chapter, we have listed some resources. Personality and interests are closely intertwined, as you will see in the next section.

PINPOINT YOUR PARTICULAR INTERESTS

When asked about your interests, do you reel off dozens of activities, causes, subjects, and so forth that you thoroughly enjoy pursuing? Some people have many different interests. Others have a few focused interests that they pursue avidly. Still others have relatively few interests and tend to fill their free time with passive activities such as watching television. You can pursue interests through TV viewing, or you can use it as a time killer by watching programs that entertain you rather than stimulate your thinking.

Interests lead to active involvement

Interests involve you in some active way. If you're a sports enthusiast, even of the spectator variety, you probably follow and root for certain teams; you may know the names of particular players and remember the team's past performance. Perhaps you watch the games with other fans or rehash them the next day with fellow enthusiasts. That's an active interest.

As part of your self-assessment, you may find it helpful to identify not only current interests but also interests you've had at different times in your life. Remembering childhood interests can be a beneficial part of self-discovery because they often contain clues about our original selves that may have been lost or thwarted over the years. Interests can provide valuable material for expanding career options.

WORK IN PROGRESS

Charles

Charles had worked successfully for many years in the restaurant business, most recently as manager in a rather exclusive establishment. Feeling burned out, Charles wanted to change careers. A major criterion for his next career was to find work that left his evenings free. During his self-assessment, Charles shared with the class that he was interested in antiques, especially 17th- and 18th-century French decorative accessories. Together, he and the group identified over 25 related occupations that Charles could investigate, including antique dealer, museum curator, cataloguer, buyer, researcher, writer, instructor, consignor, restorer, and antique show coordinator.

Charles spent several months exploring options. Eventually, he chose to become an antique dealer in a group facility where independent dealers rented stalls. Overhead was relatively low. In this setting, he could work out coverage with other dealers; this permitted him to continue restaurant work part-time until his business became profitable. His long-term goal is to own a shop in a beautiful colonial home in Maine.

Professor John Holland has made a notable contribution to the field of career development. Holland contends that people are attracted to careers by their personalities and interests. He sees career choice as a way to express yourself and extend yourself into the world of work. Holland's theory can be most easily remembered by linking it with the expression "birds of a feather flock together." We will look at Holland's work in detail, but first complete the following exercise. If you are interested in taking the Holland Assessment, please check with your instructor or your local or campus career center.

Interests Survey

WORK IN PROGRESS

Purpose: This survey will help you to identify personal interest areas. Since interests are an expression of your personality, they may suggest careers likely to be satisfying to you.

Directions: Complete the survey below to discover your current interest patterns. Do not be concerned about whether you have the skill or ability to perform each of the tasks listed. Simply answer based on how much you think you would enjoy participating in that activity.

For each item listed below, place an *x* in the appropriate column. Each column has an assigned value: 5 = like strongly, 2 = like, 0 = dislike. When you have completed the survey, go back over it to score each section. Directions for scoring appear at the end of the survey.

1. *Realistic:* Preference to work with your hands, machines, or tools

5	2	0	
		0	operate a crane, backhoe, or riding mower
		0	repair electrical appliances
	2		cut and split wood
	2		operate telecommunications equipment
	2		cook a meal for a large group
		0	cut out material from patterns
		0	make a wooden fixture
		0	repair a bicycle
		0	network computers within a company
		0	assemble a barbecue grill
	2		plant bushes and trees
	2		paint houses or furniture
		0	rebuild the engine of a car or truck
	2		troubleshoot a problem with equipment
	12	0	SUBTOTALS
12/15			TOTAL SCORE

2. *Investigative:* Interest in work that involves math and science

5	2	0	
_____	_____	_____ ⃝	solve mathematical puzzles
_____	_____	_____ ⃝	use statistical data to solve problems
_____	_____	_____ ⃝	build a model or prototype
_____	_2_	_____	learn to navigate by the stars
_____	_____	_____ ⃝	conduct laboratory experiments using chemicals
_____	_____	_____ ⃝	dissect animals
_____	_____	_____ ⃝	visit a planetarium
_____	_2_	_____	grow vegetables or flowers
_____	_2_	_____	watch shows about wildlife
_____	_2_	_____	learn theories about the origin of Earth
_5_	_____	_____	conduct research of any kind (e.g., scientific, social, economic, psychological, historical)
_5_	_____	_____	read about new discoveries in health, medicine, science, industry, or business
_____	_____	_____	develop a study to investigate an area of particular interest to you
_10_	_8_	_0_	SUBTOTALS
	_18/65_		TOTAL SCORE

3. *Artistic:* Interest that involves the production of original work using various media

5	2	0	
_____	_____	_____ ⃝	perform creative dance
_____	_2_	_____	design a magazine cover
_____	_2_	_____	sketch or paint
_____	_2_	_____	make scenery for a theater production
_____	_2_	_____	redecorate a room with flair
_____	_2_	_____	write short stories, plays, or poetry
_____	_2_	_____	play a musical instrument
_____	_2_	_____	write music
_____	_____	_____ ⃝	design original jewelry
_____	_____	_____ ⃝	make fashion statements with attire
_____	_2_	_____	visit art museums and galleries
_5_	_____	_____	collect and display beautiful objects
_____	_2_	_____	act in a play
_5_	_____	_____	take photographs of interesting things, scenes, or people

_____	2	_____	arrange a floral bouquet
5	_____	_____	design a logo
15	20	0	SUBTOTALS
35/80			TOTAL SCORE

4. *Social:* Interest in serving people's needs (personal, health, educational, social)

5	2	0	
5	_____	_____	carry on a conversation with friends
_____	2	_____	help people in trouble
_____	2	_____	belong to clubs, organizations, or teams
_____	_____	0	nurse a sick friend back to health
5	_____	_____	teach people about health or safety
5	_____	_____	study behavioral psychology
_____	2	_____	make personal sacrifices to help others
5	_____	_____	counsel people with problems
5	_____	_____	listen to both sides of an argument and mediate a solution
_____	2	_____	raise funds for a good cause
_____	2	_____	care for infants or young children
5	_____	_____	visit with an elderly person living alone
5	_____	_____	create a safe and supportive environment
5	_____	_____	work on personal growth either independently or in a group setting
5	_____	_____	feel deep concern for social ills
5	_____	_____	find ways to contribute to society
50	10	0	SUBTOTALS
60/80			TOTAL SCORE

5. *Enterprising:* Desire to work in some area related to the competitive business world

5	2	0	
5	_____	_____	canvass for a political candidate
_____	_____	0	sell products door-to-door
_____	_____	0	give public speeches
5	_____	_____	persuade others to do things my way
5	_____	_____	establish a small business
_____	_____	0	supervise other workers
_____	2	_____	invest in the stock market

_____	_____	O	discuss political issues
5	_____	_____	"wheel and deal"
_____	_____	O	search high and low for bargains
_____	2	_____	hold a leadership position in an organization
_____	_____	O	organize a committee to solve a problem
_____	_____	O	negotiate contracts
5	_____	_____	see business opportunities in everyday life
5	_____	_____	take risks for something I believe in
5	_____	_____	develop a marketing strategy for a new product
35	4	O	SUBTOTALS
	39/80		TOTAL SCORE

6. *Conventional*: Preference for well-ordered work environments involving systematic activities

5	2	0	
_____	_____	O	read or interpret construction blueprints
_____	_____	O	program a computer
_____	_____	O	produce mechanical or technical drawings by hand or by computer
5	_____	_____	appraise value of a real estate property
5	_____	_____	maintain office records and files
_____	_____	O	edit a manuscript for a publisher
_____	_____	O	process insurance claims
_____	_____	O	prepare tax returns for others
_____	_____	O	record and interpret statistical data
5	_____	_____	check bank statements for errors
5	_____	_____	make hotel and plane reservations for travelers
_____	_____	O	maintain patients' medical records for a hospital
20	O	O	SUBTOTALS
	20/65		TOTAL SCORE

Scoring the interest survey: Score each section of the survey separately. First, count the number of X's in each column and multiply by the value at the top of that column. Second, add the subtotals together and write your score for the section on the "TOTAL SCORE" line.

Transfer your total scores from each of the six areas to the categories listed below:

___12___ Realistic   ___60___ Social

___18___ Investigative   ___39___ Enterprising

___35___ Artistic   ___20___ Conventional

When you have scores recorded for all six sections, list the top three sections in descending order:

1. SOCIAL   S

2. ENTERPRISING   E

3. ARTISTIC   A

Within the work world, Holland sees certain occupational stereotypes. When you choose a career, you identify with occupational functions and work environments. Individuals experience career satisfaction when they are well matched for the job they do. Holland's major points are the following:

1. In our culture, most persons can be categorized as one of six types: realistic, investigative, artistic, social, enterprising, or conventional.

2. There are also the same six kinds of environments: realistic, investigative, artistic, social, enterprising, and conventional.

3. People search for environments that will let them exercise their skills and abilities, express their attitudes and values, and take on agreeable problems and roles.

4. People's behavior is determined by an interaction between their personality and the characteristics of their environment (Holland, 1985, pp. 2–4).

Holland provides detailed descriptions of the six personality types in the paragraphs that follow (1985, pp. 13–17). Read the description for your highest scoring type first. Look next at your second-highest preference and then your third. Some people identify strongly with a single personality type, while others seem to be a blend of two or three types. Next, read about all six of the types so you can compare your preferences to others.

Realistic Types

Realistic types are often rugged, practical, physically strong, and stable individuals. Typically, they like to work outdoors using tools, operating heavy machinery, or handling animals. They usually prefer to deal with things rather than with people or ideas. As a result, they tend to develop manual, mechanical, agricultural, electrical, and technical competencies. You will find realistic types in positions such as mechanics, construction workers, farmers, fish and wildlife managers, laboratory technicians, some engineering specialties, some military jobs, and skilled trades.

Investigative Types

Investigative types are drawn to scientific activities and solving abstract problems. Systematic observers, they are driven to understand the physical world. They often become methodical, analytical, rational, and intellectual as they develop competencies in math and science. They may also become highly creative, original thinkers. They work well with data and things and are less concerned with people. Investigative types thrive in careers as engineers, biologists, biotechnology researchers, social scientists, physicists, technical writers, and meteorologists.

Artistic Types

Artistic types prefer activities that allow them to express themselves through their particular art medium. They often prefer to work alone. They typically become competent in the areas of language, art, music, drama, or writing, and they develop personality traits of being imaginative, expressive, original, unconventional, intuitive, independent, and idealistic. They may also be sensitive and emotional. Career choices include artist, author, cartoonist, musician, singer, songwriter, drama coach, poet, actor or actress, and symphony conductor.

Social Types

Social types are humanistic, responsible, and concerned with the welfare of others. They are usually articulate and get along well with other people. Preferring to solve problems through discussions with others, they have little interest in working with machinery or analyzing data. They are drawn toward activities that train, develop, or cure other people; thus they develop competencies in human relations, education, and interpersonal communication. They are usually seen as cooperative, helpful, insightful, persuasive, and tactful. Occupational preferences include schoolteacher, marriage counselor, youth worker, clinical psychologist, speech therapist, minister, and career counselor.

Enterprising Types

Enterprising types often have great facility with words and use that ability in persuasive pursuits, such as leading and selling. They may focus on organizational goals or on personal economic or political gain, developing leadership, interpersonal, or persuasive competencies. They are often adventurous, ambitious, energetic, enthusiastic, domineering, and self-confident. They are not particularly good with details, precision work, or lengthy intellectual effort. They enjoy power, status, and material wealth. They do well in careers such as business executives, buyers, real estate practitioners, hotel managers, politicians, salespersons, sports promoters, and television producers.

Conventional Types

Holland types—
"birds of a
feather flock
together"

Conventional types prefer the highly ordered activities that comprise office work. These include the systematic manipulation of data, such as filing and maintaining records, and operating computers and business machinery. They are most comfortable in structured organizations with a well-defined chain of command and clearly stated expectations. Their competencies are in the areas of clerical, computational, and business systems. Typically, they are seen as efficient, conscientious, persistent, practical, dependable, and conforming. They frequently choose careers as bookkeepers, computer operators, inventory controllers, tax experts, statisticians, traffic managers, bank tellers, financial analysts, and some accounting positions.

Reflections: Which of the Holland "types" best described you? Were there any surprises in your results from this activity? Go back and review the characteristics of the preferences you chose. Do they fairly accurately describe you?

Holland developed a hexagonal model for his theory of types. He believed that we have more in common with types located close to us on the model and less in common with those types opposite us. Figure 4.2 is a diagram explaining this phenomenon. Are your second and third preferences next to or opposite your first choice?

This exercise linked your preferred interests with your preferred personality type and environment. To get a more accurate assessment based on this model, you will have to complete a standardized test. The Strong Vocational Interest Blank, Holland's Self-Directed Search, and the Harrington O'Shea Career Decision-Making System are all based on or normed to Holland's theory. Your instructor may be planning to give you a standardized interest inventory.

When you have your Holland type, based on one of these assessments, you can use it to look up career options that are compatible with your interests and personality, according to Holland. You can do this by using the *Directory of Holland Occupational Codes* (Gottfredson, Holland, & Ogawa, 1982) or *Making Vocational Choices* (Holland, 1985).

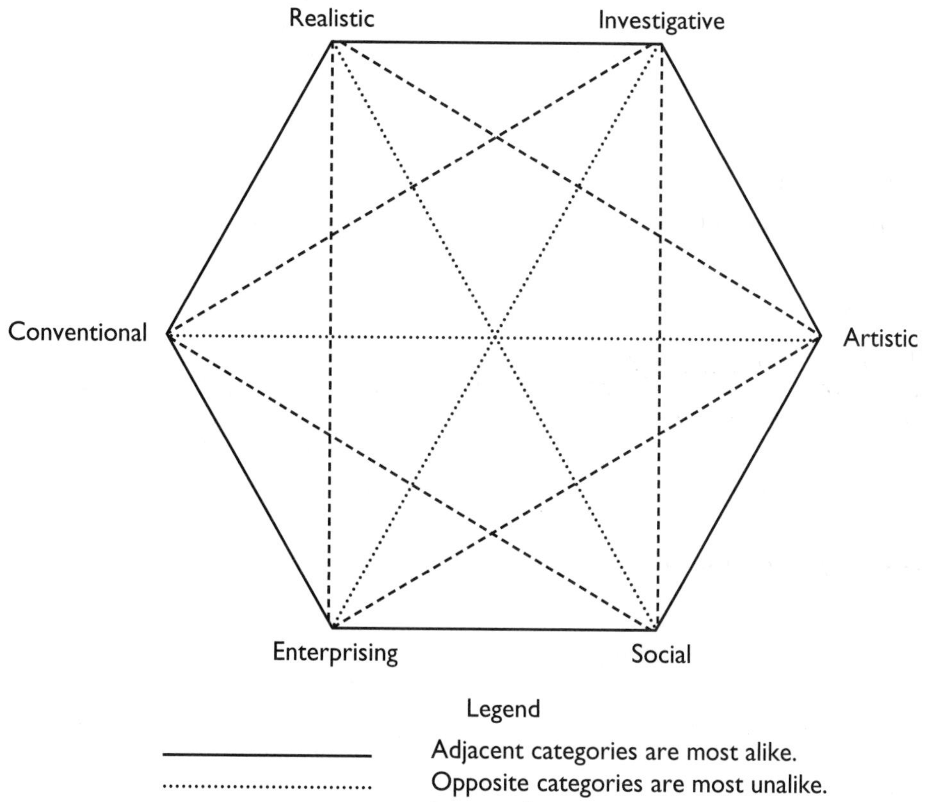
Realistic
Investigative
Conventional
Artistic
Enterprising
Social
Legend
Adjacent categories are most alike.
Opposite categories are most unalike.
Intermediate categories are somewhat alike.

FIGURE 4.2

Holland hexagon of personality types.

FIGURE 4.3

Examples of occupations and careers suggested by Holland three-letter codes.

AEI

fashion artist
package designer
patent agent
screenwriter

ISE

director of speech and hearing
nurse anesthetist
pediatrician
product safety engineer

SER

air traffic coordinator
detective
manager/supervisor
wildlife agent

REI

aircraft mechanic
building equipment inspector
quality control inspector
technician
wastewater-treatment plant operator

ISR

biologist
dietitian
food tester
mineralogist
optometrist

SEC

customer service representative
dispatcher
teacher

SEA

caseworker ✕
home economist ?
occupational therapist ?
social worker ✕

RSC

bicycle repairer
excavator
finishing machine operator
mechanical inspector

If your three-letter code is SEA, look up careers under that listing first. Then look up career options for SAE, EAS, ESA, ASE, and AES. You will find that by reordering your preferences, you can generate variations on the suggested occupations. See Figure 4.3 for sample occupations suggested by the Holland three-letter codes.

Many people choose careers because someone has told them that the field is "hot" and there will be opportunity. Remember the "plastics" scene from the movie *The Graduate*? There is nothing wrong with choosing a career based on future projections if you are selecting a field that is of great interest to you. Individuals who make career choices with no personal interest in the subject area or field chosen tend to be less satisfied and less successful than those who choose careers compatible with their interests. In classrooms and career centers, instructors and counselors see hundreds of students pursuing majors that they dislike, preparing for fields they hope will make them rich. It's sad. How much more energy they would bring to their work if they loved it. And how much more satisfaction they would experience if they were enthusiastic about what they were doing. There are millions of people who are miserable in their jobs because they chose occupations for the wrong reasons. This book will help you to know yourself better and use that self-understanding to find a career path that brings you joy and fulfillment.

The more you love your work, the less it feels like work

This chapter has focused on your personality preferences and your personal interests and will provide you with useful information and self-knowledge in your quest for a satisfying career or series of careers. The more you know about what draws your attention and why that happens, what excites your energy and challenges your mind, the better informed you will be in making life choices.

A lot of work is involved in thoroughly assessing yourself. Remember that the purpose is to get to know yourself better so you can make appropriate decisions about your future. In the next chapter, you will have an opportunity to thoroughly assess your skills and abilities, yet another "piece of the puzzle" contributing to your heightened self-awareness.

Identifying Interests

WORK IN PROGRESS

4.3

Purpose: This exercise explores your interests using different kinds of questions from the ones previously asked. Perhaps it will shed new light on what is of interest to you. These questions focus mainly on your leisure-time activities.

Directions: Relax and let your mind wander as you consider your answers to the following questions. Write your responses in the space provided.
When you pick up a newspaper, what sections do you read first?

> Art + Leisure
> Books
> Travel

What television shows do you enjoy watching? Is there a theme, such as law enforcement or comedy?

> Comedy, esp. Romantic Comedy,
> E - Ent't, etc
> 60 min

What recreational activities and hobbies do you engage in? Think of things you do outdoors as well as indoors, especially seasonal activities. What games do you play? What do you enjoy doing in your free time?

> Travel Planning, Sorting out Paperwork, Cooking
> Yoga, Travel, Hiking, Walking, Camping,
> Ocean - Gazing,

With so many people experiencing role overload these days, the notion of free time may seem elusive. If that is the case, think about the things you miss doing, the things you'd like to do if you had spare time. Suppose someone gave you a gift of two days to be spent any way you wanted *except* catching up or dealing with life's demands. The two days are for indulgence, for pleasure, for feeding your soul. What would you do with your gift of time?

> Yoga, Pottering About, Planning Travel,

When you enter a bookstore to browse, what sections are you drawn to? What kinds of books, magazines, and newspapers do you like?

> Travel, Holistic Medicine,
> Hollywood News, Latest Fiction - People's
> Exploration

What Internet sites do you regularly visit? What interests do they represent?

NetFlix, BayArea.com/Ent'T, Hotmail,

Imagine you are given a day to spend with an interesting person of your choice. Whom would you choose? The person you choose can be real or imaginary (such as a character from a novel) and can be alive or deceased. Why did you make the choice you made?

→ *My Dad -- get his guidance on my life now -- to tell him again how wonderful a person he was.*

→ *Female Entrepreneur -- ask what motivated her to get there.*

Among celebrities, famous people, or people on the world stage, whom do you find interesting? What makes them interesting to you?

Glamourous Couples -- voyeurism.
Famous People who seem to do so much -- how do they do it, I bet.
Singer/Songwriter -- magic of tune + a song all in inside you.

Which courses do/did you find most enjoyable and stimulating in school?

Math, Drama, Sociology, Languages *

What kinds of music and art appeal to you? What concerts or other kinds of performances have you been to lately? How do you express your artistic side?

Never been able to classify my artistic tastes
Folk Music -- special lyrics + gentle music

How do you express your creativity? What crafts have you tried? What new culinary wonders have you produced? What else?

Poetry, Travel, Desc, Music, Cooking,
Apt Decorate

What kinds of places do you like to visit? What do you like to do there?

Everywhere! Diff cultures, Diff ways of doing things

Imagine that you have won some kind of major sweepstakes and that money is no longer a concern for you. With complete financial independence assured, how would you spend your time?

Small cottage by ocea
Travelling
Massage Therapy in other Holistic
Gardens
Having friends + family from Cda + UK
Kona west -- help the poor the world

Reflections: What patterns can you identify in the responses given above? What clues can you find that could indicate new areas for career exploration, based on your personal interests?

Time to Explore
Social Counsellor

RESOURCES FOR FURTHER EXPLORATION
OF PERSONALITY TYPE

Hirsh, Sandra, and Jean Kummerow. *Life Types.* New York: Warner Books, 1989.

Kroeger, Oho, and Janet M. Thuesen. *Type Talk.* New York: Dell, 1989.

Tieger, Paul D., and Barbara Barron-Tieger. *Do What You Are*, 2nd ed. Boston: Little, Brown, 1995.

SKILLS IDENTIFICATION WORKSHEET
Continued.

Achievements

Predicting					
Preparing					
Prioritizing					
Streamlining					
LEADERSHIP					
Building consensus					
Coaching					
Empowering					
Envisioning					
Influencing					
Initiating					
Inspiring					
Motivating					
Navigating political waters					
Politicking					
Recruiting					
Setting/achieving goals					
Visioning					
MANAGEMENT					
Administering					
Allocating resources					
Assessing skills, priorities					
Deciding					
Delegating					
Evaluating					
Monitoring					
Negotiating					
Running meetings					
Supervising					
HUMAN DEVELOPMENT					
Coaching					
Counseling					
Empathizing					

SKILLS IDENTIFICATION WORKSHEET
Continued.

Achievements

Guiding/advising					
Healing/curing					
Intuiting					
Listening					
Rehabilitating					
Supporting					
Understanding					
PROBLEM-SOLVING					
Handling complaints					
Investigating					
Locating					
Mediating					
Observing					
Obtaining information					
Researching					
Resolving					
Troubleshooting					
CREATIVE					
Decorating					
Designing					
Developing					
Displaying					
Dramatizing					
Entertaining					
Innovating					
Inventing					
Visualizing					
ARTISTIC					
Designing					
Drawing/painting					
Illustrating					
Sketching					
Styling					

SKILLS IDENTIFICATION WORKSHEET
Continued.

Achievements

Working with shapes, colors					

PERFORMING
Acting					
Dancing					
Playing music					
Singing					

MANUAL
Adjusting					
Assembling					
Constructing					
Developing muscle coordination					
Handling with precision					
Having manual dexterity					
Installing					
Maintaining					
Operating equipment					
Repairing/fixing					
Using tools/instruments					

MAINTENANCE
Carrying out requests					
Compiling					
Handling detail work					
Record keeping					
Serving					
Setting up					
Updating					

INTELLECTUAL
Abstracting					
Analyzing					
Classifying					
Conceptualizing					
Questioning					

SKILLS IDENTIFICATION WORKSHEET
Continued.

Achievements

Reading					
Reasoning					
Remembering					
Testing					
JUDGMENT					
Appraising					
Deciding					
Editing					
Evaluating					
Examining					
Hiring and firing					
Inspecting					
Reviewing					
Weighing alternatives					
COPING					
Accepting criticism					
Asserting					
Enduring long hours					
Getting along with others					
Hurrying					
Persevering					
Waiting					
Working under pressure					
MANAGING RESOURCES					
Acquiring					
Allocating					
Budgeting					
Calculating					
Collecting					
Counting					
Estimating					
Fund-raising					

SKILLS IDENTIFICATION WORKSHEET
Continued.

Achievements

Inventorying					
Protecting					
Reconciling					
Recording					
INFORMATION					
Acquiring					
Attending to detail					
Classifying					
Communicating					
Distributing					
Evaluating					
Interpreting					
Maintaining					
Manipulating					
Organizing					
Processing with computers					
Updating					
Using					
SYSTEMS					
Applying technology					
Correcting malfunctions					
Designing					
Entering data					
Improving systems technology					
Maintaining equipment					
Monitoring performance					
Selecting technology					
Troubleshooting					
Understanding complex interrelationships					
Using graphics					
Using spreadsheets					
Word processing					

PART TWO

Directions: When you have completed the worksheet, go over the items and circle any skills that you have checked in four or five columns. To do this, scan the blocks horizontally. These skills represent your strongest functional skills. Also note skill clusters containing numerous check marks. Skill clusters are the groupings such as Leadership and Communication, with related skills listed underneath them. Looking at your strongest functional skills, which ones do you enjoy using and therefore want to use in your next career? List your 10 strongest and preferred functional skills below:

1. ....
2. ....
3. ....
4. ....
5. ....

6. ....
7. ....
8. ....
9. ....
10. ....

Reflections: Now that you have identified and evaluated your functional skills, are you surprised to find that you have many well-developed skills? Can you see their value in the marketplace?

The final list, containing your strongest and most marketable skills, will be useful when you are writing your resume and cover letters. You will also find it beneficial to emphasize these skills when you are interviewing. As you can see, you will bring many abilities to the positions for which you apply.

ADAPTIVE SKILLS

Adaptive skills describe personal qualities that affect work habits and work ethics

Adaptive skills are personal qualities you possess that make you a desirable (or undesirable) employee. Like functional skills, adaptive skills are portable. They can be transferred from one job or field to another. Adaptive skills relate to your work habits. Employers want to hire people they can rely on to produce for them. It is important to any hiring organization that its employees fulfill their responsibilities and do so in a timely manner. They must also be courteous to one another and to customers. Depending on the culture of the organization and the requirements of the job, some adaptive skills may be more important than others. While we're all different and have different skill sets, the following list will give you an idea of the kinds of qualities encompassed by adaptive skills:

conscientious	enthusiastic
trustworthy	even-tempered
energetic	self-confident
self-disciplined	tenacious
considerate	friendly
dependable	resourceful
respectful	patient
ambitious	diplomatic

Identifying Adaptive Skills

Purpose: The adaptive skills exercise that follows will help you to identify your work style and work habits.

PART ONE

Directions: Place a check mark next to each word that you feel accurately describes one of your work traits. You may want to make copies of this list before you write on it so you can ask a colleague or supervisor to evaluate your adaptive skills as well. When you have finished selecting your adaptive skills, you will find further instructions at the end of the list.

ADAPTIVE SKILLS CHECKLIST

_____ Adaptable	_____ Enthusiastic	_____ Poised
_____ Adventurous	_____ Experienced	_____ Polite
_____ Alert	_____ Expressive	_____ Precise
_____ Ambitious	_____ Firm	_____ Punctual
_____ Assertive	_____ Flexible	_____ Receptive
_____ Astute	_____ Forthcoming	_____ Reliable
_____ Authentic	_____ Frank	_____ Resourceful
_____ Aware	_____ Friendly	_____ Respectful
_____ Calm	_____ Generous	_____ Responsible
_____ Candid	_____ Genuine	_____ Responsive
_____ Committed	_____ Honest	_____ Risk-taking
_____ Competent	_____ Humane	_____ Self-confident
_____ Conscientious	_____ Imaginative	_____ Self-controlled
_____ Cooperative	_____ Initiating	_____ Self-reliant
_____ Courageous	_____ Innovative	_____ Self-starter
_____ Creative	_____ Insightful	_____ Sense of humor
_____ Curious	_____ Integrity	_____ Sensitive
_____ Decisive	_____ Judgment	_____ Sincere
_____ Democratic	_____ Loyal	_____ Sophisticated
_____ Dependable	_____ Objective	_____ Spontaneous
_____ Diligent	_____ Open	_____ Strong
_____ Diplomatic	_____ Open-minded	_____ Successful
_____ Direct	_____ Optimistic	_____ Sympathetic
_____ Discreet	_____ Original	_____ Tactful
_____ Driven	_____ Outgoing	_____ Talented
_____ Dynamic	_____ Outstanding	_____ Tenacious
_____ Easygoing	_____ Patient	_____ Thorough
_____ Effective	_____ Perceptive	_____ Tolerant
_____ Efficient	_____ Persistent	_____ Trustworthy
_____ Empathic	_____ Pioneering	_____ Versatile
_____ Energetic	_____ Playful	_____ Warm

PART TWO

Directions: When you have checked all items that apply to you, review the list and circle the five items you feel are your strongest and most marketable adaptive skills. Record these work traits below, in the column on the left. Beside each, give examples you would use in a job interview to demonstrate mastery of the skill. A sample is provided.

ADAPTIVE SKILLS	EXAMPLES
trustworthy	*Closed store every night. Cashed out registers, activated alarm system, made bank deposits.*

Reflections: Did you find any surprises when you looked at your adaptive skills? Do you see the positive qualities you have developed? If you have asked someone else to complete this assessment of your adaptive skills, how do the results compare? What do the results tell you about your self-perceptions?

Employers will be interested in knowing about your adaptive skills. You can communicate these skills in your resume, cover letters, and job interviews. Be ready with examples that illustrate how you developed or demonstrated these skills in previous work situations.

WORK CONTENT SKILLS

Work content skills are specific to jobs or occupations

Work content skills are specific skills and knowledge required for specific occupations. For example, a business applications computer programmer may be required to know COBOL or C++, both of which are computer programming languages. An accountant may be required to know how to use Lotus 1-2-3, a software package used for spreadsheets. A pharmaceutical salesperson must have in-depth knowledge of the product line, and a medical insurance adjuster must know medical terminology. An automobile mechanic must know the parts of an engine and how to maintain and repair them.

These examples give you a sense of work content skills. Some occupations require a tremendous number of work content skills, while others require fewer specific skills and less comprehensive knowledge. In some fields, the content knowledge can be learned on the job, while in other fields, entry-level applicants are expected to have specific academic training.

For many positions in the financial services industry (banking, insurance, investments), for instance, a bachelor's degree in the liberal arts is sufficient education. Specific knowledge about business practices, the industry, and the products and services of the company are gained by employees after they are hired.

Conversely, many medical and technical occupations seek candidates with degrees and certificates representing knowledge/competence in specific content areas. Examples include the engineering disciplines, such as mechanical, civil, and electrical, and medical occupations, such as nurse, radiology technician, and physical therapist. Entrance to many of these occupations is governed by state or national certification requirements, and colleges design their programs to meet these requirements.

If you are planning to change careers, analyzing your skills and carefully researching the requirements of the fields you are considering will take most of the mystery out of the process. When you understand what is needed in a new field and how your skills mesh with the requirements, you will also see the specific content knowledge you may need to acquire to become a viable candidate for hire. For example, a position advertised in the newspaper may list a degree in business as a requirement. By decoding the job, however, you may find that with your previous schooling and work experience, you may only need a series of specific courses in accounting to be able to do the job.

What work content skills do you possess? To answer this question, you will need to carefully review your educational background and work experience. Knowledge acquired through personal reading, pursuing interests and hobbies, and volunteering may also be applicable.

Debbie had a degree in dance and had taught as well as performed professionally for six years. When Debbie was 30, she and her husband decided to have children. She put her career on hold for several years and devoted her energy to managing her household and raising her family. When she was ready to reenter the workforce, she no longer wanted to dance professionally.

While a full-time homemaker, Debbie had served on the board of an arts guild in her town. She also initiated and ran an after-school program that offered courses ranging from computers to crafts. Both roles involved hiring personnel, developing and managing budgets, writing promotional literature and grant proposals, and designing programs.

These experiences had allowed Debbie to expand her functional and work content skills. After identifying her skills, she felt qualified to pursue a career in arts management.

WORK IN PROGRESS

Debbie

Work Content Skills

Purpose: This exercise is designed to help you identify, analyze, and record your work content skills.

PART ONE

Directions: Analyzing your work content skills requires detailed thinking about your experience. Review your background and assess the areas where you have acquired content knowledge. To do this, start with all of your educational endeavors. What knowledge did you gain from courses, seminars, training programs? Next, look at all of your previous work experience and volunteer experiences in chronological order. What did you learn in each position? Finally, consider interests, hobbies, and independent reading. What have you learned through these pursuits?

The form provided below will help you to organize this information. If you have difficulty figuring out where your content knowledge is usable (third column), ask for help in class. Your instructor and your classmates may have useful input. Sample entries are provided to help you get started.

WORK IN PROGRESS

5.4

Knowledge Areas	How Acquired	Where Usable
Mutual funds	On the job at State Street Bank	Other banking jobs; investment companies; consultant on financial services
Statistics	Took 2 courses	Most business positions; some nonprofit jobs; research and analysis positions
U.S. Army inventory systems	20 years' experience; enlisted	Manufacturing companies, especially defense industries

WORK CONTENT SKILLS WORKSHEET

Knowledge Areas	How Acquired	Where Usable
(from educational pursuits)		

(from work experience and volunteer activities)

(from interests, hobbies, and independent reading)

....
....
....
....
....
....
....
....
....
....
....

PART TWO

Directions: When you have identified your work content knowledge, your final analysis involves deciding on the work content skills you want to take with you into your next career. On your list, circle the items you most want to use in your next position.

Reflections: As you have probably discovered in this exercise, you have learned a great deal over the years, and you have learned in many different ways. How do you feel about the work content skills you have gained? Do you have more knowledge than you first expected? Is the knowledge you have gained marketable to employers in today's marketplace? This last question will be an important one to reflect on, but you may not know the answer immediately. The next section provides some important information in this area. In the career exploration work in Chapter Six, you will have an opportunity to do more extensive research into the needs and requirements of employers and the marketplace.

SKILLS EMPLOYERS WILL REQUIRE IN WORKPLACE 2000

In the late 1980s, the U.S. Department of Labor and the American Society of Training and Development jointly researched the needs of employers and uncovered interesting results. The skills that employers expected to continue or increase in demand fell into seven categories:

1. *Learning to learn.* American workers must continually learn new skills. They must, therefore, know how they learn best and take responsibility for updating their skills.

2. *Competence.* Beyond basic reading, writing, and math, workers must be able to read and interpret graphs, diagrams, and charts; digest complex material; and apply information to solving problems. They must also write business documents that are clear, concise, accurate, logical, and easy to read and understand. Knowledge of higher-order math, including business statistics, is essential.

3. *Communication.* Verbal and listening skills are critical because the fast-paced work environment puts less and less in writing. Workers must be able to share information and ideas quickly and effectively, and to listen actively to their coworkers.

4. *Personal responsibility.* Workers must be internally motivated to do their jobs, take pride in their achievements, and recognize their limitations. They need to assume responsibility for setting goals and managing their careers. There will be less supervision provided.

5. *Adaptability.* Increasingly, decision-making and problem-solving responsibilities fall on employees, both individually and as team members. The ability to think creatively and find innovative approaches to problems is sought by employers.

6. *Group effectiveness.* The ability to work effectively in groups requires skills in negotiating, resolving conflicts, handling stress, sharing task accomplishment, and building positive working relationships with others.

7. *Influence.* Understanding how organizations work and how to effectively lead others toward achievement of the organization's goals are key strengths.

The above list does not contain the hardware, software, and systems skills you might have anticipated, but it contains skills that allow the worker to acquire specific technical skills when needed. Since technical knowledge becomes obsolete rapidly, the ability to learn new technology surpasses specific knowledge in importance. When it comes to hiring individuals for positions, however, specific technical skills are frequently required. Many readers are likely to be intimidated by the reference to "higher-order math" in item 2 above. Using mathematical modeling is becoming prevalent in many fields. If you are concerned about math requirements, watch for them as you research specific occupations.

Another study from the Secretary of Labor and the Secretary's Commission on Achieving Necessary Skills, called the SCANS Report, has identified five competencies needed in all industries and at every level of organizations, from production floor to executive suite. Figure 5.1 lists and defines these five competencies.

The SCANS Report also identified a three-part foundation of intellectual skills and personal qualities that support each of the five competencies. Figure 5.2 enumerates and describes five basic skills considered to be the irreducible minimum a worker needs for even a low-skill job, six thinking skills that give workers mastery of their work, and five essential personal qualities. The foundation and the competencies identified in the SCANS Report suggest ideals for our educational systems to strive toward; they are being used across the country as guidelines in the development of new educational programs.

Employees need a foundation of basic skills, thinking skills, and essential personal qualities

You have completed several exercises to help you to identify the skills you possess and to determine which are your strongest and most marketable. You have also had a chance to consider the skills you most want to use in your next career. You may be an ace computer programmer and not want to write another line of code as long as you live. Or you may be a top-notch private secretary who doesn't want to type one more letter for someone else's signature. It will be important for you to recognize these attitudes about your skills.

We have also looked in a general way at the skills predicted to be required in the workplace as we move to an increasingly competitive global economy. You will have a chance to examine the marketplace more closely in Chapters Six and Seven.

FIVE COMPETENCIES IDENTIFIED BY SCANS

FIGURE 5.1

Resources: Identifies, organizes, plans, and allocates resources

A. *Time*—Selects goal-relevant activities, ranks them, allocates time, prepares and follows schedules

B. *Money*—Uses or prepares budgets, makes forecasts, keeps records, makes adjustments to meet objectives

C. *Material and Facilities*—Acquires, stores, allocates, and uses materials or space efficiently

D. *Human Resources*—Assesses skills and distributes work accordingly, evaluates performance, provides feedback

Interpersonal: Works with others

A. *Participates as Member of a Team*—Contributes to group effort

B. *Teaches Others New Skills*

C. *Serves Clients/Customers*—Works to satisfy customers' expectations

D. *Exercises Leadership*—Communicates ideas to justify position, persuades and convinces others, responsibly challenges existing procedures and policies

E. *Negotiates*—Works toward agreements involving exchange of resources, resolves divergent interests

F. *Works with Diversity*—Works well with men and women from diverse backgrounds

Information: Acquires and uses information

A. *Acquires and Evaluates Information*

B. *Organizes and Maintains Information*

C. *Interprets and Communicates Information*

D. *Uses Computers to Process Information*

Systems: Understands complex interrelationships

A. *Understands Systems*—Knows how social, organizational, and technological systems work and operates effectively with them

B. *Monitors and Corrects Performance*—Distinguishes trends, predicts impacts on system operations, diagnoses deviation in systems' performance and corrects malfunctions

C. *Improves or Designs Systems*—Suggests modifications to existing systems, develops new or alternative systems to improve performance

Technology: Works with a variety of technologies

A. *Selects Technology*—Chooses procedures, tools, or equipment, including computers and related technologies

B. *Applies Technology to Task*—Understands overall intent and proper procedures for setup and operation of equipment

C. *Maintains and Troubleshoots Equipment*—Prevents, identifies, or solves problems with equipment, including computers and other technologies

---

When you have completed this chapter and any additional assessment tools that your instructor may introduce, you will be ready for the next step in the career development process, career exploration. Then in Chapter Eight you will have a chance to review and integrate your self-knowledge with your deeper understanding of the marketplace. At that point, you will be ready to make your next career decision.

FIGURE 5.2 THREE-PART FOUNDATION IDENTIFIED BY SCANS

Basic Skills: Reads, writes, performs arithmetic and mathematical operations, listens, and speaks

A. *Reading*—locates, understands, and interprets written information in prose and in documents such as manuals, graphs, and schedules

B. *Writing*—communicates thoughts, ideas, information, and messages in writing; creates documents such as letters, directions, manuals, reports, graphs, and flow charts

C. *Arithmetic/Mathematics*—performs basic computations and approaches practical problems by choosing appropriately from a variety of mathematical techniques

D. *Listening*—receives, attends to, interprets, and responds to verbal messages and other cues

E. *Speaking*—organizes ideas and communicates orally

Thinking Skills: Thinks creatively, makes decisions, solves problems, visualizes, knows how to learn, and reasons

A. *Creative Thinking*—generates new ideas

B. *Decision Making*—specifies goals and constraints, generates alternatives, considers risks, and evaluates and chooses best alternative

C. *Problem Solving*—recognizes problems, and devises and implements plan of action

D. *Seeing Things in the Mind's Eye*—organizes and processes symbols, pictures, graphs, objects, and other information

E. *Knowing How to Learn*—uses efficient learning techniques to acquire and apply new knowledge and skills

F. *Reasoning*—discovers a rule or principle underlying the relationship between two or more objects and applies it when solving a problem

Personal Qualities: Displays responsibility, self-esteem, sociability, self-management, and honesty/integrity

A. *Responsibility*—exerts a high level of effort and perseveres toward goal attainment

B. *Self-Esteem*—believes in own self-worth and maintains a positive view of self

C. *Sociability*—demonstrates understanding, friendliness, adaptability, empathy, and politeness in group settings

D. *Self-Management*—assesses self accurately, sets personal goals, monitors progress, and exhibits self-control

E. *Integrity/Honesty*—chooses ethical courses of action

WORK IN PROGRESS

Success Chart

Purpose: By the time you finish this exercise, you will take justifiable pride in past achievements and will have learned to define success in your own terms. Ideally, you will prepare your chart on your own and share it with classmates who will work with you to interpret the results. Have fun with this one!

PART ONE MAKING YOUR CHART

Directions: If possible, complete this exercise on a large piece of paper (i.e., 27″ x 34″ newsprint). Hold your paper horizontally and divide it vertically in thirds. Draw columns. Label the top of the first column *What I did*. Label the middle column *What it took*, and the third column *What I got*. Next, divide the page in thirds horizontally. Now your page is set up for the exercise. See the sample in Figure 5.3.

	WHAT I DID (Achievements)	WHAT IT TOOK (Skills)	WHAT I GOT (Personal rewards)
First third of life			
Second third of life			
Third third of life			

FIGURE 5.3

Success chart.

This exercise involves identifying achievements. As indicated in the body of the chapter, achievements are events or activities that have given you a good feeling, a feeling of accomplishment. Whether small or large, they are meaningful to you. Don't get hung up on someone else's judgment of your achievement. If you did something that you recall with satisfaction, it is worthy of being on your chart.

The left-hand column of the chart is for recording your achievements. In order to identify achievements from your whole life, divide your age by three. In the upper left block, list three achievements from the first third of your life. (For example, if you are 45, your first three achievements will span ages 0–15.) They might include things like learning to ride a bike or learning to read. In the second block in the left-hand column, list achievements for the second third of your life (e.g., ages 16–30). In the lower left block, list three achievements for the third third of your life (i.e., 31–45).

The second column is for recording skills involved in the achievements. Taking each achievement separately, list the skills you used or learned and the tasks you performed. Breaking down the achievement into skills will involve the same thinking that went into analyzing returning to school in the body of the chapter. See the skills lists in other exercises for inspiration.

The third column of your success chart is for recording the personal rewards you enjoyed from each achievement. Perhaps what made you feel good about the achievement was the recognition you got from a parent or teacher. On the other hand, your reward may have been inclusion in a different social group or a sense of personal mastery. Try to identify what made each of your accomplishments meaningful to you personally.

PART TWO ANALYZING SUCCESS PATTERNS

Directions: Sharing and interpreting the success charts provides support and affirmation for each individual's achievements. Your instructor may do this with the whole class or in groups of five or six. If the class is being divided,

FIGURE 5.4

Form for identifying
success patterns.

> Jose feels successful when . . .
>
>
>
> Success to me is . . .

one chart should first be presented and interpreted to the whole group as a demonstration.

The chart will be displayed on the wall. Next to it is placed a second piece of paper for identifying success patterns, prepared as indicated in Figure 5.4.

Your instructor will ask for a volunteer to present his or her success chart. You and your fellow students in the listening audience must listen carefully to the presentation and be prepared to suggest skills that may have been involved in the achievements but were not mentioned by the presenter. The presenter is also free to add skills that were omitted.

Reflections: The reflections for this activity are done with the group. The class will next complete the second piece of paper, recording the patterns observed in the rewards described by the presenting student. Someone may suggest, for example, "Tom feels successful when he wins trophies," and someone else, "Tom feels successful when he sets a long-term goal and works diligently toward its completion." Each observation must be confirmed by the presenter before being recorded. Sometimes the presenter will want to change the wording so that it fits with his or her personal experience.

When the patterns have been identified, they are read aloud. Then the presenter is asked to complete the sentence, "Success to me is . . ." This response is also recorded. Your instructor will return your success charts and success patterns to you after the presentations are completed.

When we analyze the success chart, we usually discover that there is a consistent pattern throughout a person's life in the kinds of experiences that evoke a feeling of success. . . . The group helps each participant identify areas of satisfaction that previously may not have been realized.

(*Author's note:* The Success Chart is one of the best self-assessment exercises I know of; each time I complete it, I learn something more about myself. I was first led through the activity at a conference workshop led by Thaddeus Raushi and Janet Robbins from Schenectady County Community College. Their material was based on two works: Chitayat, D., and G. Berens, *Motivation Advance Process.* New York: Institute for Research and Development in Occupational Education, CUNY; and Nash, K., *Get the Best of Yourself.* New York: Grosset & Dunlap, 1976.)

EXPLORING CAREER ALTERNATIVES

By now you have probably heard: The rules have changed. The assumptions we've made in the past about the world of work and how to navigate within that world are, for the most part, outmoded. New rules, new assumptions, new economic realities, new organizations and structures, and new technologies are rapidly replacing the old and familiar. In order to redirect your career, you need to be aware of the shifts taking place in the labor market and anticipate steadily accelerating change. This chapter and the one following will guide your exploration of career alternatives and help you to make sense of the changing workplace.

LOOK AT MANY OPTIONS

At this point, you have assessed your strengths, talents, interests, and preferences. Now you need to learn about the many different options that exist within the marketplace. While you have had exposure to the work world through your jobs and your interactions with service providers, in reality you have come in personal contact with only a small percentage of the workforce. Cities are filled with high-rise office buildings and surrounded by industrial parks employing thousands of workers you never see on the job. How can you know what goes on inside those structures, and what your employment options might be? Even familiar institutions such as hospitals are changing dramatically and employing workers in entirely new roles. How can you learn about these changes? And how can you know what occupations are likely to emerge in the future, providing opportunities for employment?

There are different ways of approaching career exploration. Some people try reading help-wanted advertisements in newspapers and become discour-

New rules, new realities, and new technologies in the world of work

aged because the listings are filled with technical jargon. While this source is informative, it is also limited because most available positions are never advertised in the newspaper.

The best way to become fully informed about the marketplace is to visit the career resource center at your college or your local library and start browsing through career literature. Most people are unaware of the print, video, and computer resources available for learning about career options. We will take a close look at a few of the standard resources for career information and list many additional sources at the end of the chapter.

Self-assessment activities you completed in Chapters Three, Four, and Five have suggested career possibilities for you, given your interests, personality preferences, and skills. With the help of your instructor, review this material and identify specific careers to explore.

It is preferable at this stage for you to look at a wide variety of possibilities. If you are like most people, you have never done this before. For now, consider all the options that appeal to you for whatever reason. You will have plenty of time later to narrow your focus.

For those readers who are Internet-savvy, you probably prefer to do as much research as possible online. Listed below are some Web sites that offer occupational information. If you are unfamiliar with the Internet, see Chapter 10, where we walk first-time users through the process of getting started with career research on the Internet.

America's Career InfoNet
http://www.acinet.org

Sponsored by the U. S. Employment and Training Administration, this site contains occupational information that will assist you in your employment search and increase your understanding of the job market. You can find information about both the employment outlook and the earnings and training for specific occupations, as well as geographic profiles for each state. A substantial career resource library offers extensive links for career exploration, employment trends, location of and research on employers, salary and relocation information, and education/training sources. Another handy resource is a collection of state career information sites.

JobSmart
http://www.jobsmart.org

Don't be misled by the descriptors at this site defining it as a "California Job Search Guide." This site contains rich career information, and the majority of it is not geographically specific. There is an excellent collection of links to career guides on the Internet, as well as links for researching industries and companies. Information also exists on both how to tap into the hidden job market and networking tips. A collection of links also exists to over 200 salary surveys on the Internet.

JobWeb
http://www.jobweb.org

This site, sponsored by the National Association of Colleges and Employers, is one of the best sources of information on career planning and employment for the college-educated workforce. It is an exhaustive resource for career planning issues, with numerous links relating to the process of making career choices. An extensive career library exists with links to reference sources, including books, directories, and periodicals. Another notable feature is the site's links to international career planning resources.

Occupational Outlook Handbook
http://stats.bls.gov/ocohome.htm

Produced by the Bureau of Labor Statistics, this online version of the *Occupational Outlook Handbook* is a nationally recognized source of career information. The *Handbook* is a searchable database of approximately 250 occupations accounting for about 6 out of every 7 jobs in the economy. Descriptive information covers workers, tasks, working conditions, training and education needed, earnings, and expected job prospects for each occupation.

Many resources are available for career exploration

If you prefer books to screens, you can start exploring by looking up occupations in standard career reference books (such as the *Occupational Outlook Handbook*, the *Dictionary of Occupational Titles*, the *Encyclopedia of Careers*, the *Professional Careers Sourcebook*, and the *Guide to Occupational Exploration*) to learn specific information. These reference books describe job functions, training requirements, advancement possibilities, outlook for future employment, and sources of further information for each occupation covered.

The *Guide to Occupational Exploration (GOE)* is organized into 12 broad interest areas: artistic, scientific, plants and animals, protective, mechanical, industrial, business detail, selling, accommodating, humanitarian, leading-influencing, and physical performing. Interest areas are divided into 66 work groups. Within each work group, information is provided about what kind of work you would do, what skills and abilities are needed, how you would know if this is the right field for you, how you can prepare to enter this field, and what specific jobs are found in the field. Once you have identified possible jobs within the groups, you are referred to the *Dictionary of Occupational Titles* by code number for more specific job information.

The *Dictionary of Occupational Titles (DOT)* is a reference book published by the federal Department of Labor. It contains thousands of job titles, with industry designations and task descriptions; each highly detailed entry is one paragraph in length. This volume, published approximately every 10 years, is a little harder to use than the *GOE* because entries are organized according to a nine-digit numerical code. If you began with the *GOE*, you can go directly from that reference to occupations in the *DOT* using the numerical codes. If you are beginning your exploration with the *DOT*, you will find detailed instructions in the front of the book. Take the time to read the instructions; otherwise, you may feel frustrated, since this is not a book that is conducive to browsing.

The *Occupational Outlook Handbook (OOH)* is another publication of the Department of Labor; it is published every two years and contains detailed information on over 250 occupations that employ approximately 85 percent of all the workforce. The volume is user-friendly and filled with photographs that help make the written material come alive. It contains an alphabetical index of occupations. If you read brief descriptions in the *DOT* that appealed to you, the *OOH* is the next reference to use for additional information.

When you are looking in the *OOH* for ideas about possible occupations, start by reading the front matter entitled "Tomorrow's Jobs." This material contains valuable information about employment projections for the next 10 years. Then read the alphabetical index. Make a list, with page numbers, of all occupations that attract your interest for any reason. After reading the index, you may have a list of 15 or 20 careers that appeal to you. Look up each of the entries. The book provides a page or two of text on each occupation, enough to decide either "That's not for me" or "That sounds interesting. I need to learn more."

Vocational Biographies are four-page leaflets that many career centers collect by subscription. These publications focus on individuals in particular occupations. The people are pictured in their work settings. The text contains their stories about selecting their occupation and the details of their jobs. They are personal accounts and individual perspectives that appeal to many people exploring career options.

We have described several resources that you may encounter in your exploration. It is beyond the scope of this book to mention them all. There are many excellent resources available, and new ones are being released all the time. Your reference librarian can introduce you to the resources available in your locale.

RESEARCH ALTERNATIVES THOROUGHLY

As you read about occupations in career reference guides, you can decide if a particular occupation interests you enough to obtain more information. If you're interested in a general field, but not in the specific job you've looked up, the source will refer you to related occupations. Careful research is especially critical today because change is occurring so rapidly and because the demands of the marketplace are confusing. On the one hand, you are told to develop more specialized skills; on the other hand, you are urged to become a generalist. It is important that you have *current* information about career fields and specific jobs within them.

Once you have identified occupations that strongly interest you, you can further research them in books dealing specifically with the particular field(s); a list of career-specific books appears at the end of the chapter. If you have difficulty finding the career-specific book you need in your library, you can either request that the library order it or contact the publisher directly to purchase your own copy. These books are relatively inexpensive.

You can also learn a lot about careers by reading professional journals and trade publications produced for professionals in the particular field. For example, people in marketing often belong to the American Marketing Association and subscribe to its quarterly publication, the *Journal of Marketing*. Articles in this publication address critical issues and new developments within the marketing field. If you are seriously interested in this field, you will likely find these articles absorbing. If the articles don't hold your attention, the field is probably one you can eliminate from consideration. The *Job Hunters Source Book* identifies professional associations and their publications by field.

NARROW YOUR FOCUS

You began the exploration process by opening up possibilities. The next step involves narrowing your focus. As you read about different career possibilities, you will notice that some fields compel you to learn more, while other fields do not hold your interest. Some career options utilize more of your skills, match better with your personality, or are more compatible with your previous experience and education. Each of these factors needs to be care-

Dorothy taught elementary school for 23 years and, at the age of 45, took a retirement buyout. Her retirement income was not sufficient to support her, so she began to explore alternative careers. At first, she did seasonal work in retail sales and temp work in offices, but these jobs were not satisfying; neither job adequately supplemented her retirement income.

After a year of marginal employment, Dorothy returned to her college career office for advice and was guided through several self-assessment activities. The assessment confirmed that Dorothy worked well with people, had strong organizational and administrative skills, enjoyed planning large projects, and was a creative program developer.

Then she began to explore a wide range of alternative careers. She did not like the process much and sometimes disappeared for a few months into another temporary solution. Eventually, she was able to identify appealing career options. They included special events planner and trade show coordinator working in a corporation, customer service specialist and trainer working for a telecommunications company, conference planner working with a hotel, and trip coordinator working with a travel bureau.

Through library research and informational interviews with professionals in these areas, Dorothy was able to narrow her choices down to the special events planner and trade show coordinator. Having planned class trips, directed school plays, and run career fairs, she had many transferable skills for this choice. The position also matched the setting Dorothy desired: she wanted to work in a fast-paced corporate environment. Conference planning positions in hotels and coordinator positions in travel bureaus turned out to be sales positions, which did not appeal to her, and the customer service and training positions were too much like teaching. Dorothy wanted a change!

Dorothy discovered through further research that most large corporations have people who coordinate trade shows and plan special events. She joined the International Association of Meeting Planners, where she met many of these professionals. Next she conducted informational interviews to learn about the demands of these positions. Fortunately, her lifestyle meshes well with the frequently required travel.

Dorothy's final act before making the transition was taking a long-term temporary assignment with a company that ran trade shows for small organizations. In the role of receptionist, she observed all aspects of the business. To her delight, her temp position led to a job offer, and Dorothy has successfully made the transition.

fully weighed. Eventually, you will have a list of three or four career options that strongly appeal to you, based on your research.

CONSIDER NONTRADITIONAL CAREERS

Most of us have been subtly conditioned to consider certain careers either "male" or "female." This phenomenon, called sex-role stereotyping, causes women to choose the paralegal profession while men become lawyers, or women to become hygienists while men become dentists. By paying attention to stereotyping, you will see how it has influenced your thinking about yourself and your career options.

As a woman, you may automatically have eliminated engineering as an option even though you are good at math. As a man, you may have discounted nursing, although you excel in the sciences and want to help people in a hands-on profession. Beware of stereotyping yourself!

Juanita was always a good student, particularly in math. In high school, she had one teacher who recognized her talent and encouraged her to consider going on to college to study engineering. Juanita's father wouldn't hear of this and only reluctantly let her go to the local community college to prepare to be a teacher. She completed her associate degree and transferred to a state college, where she majored in secondary education with a specialty in math. She became a little more enthused as she took the higher-math courses.

When she graduated, Juanita found a teaching job close to home. She taught for two years, married, stayed home with her children for six years, and eventually returned to teaching math for another nine years.

In her late 30s, Juanita saw an advertisement for a graduate program at a nearby university. Described as a career change program, the college of engineering was recruiting women with high math aptitude and nontechnical undergraduate degrees for a master's program in information systems. For the first time in nearly 20 years, Juanita felt deeply inspired to take the next step in her career.

Although she was terrified, she contacted the school, gathered more information, and visited and spoke both with students in the program and with a woman who had completed the program and changed careers. Juanita arranged to take the required GRE (Graduate Record Examination) and applied for admission. Her family's reaction to her plan was mixed. Her husband was initially concerned about finances, the well-run household, and the children, but when Juanita demonstrated how some of the household responsibilities could be redistributed, his real concerns surfaced. Was Juanita going to become a "big shot"? Was she going to become a "corporate type" or maybe even meet another man more interesting than himself? These issues needed careful attention. Meanwhile, Juanita's father just shook his head. Why would his daughter want an engineering degree now? She had a nice family and a perfectly good job. He had to admit that she never was the stay-at-home type he thought she should have been all along.

Eventually, Juanita entered and completed the graduate program and went on to become a software engineer in a high-tech company. Over time, she won her family's support as they observed the joy and satisfaction she experienced.

Beware of your own attitudes that may support stereotypes and limit your career options

Juanita's case illustrates many issues. Stereotyping is certainly one. Clearly Juanita had the aptitude for engineering in high school; with encouragement from her teachers and family, she might have pursued engineering for her bachelor's degree. However, society at that time considered engineering a male bastion. Teaching, on the other hand, was seen as a practical endeavor for women. Juanita's family expected her to work for only a few years and then to stay home raising her family. They saw teaching as something she could fall back on only if, heaven forbid, something happened to her husband.

Although innumerable changes have occurred in our society in the last few decades, many stereotypes remain. You may be unaware of limiting beliefs or attitudes of your own that are subtly working to steer you in some directions and away from others. Get to know the hidden attitudes that may be limiting you.

CONSIDER WORK AND FAMILY BALANCE

As a society, we are closer to the ideal of women being willing and able to pursue their career aspirations, but we still have a long way to go. Women walk a tightrope when it comes to work and family issues. When they stay home to raise a family, women often feel guilty because they think they "should" pursue a career. When they place children in day care to pursue careers, they feel guilty about not being at home. Women must be free to make decisions that are best for them and their individual family situations.

When two partners work outside the home, especially when young children are involved, typically both individuals also need to assume household and family responsibilities. Unfortunately, old stereotypes are still played out, with women having most of the household and child-care responsibilities. Furthermore, in households headed by single mothers, women report extremely high stress levels because of the many roles and responsibilities they juggle.

The workplace is slowly becoming more responsive to the personal and family needs of today's workers. The most enlightened organizations offer some of these sought-after options: flexible hours, working at home, job sharing, on-site child care or child-care backup, advisory services for dealing with aging parents, and so forth. The issue of "face time," the pressure to be seen in the office from early in the morning until late in the day, has gradually been replaced by a measuring of contributions or results produced. As the unemployment rate has fallen, leaving a depleted reserve of available workers, employers have been forced to respond to workers' needs for balance.

However, sometimes we lag behind when it comes to our own attitudes, behaviors, and expectations. Fathers turn down opportunities for paternity leave, concerned about how they will be perceived by fellow workers. Mothers strive to be superwomen, making unreasonable demands on themselves, often at the expense of the very family they are trying to do everything for. The intention of the women's movement was to offer choice for women, so they could have parity in the workplace if they chose to pursue careers, and respect for their role as homemakers if they chose that option. Instead, it seems women are damned if they do and damned if they don't! Whether you're a woman or man, remember to keep your work life in perspective with your many other roles and responsibilities when exploring your career alternatives.

CONDUCT INFORMATIONAL INTERVIEWS

At this point, you have explored career options using general occupational guides and career-specific literature. You have no doubt become excited about new possibilities while eliminating options that do not appear to be a good fit. The next step is to further explore the career options on your newly shortened list by conducting informational interviews with people in your fields of interest. In Chapter Eight, you will learn how to assess all of the information you have gathered in order to make a sound decision about your future career direction.

Informational interviews are conversations that you arrange with people who have information that could be helpful to you. People who have worked for many years in an occupation that you are considering will be able to tell you a great deal about the realities of the work. Ideally you should meet with them at their work settings so you can observe the work environment as well as discuss their experience. Telephone interviews and online conversations using e-mail are acceptable alternatives. Chat rooms may be less reliable sources since communications are anonymous.

Informational interviews provide firsthand information on the realities of the work

Many adult students are initially resistant to the idea of approaching someone they don't know and requesting an informational interview. It may surprise you to discover, as countless students have, that people like to talk about themselves. If you approach them politely, and explain to them how they can be of help to you in making important career decisions, they are usually willing to comply. Emphasize that you are interested in knowing about their experience.

To find appropriate people, speak with relatives and friends, teachers and classmates, to see if anyone knows someone in the field you are exploring. Go to your school's career center to see if it has an alumni/ae network. You can also contact the local chapter of the professional association to find out when it is meeting next and whether you may attend as a guest. By attending the meeting of a professional association, you will have a chance to speak informally with several professionals in the field. After this initial meeting, you can ask some individuals about talking further at another time.

Another way to find people to interview is through the telephone directory. If you are interested in the field of publishing, for example, you can find a list of publishers in the business directory. You will have to make a "cold call" to find someone who is willing to talk with you about his or her occupation. Be clear about the role of the person with whom you wish to speak; in publishing, you may want to talk with a proofreader or an editor.

It is not appropriate to call the human resources office of a hospital and ask to speak with someone about careers in health care. You must do this research on your own. Once you have researched a specific occupation, you may then call an organization to request to speak with someone in that role. For example, "I'd like to speak with someone in your purchasing department" or "I would like to speak with someone in admissions."

Some of you may find it easier to walk into an organization than make a cold call on the phone. You may be able to walk into a furniture store to speak with an interior decorator or an animal clinic to speak with a veterinarian, but in most instances, it is more appropriate to make an appointment in advance.

Once you have the names and numbers of people in the field you wish to explore, call them to ask about the possibility of meeting with them so that you can learn more about their occupation. When you don't know the individuals personally, you may feel uncomfortable about asking them for a favor. You will find, however, that many people enjoy the opportunity to share their experiences and insights. Making the call to request the interview is often the hardest part.

Some possible introductory scripts are:

Hello, Ms. Chang, my name is Felix Hernandez, and I'm a student at Three Rivers College. I'm taking a career management course, and one of my assignments is to interview a professional in the career field I'm exploring. Since I'm very interested in the field of accounting, I'd like to talk with you about your work. I would need no more than 20 minutes of your time. Would you be willing to meet with me?

Hello, Mr. Wiezel, my name is Nicole Bondeau. I got your name from my friend John McCord, who works in your department. I'm exploring career alternatives and have reached a dilemma: should I stay in sales or move in the direction of sales management? Since you have made the transition into sales management, I wonder if you would be willing to tell me about your job? I'd be happy to meet you in your office and would need only about 30 minutes of your time. Your insights could be a big help to me. Can you spare some time next week?

Hello, Michelle, this is Alice Frasier. I enjoyed talking with you at the ASTD meeting Wednesday night. I was wondering if I could make an appointment to talk with you further about your work. Your team-building training program sounds fascinating.

Some students prefer to write a letter first, especially if they are contacting someone they have never met before. This is a fine approach, too. However, it creates a little more work because you have to compose the letter and then call to follow up. A letter of introduction would look something like the one in Figure 6.1. You will have to tailor the content to your own situation.

After a letter of introduction, follow up with a phone call one week later. Thomas will call Ms. Nielsen to request an informational interview. He will remind her of his letter and that he was referred to her by his professor. How can she possibly refuse?

Once you have scheduled the appointment, you will need to prepare for the informational interview. *This is not a job interview, nor are you campaigning for a job at this time.* It is an interview initiated by you to learn more about the individual's work and employer organization, as well as the overall field. The person's time is valuable, so use it well.

Since it is your responsibility to conduct the informational interview, prepare a list of questions and become familiar with it. Read all you can about the field beforehand. Do your library research prior to the informational interview so you will not waste time asking basic questions such as, "What exactly does a toxicologist do?" Instead, you will be asking more insightful and information-generating questions: "What made you decide to

---

Ms. Karyn Nielsen
Public Relations Group
Manchester Community Hospital
Manchester, Ohio 45887

January 8, 2000

FIGURE 6.1

Sample letter requesting an informational interview.

Dear Ms. Nielsen:

My professor, Dr. Giordano, suggested that I contact you. I am in my second year in a marketing/public relations concentration at Ohio State and am exploring career options after graduation.

Having worked in hospitals since graduating from high school, I am considering occupations in a medical environment. Public relations appeals to me. Another option is pharmaceutical or medical equipment sales. I realize that I know very little about the realities of public relations. I've read all I can and it sounds exciting, but it must be different behind the scenes.

My hope is that you can spare 30 minutes of your time in early February to tell me about your work. What's involved in developing and maintaining the positive public image of Manchester Community Hospital? I will call you next week to see if we can arrange a time to meet.

Thank you for considering my request.

Sincerely,

Thomas Freeman

become a toxicologist?" "What are the things you like best about your work?" "What are the things you like least?" "What are the greatest challenges in your field today?" See Figure 6.2 for additional suggested questions.

Some of your questions should be addressed to your interview subject's personal career experience. Other questions may relate to the organization the

---

FIGURE 6.2

Possible questions for an informational interview.

Information about the person's career
- How did you choose this profession?
- How did you prepare to enter this field? Where did you go to school?
- What was your major?
- How has your career progressed?
- Are you happy in your work?

Information about the person's current position
- What do you like about what you do?
- What don't you like about your work?
- What is a typical workday like? How about a typical week? Year?
- How has technology changed your work?
- How much work do you take home? How many hours do you work each week?
- How much do you travel? How often and for how long?
- What are some of the toughest situations you have encountered?
- What percentage of your time do you spend in meetings or working with people on teams?
- What percentage of your time do you spend working independently?

Information about the company or organization
- How would you describe the culture of your company?
- Where do you see the company heading? How is it being positioned for the future?
- What kind of people does your organization hire?
- What are the minimum qualifications for a person entering this field at your company?
- Does your organization promote from within?
- Is your company receptive to career changers?

Information about the field
- What are some of the possible career paths within this field?
- What are some of the challenges and major issues confronting professionals in the field today?
- What are the leading professional organizations in this field? Are nonmembers permitted to attend meetings?
- Is there an active local chapter?
- What journals do you recommend I read?
- Where do you see the future opportunities within this field?
- Are there others with whom I should speak for additional information? May I use your name when I contact them?

Advice
- What advice do you have for me as I consider a career in this field?
- What do you wish you had known before you entered this field?
- What courses, certifications, or other credentials do you recommend I pursue?
- How does someone get into this field through the "backdoor," when they are changing careers and have transferable skills?
- When I'm ready to enter this field, what job hunting strategies do you recommend?

Be prepared to talk about my "transferable skills" + what specific direction I'm interested in.

individual is affiliated with and its products or services, plans for the future, and potential future needs for employees. It may be appropriate to ask for a tour of the facility. Still another area to address is the future of the field: What new technologies are being developed? What new markets are they opening? What people may be needed in the future, and with what kind of training?

The last area to address in your informational interview is additional contacts. If the information shared with you confirms that this is a good field for you, ask your interview subject for names and numbers of people you might contact for more information.

Immediately after the interview, write down everything you have learned

After the interview, write down everything you learned. The experience will fade quickly, so start writing as soon after the interview as possible. Some of the information will be objective (factual) and some will be subjective (the opinions of the person you interviewed). Write down both the information you learned and your own impressions. What is your assessment of this person's view? Is it fair or biased? You may need to talk with a few more people before you have the real lowdown on this occupational choice.

Informational interviewing may confirm an occupational choice for you. If so, the contacts you have made could be valuable to you in the future when you are ready to seek employment in the field. A warm and enthusiastic thank-you letter is an appropriate follow-up. A sample is provided in Figure 6.3.

If you connect strongly with your interview subjects and they encourage you to keep in touch, you have the beginnings of a new professional network. If you have a network already, then perhaps you have developed a new branch to that network. We will talk about networks in more detail in Chapter Ten.

In this chapter, we have introduced career exploration by giving many sources of occupational information: reference books and other print resources,

---

FIGURE 6.3 Sample follow-up letter to interview.

Ms. Karyn Nielsen
Public Relations Group
Manchester Community Hospital
Manchester, Ohio 45887

February 15, 2000

Dear Karyn:

Thank you for taking the time to speak with me on Friday. Your insights about the field of public relations helped me to separate the glamour from the day-to-day challenges. The complex and sticky problems you described encouraged me to strongly consider this field.

I have already arranged another informational interview with someone handling corporate public relations so I can compare the profit and nonprofit sectors. I've also scheduled a meeting with a faculty advisor to explore changing my major. Your suggestion that I study public relations in combination with communications appeals to me far more than the public relations/marketing track I thought I needed to follow.

All in all, our conversation filled many gaps in my knowledge and perceptions. You've helped me to make a pivotal decision in my life. Again, my thanks for your guidance. I'll give you a call in a few months and let you know how I'm progressing.

Warmest regards,

Thomas Freeman

videos, computer resources, and people who share their personal perspectives. These sources provide information on specific careers and occupational fields. In Chapter Seven, we will explore resources for getting "the big picture": economic indicators and market trends.

WORK IN PROGRESS

Presentation Piece

Purpose: The purpose of this exercise is to prepare an introductory script for meeting new people as you explore career possibilities.

Directions: Answer the following simple questions in the space provided. Then weave the answers into a brief paragraph that you can use when introducing yourself to someone during a professional first encounter. Develop one version for a telephone "cold call" in which you get the person's voice mail and another for a meeting in person, such as at a professional association meeting or a job fair.

Who am I?

....

....

What do I do?

....

....

Where do I do it?

....

....

What do I want to do next?

....

....

Why am I making a change?

....

....

What do I want from this person?

....

....

....

Sample final telephone script: Hello, Mr. Harrington. My name is Valerie Martin. I'm a social worker in New Jersey where I'm affiliated with St. Mary's Hospital Outpatient Services. I'm planning to relocate to the Baltimore area six months from now, and I would like to meet colleagues in the area. Could you spend some time with me next week to tell me about your practice in the Baltimore schools?

When you have developed your scripts, practice them with a partner until they sound natural and feel right. When you have the scripts perfected, use them for your career exploration. Write your first draft below.

....
....
....
....
....
....
....
....
....
....

Reflections: Are you comfortable with your script? In general, are you satisfied with your telephone technique? How do you need to improve your telephone skills?

Own Your Expertise

Purpose: This exercise is designed to warm you up for informational interviews and help you learn to formulate questions that stimulate discussion. Everyone will experience the roles of interviewer and interviewee. When interviewing a member of the class, you will have an opportunity to practice asking probing questions about your classmate's area of expertise.

Directions: Each of us is an expert at something. What is your specialty? It could be hunting, packing lunches for kids, or line dancing. Anything goes in this activity. Start by claiming an area of expertise.

Your instructor will set up a demonstration interview, placing two chairs in the front of the room. One student volunteers to be the expert and takes one of the two seats. The second seat, the "Barbara Walters chair," should have rotating occupants. The instructor introduces the student expert, and his or her area of expertise, and invites members of the class to take turns occupying the other chair and asking questions. The entire interview should last for about 10 minutes. When it is over, process the demonstration with the expert and participants. What kind of questions generated interesting discussion? Ask the expert how it felt to claim expertise and to be interviewed.

Now pair off for simultaneous interviews. The first interviewer may take five minutes; then reverse roles. Afterward, your instructor will help you process the activity and tie it to informational interviewing.

Reflections: How did you feel about claiming an area of expertise? How did you like being interviewed? How did you feel about asking your partner questions? Which questions generated more interesting discussion?

Major Career Research Project

Purpose: This project will provide you with an opportunity to conduct career research in a field of your choice. The written report will give you a chance to develop or refine your writing skills, so important in today's workplace. The oral presentations of the results of your classmates' research will provide you with valuable information about a variety of careers, while your own presentation will offer you a chance to build marketable presentation skills. You will be allowed at least four weeks for this assignment.

Directions: Conduct research on careers of interest to you. Start by doing some general reading, especially in reference books like the *Occupational Outlook Handbook*, to get a sense of the many options open to you. You may also use online resources available on the Internet. Gradually focus in on areas that make the most sense, given your experience, skills, personality and lifestyle preferences, current interests, and values.

When you have narrowed your options to one or two, do more in-depth research in those areas. Then conduct a minimum of two informational interviews with people in these fields. Write a detailed report that summarizes your library and computer research and your interviews, and prepare a 10-minute presentation for class.

The written report should contain the following:

A. Summary of background research
   1. Description of the specific occupation and the career field
   2. Preparation required: education, training, and/or certification
   3. Nontraditional entry routes for career changers
   4. Salary range
   5. Advancement possibilities/growth potential/career development options
   6. Places of employment and typical working conditions
   7. Future outlook, including labor market information
   8. Related occupations
   9. Sources of further information
   10. List of resources used

B. Summary of interviews
   1. Who you saw, where they work, what they do, how they got there, why they chose their career and their current position
   2. Specific information gained about the field and the occupation
   3. Information gained about the organizations visited
   4. Insights gained from the interviews

C. Conclusion
   1. Your objective assessment of this career option
   2. Your feelings about this career option
   3. An evaluation of the match between your self-knowledge (include personality and lifestyle preferences, values, interests, skills) and this career option
   4. Additional information needed, next steps

Your class presentation should not exceed 10 minutes. Include the same topics outlined above but in less detail. Whatever you do, *do not* try to read your paper to the class. Just tell them about it. By the time you have completed the paper, you will be an expert on the field(s) you researched. Plan to talk with only an outline or note cards. Be sure to rehearse your presentation beforehand so your delivery will be smooth.

GREAT BOOKS FOR RESEARCHING CAREER OPTIONS

Few people are aware of the vast amount of literature available on occupations. Most of these books are appealing and easy to read. They provide the reader with useful factual information about a field and describe a variety of occupations within a given field. Typically, they also give you resources for further information. This material can help you determine if a particular career is right for you.

VGM Career Horizons has published a delightful series of books, one of which is bound to inspire even the most frustrated, turned-off, resistant career changer. If you do not find the book you want at your library, you can order it from the publisher by calling 1-800-323-4900.

Careers for Animal Lovers & Other Zoological Types (Miller, Louise, 1991)

Careers for Bookworms & Other Literary Types (Eberts, Marjorie, & Margaret Gisler, 1995)

Careers for Computer Buffs & Other Technological Types (Eberts, Marjorie, & Margaret Gisler, 1993)

Careers for Culture Lovers & Other Artsy Types (Eberts, Marjorie, & Margaret Gisler, 1992)

Careers for Foreign Language Aficionados & Other Multilingual Types (Seelye, H. Ned, & J. Lawrence Day, 1992)

Careers for Good Samaritans & Other Humanitarian Types (Eberts, Marjorie, & Margaret Gisler, 1991)

Careers for Nature Lovers & Other Outdoor Types (Miller, Louise, 1992)

Careers for Numbers Crunchers & Other Quantitative Types (Burnett, Rebecca, 1993)

Careers for Sports Nuts & Other Athletic Types (Heitzmann, W. Ray, 1998)

Careers for Travel Buffs & Other Restless Types (Plawin, Paul, 1992)

The same publisher has another popular series that covers dozens of occupational options. These quick reads give a comprehensive overview of the field. If the one you are interested in is not available in your local library, contact the publisher at 1-800-323-4900. The cost to purchase one of these paperbacks is about $12. If the occupation you want information on is not included in the list, check with the publisher, which is constantly expanding and updating this series. *One other note:* These books contain information about the occupations, not job listings.

Opportunities in Accounting Careers (Rosenberg, Martin, 1996)

Opportunities in Acting Careers (Moore, Dick, 1993)

Opportunities in Aerospace Careers (Maples, Wallace R., 1995)

Opportunities in Animal and Pet Care Careers (Lee, Mary Price, and Richard S. Lee, 1993)

Opportunities in Architectural Careers (Piper, Robert J., 1993)

Opportunities in Automotive Service (Weber, Robert M., 1997)

Opportunities in Banking Careers (Paradis, Adrian A., & Philip A. Perry, 1993)

Opportunities in Biological Science Careers (Winter, Charles A., 1996)

Opportunities in Biotechnology Careers (Brown, Sheldon S., 1990)

Opportunities in Broadcasting Careers (Ellis, Elmo I., 1992)

Opportunities in Business Management Careers (Place, Irene, 1998)

Opportunities in Cable Television Careers (Bone, Jan, 1993)

Opportunities in CAD/CAM Careers (Bone, Jan, 1993)

Opportunities in Chemistry Careers (Woodburn, John H., 1997)

Opportunities in Child Care Careers (Wittenberg, Renee, 1995)

Opportunities in Civil Engineering Careers (Hagerty, D. Joseph, and Louis F. Cohn, 1997)

Opportunities in Commercial Art/Graphic Design Careers (Gordon, Barbara, 1998)

Opportunities in Computer Maintenance Careers (Kanter, Elliot S., 1995)

Opportunities in Counseling and Development Careers (Baxter, Neale J., 1997)

Opportunities in Customer Service Careers (Ettinger, Blanche, 1992)

Opportunities in Data and Word Processing Careers (Munday, Marianne, 1996)

Opportunities in Dental Care Careers (Kendall, Bonnie L., 1991)

Opportunities in Direct Marketing Careers (Basye, Anne, 1993)

Opportunities in Drafting Careers (Rowh, Mark, 1993)

Opportunities in Energy Careers (Woodburn, John H., 1992)

Opportunities in Engineering Careers (Basta, Nicholas, 1995)

Opportunities in Environmental Careers (Fanning, Odom, 1991)

Opportunities in Eye Care Careers (Belikoff, Kathleen, 1998)

Opportunities in Film Careers (Bone, Jan, 1998)

Opportunities in Financial Careers (Sumichrast, Michael, and Dean Crist, 1998)

Opportunities in Fire Protection Services (Colemen, Ronny J., 1997)

Opportunities in Fitness Careers (Miller, Mary, rev. by Lewis Baratz, 1997)

Opportunities in Food Service Careers (Chmelynski, Carol Caprione, 1992)

Opportunities in Foreign Language Careers (Rivers, Wilga M., 1993)

Opportunities in Gerontology Careers and Aging Services (Williams, Ellen, 1995)

Opportunities in Health and Medical Careers (Snook, I. Donald, 1996)

Opportunities in High Tech Careers (Colter, Gary E., & Deborah Yanuck, 1995)

Opportunities in Homecare Services Careers (Cardoza, Anne deSola, 1993)

Opportunities in Hospital Administration Careers (Snook, I. Donald, 1997)

Opportunities in Hotel and Motel Careers (Henkin, Shepard, 1992)

Opportunities in Human Resources Management Careers (Traynor, William J., and J. Steven McKenzie, 1994)

Opportunities in Information Systems Careers (Hoyt, Douglas B., 1991)

Opportunities in Insurance Careers (Schrayer, Robert M., 1993)

Opportunities in International Business Careers (Arpan, Jeffrey S., 1995)

Opportunities in Journalism Careers (Ferguson, Donald L., & Jim Patten, 1993)

Opportunities in Law Careers (Munneke, Gary A., 1994)

Opportunities in Law Enforcement and Criminal Justice Careers (Stinchcomb, James, 1996)

Opportunities in Library and Information Science Careers (McCook, Kathleen, 1996)

Opportunities in Marketing Careers (Steinberg, Margery, 1994)

Opportunities in Medical Imaging (Sherry, Clifford J., 1994)

Opportunities in Modeling Careers (Gearhart, Susan Wood, 1991)

Opportunities in Music Careers (Gerardi, Robert, 1997)

Opportunities in Nonprofit Organizations (Paradis, Adrian A., 1994)

Opportunities in Nutrition Careers (Caldwell, Carol Coles, 1992)

Opportunities in Occupational Therapy Careers (Weeks, Zona R., 1995)

Opportunities in Paralegal Careers (Fins, Alice, 1990)

Opportunities in Performing Arts Careers (Bekken, Bonnie Bjorguine, 1991)

Opportunities in Petroleum Careers (Krueger, Gretchen Dewailly, 1990)

Opportunities in Pharmacy Careers (Gable, Fred B., 1998)

Opportunities in Photography Careers (Johnson, Bervin, Robert E. Mayer, and Fred Schmidt, 1991)

Opportunities in Physical Therapy Careers (Krumhansl, Bernice R., 1993)

Opportunities in Physician Careers (Sugar-Webb, Jan, 1991)

Opportunities in Plastics Careers (Bone, Jan, 1991)

Opportunities in Printing Careers (Borowsky, Irvin J., 1998)

Opportunities in Property Management Careers (Evans, Mariwyn, 1990)

Opportunities in Psychology (Super, Donald E., & Charles Super, 1994)

Opportunities in Public Health Careers (Pickett, George E., and Terry W. Pickett, 1995)

Opportunities in Public Relations Careers (Rotman, Morris B., 1995)

Opportunities in Real Estate Careers (Evans, M., 1997)

Opportunities in Recreation & Leisure Careers (Jensen, Clayne R., and Jay H. Naylor, 1990)

Opportunities in Restaurant Careers (Chmelynski, Carol Caprione, 1998)

Opportunities in Robotics Careers (Bone, Jan, 1993)

Opportunities in Sales Careers (Dahm, Ralph M., & James Brescoll, 1995)

Opportunities in Social Science Careers (Marek, Rosanne J., 1997)

Opportunities in Social Work Careers (Wittenberg, Renee, 1997)

Opportunities in Speech & Language Pathology Careers (Hicks, Patricia Larkins, 1995)

Opportunities in Sports Medicine Careers (Heitzmann, W. Ray, 1993)

Opportunities in Teaching Careers (Fine, Janet, 1995)

Opportunities in Telecommunications Careers (Bone, Jan, 1995)

Opportunities in Television & Video Careers (Noronha, Shonan F. R., 1998)

Opportunities in Transportation Careers (Paradis, Adrian A., 1997)

Opportunities in Travel Careers (Milne, Robert Scott, 1996)

Opportunities in Veterinary Medicine (Swope, Robert E., 1993)

Opportunities in Visual Arts Careers (Salmon, Mark, 1993)

Opportunities in Vocational & Technical Careers (Paradis, Adrian A., 1992)

Opportunities in Waste Management Careers (Rowh, Mark, 1993)

Many more publications are available. Additional books are included below in the hope of offering one that will grab you. Be sure to visit your library to find additional resources beyond the scope of this list. Reference librarians will help you to locate material—that's their job!

Becoming a Helper (Corey, Marianna Schneider, & Gerald Corey, Brooks/Cole Publishing, 3rd ed., 1997)

Careers in Medicine: Traditional and Alternative Opportunities (Rucker, T. Donald, Martin D. Keller, and collaborators, Garrett Park Press, rev. ed., 1990)

Careers in Social and Rehabilitation Services (Garner, Geraldine O., VGM, 1993)

Creative Careers: Real Jobs in Glamour Fields (Blake, Gary, & Robert Bly, John Wiley & Sons, 1985)

Environmental Jobs for Scientists & Engineers (Basta, Nicholas, John Wiley & Sons, 1992)

Health Care Careers in Transition: An Industry Overview (Harrison, The Nicholson Partnership, 1993)

Jobs in Paradise (Maltzman, Jeffrey, Harper & Row, 1993)

Jobs in the Arts and Media Management: What They Are and How to Get One (Langley, Stephen, & James Abruzzo, 1992)

Liberal Arts Jobs: What They Are and How to Get Them (Nadler, Burton Jay, Peterson's Guides, 2nd ed., 1989)

Liberal Education and Careers Today (Figler, Howard, Garrett Park Press, 1989)

Making a Living While Making a Difference: A Guide to Creating Careers with a Conscience (Everett, Melissa, Bantam, 1995)

New Careers in Hospitals (Sigel, Lois S., The Rosen Publishing Group, 1990)

Offbeat Careers: The Directory of Unusual Work (Sacharov, Al, Ten Speed Press, 1988)

Profitable Careers in Nonprofit (Lewis, William, & Carol Milano, John Wiley & Sons, 1987)

CHAPTER SEVEN

WATCHING ECONOMIC INDICATORS AND MARKET TRENDS

In the last chapter, you explored a variety of careers by doing library and computer research and by talking with people in those fields that interested you. You are assembling a realistic picture of your options. In this chapter, you will look at economic forces that may have an impact on your work life and at trends occurring in the marketplace that may influence the direction you choose to pursue.

NOTE ECONOMIC INDICATORS

As a job hunter or career changer, you may become more attuned to news about the U.S. and world economies. You may also find yourself curious about the economic shifts you have witnessed: Why was there a recession in the late 1980s? Will the current economic growth continue? What will be the impact of government monetary policies on your pocketbook? Most directly, how do all of these things relate to your career? If you have never taken a course in economics, this may be an ideal time to study the subject. The brief explanation that follows is intended to introduce the topic to those unfamiliar with how our capitalist economic system works.

The Federal Reserve System is a central banking system established in 1913 to strengthen the banking activities of the nation. Under this system, the country is divided into 12 districts, each having a Federal Reserve Bank owned by the member banks of that district. The 12 Reserve Banks are coordinated by the Federal Reserve Board, a seven-member board located in Washington, D. C. Members of the board are appointed to staggered 14-year terms by the President of the United States, with the advice and consent of the Senate. The board operates as an independent monetary authority (Heilbroner & Thurow, 1994).

In simple terms, the goal of federal monetary policy is to "assist the economy in achieving a full-employment, noninflationary level of total output" (McConnell & Brue, 1990, p. 339). The Federal Reserve Board controls the supply of money and interest rates in three ways. First, the board establishes reserve ratios for banks, requiring that they keep on hand a certain percentage of the money they have accepted on deposit from customers. By changing the reserve ratio, the board can control the amount of money available for loans, which then raises or lowers the interest rate.

Second, the board lends money to its member banks. It can raise or lower the interest rate it charges, called the discount rate, and these fluctuations affect the interest rates the member banks charge their customers.

Third, the board buys and sells U.S. government securities from dealers in the open market. These transactions pass through member banks, changing the supply of money available for loans and raising or lowering the interest rate.

Keynesian economists (named for the influential English economist John Maynard Keynes, 1883–1946) view monetary policy as operating through a complex cause–effect chain. Policy decisions of the Federal Reserve Board affect commercial banking reserves. Changes in reserves affect the supply of money by altering the interest rate charged by lending institutions. Changes in the interest rate affect investment (such as a corporation's decision to purchase capital equipment and hire workers), disposable income (the money from earnings that consumers have available to spend), and prices (McConnell & Brue, 1990, p. 342).

When we apply Keynesian theory to a specific economic reality, we find that it plays out in a way that directly affects us. Suppose, for example, that the nation is grappling with high unemployment and a recession. The Federal Reserve can increase the supply of money, causing interest rates to fall, thus stimulating investment spending, which creates jobs. Then disposable income increases. This is called an "easy money policy" (McConnell & Brue, 1990, p. 334).

The reverse would work for an economy plagued by inflation. The Federal Reserve can limit the supply of money, which causes interest rates to rise; investment spending (by corporations) decreases and inflation declines. Increased unemployment is a likely side effect. This second scenario is called a "tight money policy" (McConnell & Brue, 1990, p. 334).

An easy money policy usually increases jobs, while tight money increases unemployment

The economic problems of the 1980s and early 1990s were particularly confounding to the makers of monetary policy. Dubbed "stagflation," this economic condition, marked by rising prices (inflation) as well as rising unemployment (stagnating economic growth), responded to no simple cures and showed little indication that monetary policy would produce desired results (Heilbroner & Thurow, 1994, p. 142). As recession gave way to economic recovery, the Federal Reserve occasionally lowered interest rates slightly to stave off inflation at home and to stimulate investment abroad.

As you can see, federal monetary policies directly or indirectly affect workers. Understanding economic indicators and market realities can inform your timing for making a job or career change. These and other statistical indicators are calculated by federal agencies and reported in the media, often with little explanation. They are also summarized each year in the *Economic Report of the President*, which includes the Annual Report of the Council of Economic Advisors. This report, available in most public libraries, presents the current administration's assessment of the economy and plans for future development.

Economic indicators include current interest rates, the inflation rate, the unemployment rate, and new housing starts, among others. We will look at these four to get an idea about how they relate to you personally.

Interest rates are established by the Federal Reserve Board to control the availability of money for commercial loans and home mortgages and to regulate the rate of inflation. Generally speaking, low interest rates increase investment and expand the economy; high interest rates deter investment and constrain the economy (McConnell & Brue, 1990, p. 621). While you are probably more aware of how interest rates affect your own ability to secure loans, you also need to know that they have an indirect effect on you through their impact on the business sector. In order for businesses to decide to invest in new plants, capital equipment, machinery, and so forth, the expected rate of return of the investment must be greater than the real interest rate. When the investment climate is favorable, companies make capital purchases, create jobs, and hire employees to produce goods or services.

The consumer price index (CPI) measures the rate of inflation by comparing the prices of a "market basket" of approximately 300 goods and services commonly used by urban consumers against the fixed 1982–1984 prices for the same goods and services. Changes in the prices reflect changes in the "costliness of a fixed standard of living" (McConnell & Brue, 1990, p. 153) and determine the rate of inflation. While the CPI has shortcomings, it is a standard measure used to calculate cost-of-living increases in salaries, among other things. If you are making a career transition, the inflation rate may influence your income requirements. You may be aware that during the last recession, wages decreased in many industries and geographic areas.

The unemployment rate is measured monthly by the Department of Labor's Bureau of Labor Statistics (BLS) and reported both nationally and by state. The figures document the proportion of the measured labor force that is unemployed. The term *labor force* refers to the number of workers employed and unemployed. The unemployed are defined as adults who are willing and able to work and are actively looking for a job but have not found one. Discouraged workers, those who have been unemployed for a long time, and those who have exhausted unemployment benefits are not counted.

While the trough of the recession occurred in March 1991, it was not until July 1992 that the unemployment rate began to fall. At the end of 1994, the unemployment rate was 5.4 percent; in the fall of 1998, the unemployment rate was 4.5 percent, the lowest in 30 years. During good times, the rate falls below 4 percent; during the Great Depression of the 1930s, it reached 25 percent.

A falling unemployment rate signals a growing economy—a good time to look for new employment opportunities. When the unemployment rate is rising, the labor market becomes flooded with laid-off workers, and competition for jobs increases. Career changers may have more difficulty during rising unemployment because they are competing for jobs with the abundant number of available workers who have direct experience. However, this is not to say it can't be done. People change careers when they are personally ready to make the transition.

Economic indicators of a growing economy include low interest rates, low inflation, rising employment, and increased housing starts

Looking ahead, the BLS predicts continued overall growth in jobs. Projections are also available for particular industries and occupational areas. This information is published in "Tomorrow's Jobs" in the front of the *Occupational Outlook Handbook*. Samples are provided in Figure 7.1. Other BLS publications include the *Monthly Labor Review*; see the November 1997 issue for occupational and employment projections to 2006. You can also visit the BLS online at http://stats.bls.gov.

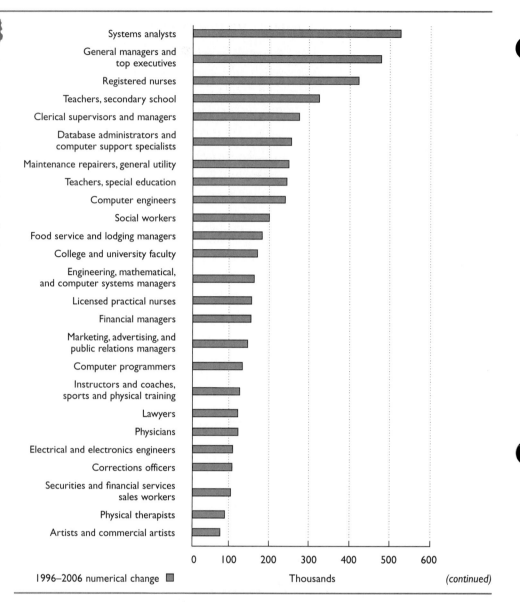

FIGURE 7.1

Occupational Outlook Handbook projections on industries and occupational areas.

Of the 25 occupations with fast growth, high pay, and low unemployment that have the largest numerical growth (projected 1996–2006), 18 require at least a bachelor's degree.

Systems analysts
General managers and top executives
Registered nurses
Teachers, secondary school
Clerical supervisors and managers
Database administrators and computer support specialists
Maintenance repairers, general utility
Teachers, special education
Computer engineers
Social workers
Food service and lodging managers
College and university faculty
Engineering, mathematical, and computer systems managers
Licensed practical nurses
Financial managers
Marketing, advertising, and public relations managers
Computer programmers
Instructors and coaches, sports and physical training
Lawyers
Physicians
Electrical and electronics engineers
Corrections officers
Securities and financial services sales workers
Physical therapists
Artists and commercial artists

0   100   200   300   400   500   600

1996–2006 numerical change ▣   Thousands   *(continued)*

Another interesting economic indicator is the monthly report on new housing units started. This figure reflects the number of new houses on which construction starts during the month. Housing starts on the rise usually indicate that the rest of the economy will follow: new houses require the purchase of lumber, cement, roofing materials, lighting and plumbing fixtures, appliances, furniture, carpeting, and so on. If housing starts are high and concentrated in certain geographic areas, they could stimulate construction of roads, schools, and shopping malls, as well as growth of new businesses. In other words, housing starts stimulate activity in many other areas of the economy.

Additional statistical indicators are reported regularly by the media. Select a few that interest you and track them. You will find that you better understand what's going on in our economy and that you can use the information to make career decisions and time your moves. For instance, you might acquire new skills by returning to school when the economy is slow in your geographic area. When the economy picks up and organizations are hiring, you will be ready to seek employment, armed with your new credentials.

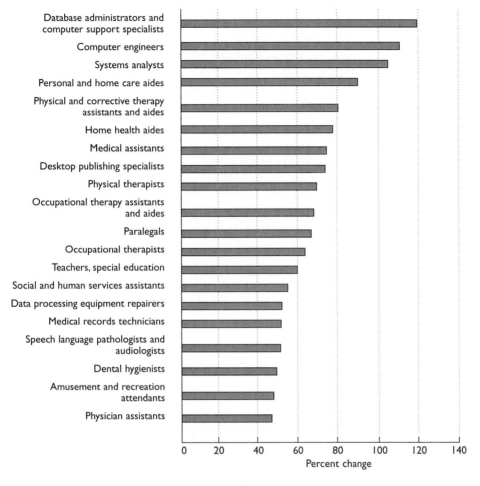

FIGURE 7.1

Continued.

Occupations projected to grow the fastest, 1996–2006.

The fastest-growing occupations reflect growth in computer technology and health-care services.

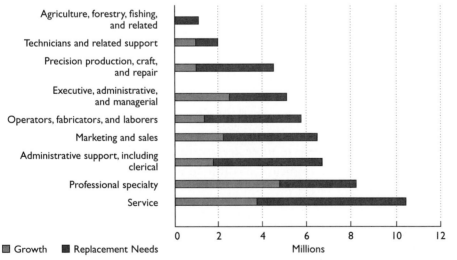

Job openings due to growth and replacement needs by major occupational group, projected 1996–2006.

Service and professional specialty occupations will provide 2 out of every 5 job openings—primarily due to high replacement needs

Source: Bureau of Labor Statistics, "Tomorrow's Jobs," *Occupational Outlook Handbook,* 1998–1999.

Some individuals may be tempted to use discouraging economic indicators as an excuse to postpone dealing with their career issues. These individuals are making a mistake. Keep in mind that even in the worst of times, organizations hire new workers and individuals make transitions. It is not unusual for an organization to lay off hundreds of workers and simultaneously hire some new people. The organization is redirecting its efforts and needs new talent, people with different sets of skills from those they have terminated. While it may be easier to make a career transition during a period of rapid economic growth, you can do it at any time. Knowing what the climate is will help you to establish appropriate expectations.

FOLLOW EMPLOYMENT TRENDS

Another area you will need to research is the labor market. A complete restructuring is taking place in the workplace, and that process is dramatically changing how we define work and career in our society. In comparison with the Industrial Revolution, the current shifts are occurring much more rapidly. It took roughly 100 years for our nation to change from an agricultural society to an industrial society, but only 10 years to transform from an industrial to an information-based society. While change has always been part of life, the pace of change has accelerated significantly. Because change is occurring so rapidly, it is difficult to stay on top of the emerging patterns and even more difficult to predict where the changes will lead.

In all of human history, there may never have been a more exciting time to be alive, and there may never have been more opportunity than exists today. As a career changer, it is in your best interest to let go of the past, including disappointments over past career losses, and look ahead at the multiplicity of possibilities that exists today. Some of the trends sound scary because they reflect such fundamental change in what we know; however, change can lead to positive and desirable outcomes that go beyond our imaginations. Stay tuned!

So much is happening so quickly, on the world stage as well as nationally and regionally, that it is impossible to offer a comprehensive list of all the important trends. The trends presented here are intended to raise awareness and stimulate thought and discussion. As you review them, note those you have seen personally. Feel free to add any patterns you've observed that may have emerged since this list was compiled.

TRENDS IN THE WORKPLACE

- Global economic issues impact the U. S. economy.
- Mergers and acquisitions pepper the headlines as companies combine forces to dominate markets, increase profits, and beat the competition.
- Companies have restructured their organizations, moving from hierarchies to teams, and giving workers more responsibility for decision making.
- Employers are using every means possible to attract and keep good people.
- Hiring decisions are based on demonstrated competency in "hot" skills.
- The use of the Internet for the purpose of commerce is exploding.
- Quality customer service has expanded into the realm of customer relationship management and customization of products and services.
- Work/life balance issues have finally made it onto the radar screen of corporate America.
- Savvy employees today actively manage their work lives and learning.

WHERE THE OPPORTUNITIES ARE

- Long-range projections indicate strong growth in jobs in computer systems, health care, and education.

- Organizations are hiring temporary and contractual workers, which creates opportunities for self-employment.

- Organizations are "outsourcing" many functions, which creates new business opportunities.

- Job opportunities are expanding in small- and medium-size companies.

- Job opportunities have shifted from the manufacturing sector to the service sector.

- Entrepreneurship is on the rise.

- Opportunities for part-time employment have increased dramatically.

- Changes in public policy, especially deregulation of some industries, have created opportunity.

- Despite low unemployment and overall economic growth, the job market remains a mixed bag.

We will look at each of these trends in more detail. We will also discuss how to apply this information in planning for careers now and into the next millennium. An understanding of the big picture will help you to see how you can fit into the evolving workplace.

Trends in the Workplace

Global economic issues impact the U.S. economy.

In 1993, the country was reeling from an economic recession. The federal deficit was out of control, unemployment was unacceptably high, and wages were stagnant. In contrast, economic growth during 1997 was the strongest in a decade: 14 million new jobs were created that year, unemployment was the lowest in 24 years (it subsequently hit a 30-year low), poverty had dropped, and core inflation was at its lowest level in 30 years. The deficit, $290 billion in 1993, had been reduced to $22 billion in 1997, and a balanced budget will soon be a reality.

A major player in the global marketplace, the U.S. economy is currently feeling the impact of recessions and monetary crises in Asia, Russia, and, more recently, Latin America. During the summer of 1998, declining sales abroad and slowing profits among U.S. corporations led to great turbulence in the stock market and fear of a major economic downturn at home. Additional speculation concerned the possibility of a worldwide recession. In September, President Clinton suggested that the major world powers consider a global lowering of interest rates to stave off a global recession. The possibility that the major powers could make economic policies collaboratively underscores a new level of recognition of our global interconnectedness. Because globalization is such a dominant aspect of the economy and work today—and drives many of the other trends—it may be useful to review earlier history.

When World War II ended, much of the industrial world (Europe, Japan) had been destroyed. The United States, on the other hand, was relatively unscathed by the war and was booming industrially. Tremendous industrial growth had occurred during the war as industries converted plants to manufacture munitions. After the war, manufacturing companies successfully converted back to a peacetime economy, helped to rebuild Europe and Japan, and flooded the world market with American-made consumer products. They exploited the tremendous, pent-up demand for consumer goods within the United States as well. During the war, the production of washing machines, automobiles, furniture, and countless other consumer products had been suspended.

Meanwhile, almost no competition for market share came from outside the United States. The 40 years following World War II were the "glory years" of American industry. As Japan and the countries of Europe recovered from the war, they concentrated on producing goods for their own consumption and only gradually entered international markets. Today, however, the competition has become intense.

Many European and Pacific Rim countries are exporting their products worldwide. Relatively low wages, favorable exchange rates, highly trained technical workers, and automated industrial plants provide advantages to these countries and their industries. In recent years, these countries have been able to produce and transport products to international markets at prices below those charged by U.S. manufacturers. Until recently, this was in part due to the relatively high exchange rate for the U.S. dollar, a situation favorable to competing countries. Another factor is the comparatively low wages of competing countries.

For example, consider the production of automobiles in the United States. In the 1980s, prices became so high for American-made cars that a huge percentage of U.S. car buyers purchased cars manufactured in other countries, primarily Japan. As U.S. automobile manufacturers fought to regain market share, they found they could not compete with the Japanese. The quality of Japanese cars was higher and the price was lower than that of American cars, even after import taxes were paid. For U.S. automakers to get their prices down, they had to significantly reduce their costs. This involved downsizing their companies and reengineering their manufacturing operations. In the early 1990s, it looked like U.S. automakers might not be able to get back in the game, but they have truly revolutionized their industry. General Motors, for example, lost $10.7 billion in 1991 but made a $362 million profit in 1993; that's an $11 billion turnaround in two years (Taylor, 1994, p. 55). In 1997, GM ranked number one in the *Fortune 500* with profits of $6.7 billion. Since then, the popular sports utility vehicles have dominated the industry.

It remains to be seen how global economic and political developments will evolve and impact the U.S. economy in the years ahead. One thing is certain: the U.S. will remain a major player on the world stage.

The global economy presents new challenges and opportunities for cvareer changers

Today's career changer who is aware of global economic issues will have an advantage in the job market. Knowledge of international trade and the ability to speak different languages and adapt to different cultures provide a competitive advantage for someone interested in building an international career. Abilities needed in the domestic marketplace also reflect globalization: the ability to develop international marketing strategies for U.S. products and services; the ability to speak different languages; and the ability to develop new manufacturing processes or financial strategies that lower costs.

Mergers and acquisitions pepper the headlines as companies combine forces to dominate markets, increase profits, and beat the competition.

A growing economy, rising stock market prices, and plentiful cash from corporate profits provide the perfect ecosystem for mergers and acquisitions in the business world. The late 1990s have seen record-setting activity, dubbed "merger mania," as companies large and small combined forces. Among the most notable recent marriages are MCI and Worldcom, Bank America and Nation's

Bank, Compaq Computer and Digital Equipment, Raytheon and Hughes Aircraft, Travelers Group and Solomon, and Mobil and Exxon. In 1998, British Petroleum took over Amoco in a $48 billion deal described as the biggest ever industrial merger and the biggest purchase of an American firm by a foreign one ("Mergers & Acquisitions," *Economist*, August 15–21, 1998).

"Merger motivations range from survival to protection to diversification to growth," according to Hisrich and Peters (p. 433). Mergers and acquisitions create a frenzy in the market that seems to breed even more "M & A's" as companies look for ways to expand before other companies gobble them up. To borrow a sports cliché, the best defense is a good offense.

Hisrich and Peters describe five basic types of mergers: horizontal, vertical, product extension, market extension, and diversified activity. Understanding these illuminates the vigorous activity we are witnessing. A horizontal merger involves two firms that produce one or more of the same products in the same geographic area. They are motivated by economies of scale in marketing, production, or sales.

A vertical merger involves two or more firms in successive stages of production; they usually have a buyer–seller relationship. The merger stabilizes and controls supply and production. A product extension merger occurs between companies that have related production and/or distribution activities but no competing products. A market extension merger combines two firms that produce the same products but sell them in different geographic markets. This pairing saves money on marketing, production, and management. A diversified activity merger is a conglomerate merger consolidating two unrelated firms with limited transfer of skills and activities (Hisrich & Peters, pp. 568–572).

Mergers typically occur when there is synergy, the magic that makes the two firms worth more together than apart. Factors that cause synergy include economies of scale, tax benefits (e.g., when one of the companies involved has net losses that can reduce the taxable income of the other), and advantages derived from combining complementary resources (e.g., acquiring a firm's new technology or keeping a firm's product from being a competitive threat).

The Sherman Antitrust Act (1890) and the Clayton Act (1973) were designed to protect small businesses against the competitive advantages of large ones. The U. S. Department of Justice and the Federal Trade Commission are charged with antitrust enforcement, and they've been extremely busy. Microsoft, Toys "R" Us, Archer Daniels Midland, Lockheed Martin, and Northrop Grumman were among the firms recently hauled into court; Staples and Office Depot were prevented from merging.

One of the most troubling aspects of mergers is that they often lead to layoffs. In a *Fortune* article, Geoffrey Colvin points out, "The startling reality is that most takeovers have never been about saving money by firing people and that's truer than ever today, when the whole point of many acquisitions is getting people. . . . In an economy based increasingly on intellectual capital, a company's assets are in the employees' heads . . . especially in pure-intellect industries like infotech, biotech, and consulting" (Colvin, *Fortune*, June 22, 1998). The banking industry is expected to continue major consolidation; in this industry, layoffs are typically a component of the deals.

The nonprofit world has had its share of mergers and acquisitions as well, most notably with hospitals. Under the tight grip of managed care (with its focus on cost containment), hospitals have been joining forces to take advantage of economies of scale. This shift has involved large teaching hospitals, small community hospitals, and those in between.

As job seekers, you can't really avoid mergers and acquisitions, but you can be informed about them. Reading the business press is the best way to stay on top of what is occurring within organizations. If you interview with an organization that is undergoing a merger, find out all you can about the motivation for the merger and whether the company expects to lay off workers.

Companies have restructured their organizations, moving from hierarchies to teams, and giving workers more responsibility for decision making.

Many U.S. corporations have transformed their traditional hierarchical structures into horizontal structures based on individual specialties and composed of self-directed work teams. This approach permitted companies to eliminate layers of middle management because workers manage themselves and are accountable to one another.

Associated with the TQM (total quality management) movement, this trend reflects yet another response to global competition. Products manufactured in other countries were frequently found to be superior to American-made products. Upon examination, it was found that companies overseas were organized differently and that their workers were involved in decision making and quality assurance. The organizational structures of these companies were modeled after the work of an American named W. Edwards Deming. Unable to implement his ideas in the United States, he had found a receptive audience in Japan.

New organization structures demand communication, problem-solving, and decision-making skills

In the new flattened organizations, workers become more fully informed about the company and their individual contributions. They learn about the entire manufacturing process for the products they make and perform many functions within that process, not just a single function on an assembly line. As a result, workers take more interest in their jobs and assume broader responsibility. They make decisions about production schedules. They also make improvements to the production process that result in fewer defective parts; these improvements lower costs and eliminate waste.

Communication has also been streamlined in companies as workers talk with one another and with workers on other teams rather than communicating upward through middle management. This horizontal approach to organizational processes, sometimes referred to as the networked organization, is more efficient. As a result of these changes, jobs have changed. They are no longer clearly defined; workers are expected to be flexible, to do what needs to be done. The job as we have known it is disappearing. Workers with broad skills, especially in communicating, decision making, and problem solving, are needed and valued in today's emerging organizations.

Some of these changes directly challenge the practices and protections of organized labor. A historic union vote took place at Maine's Bath Iron Works in August of 1994. The new union contract changed the relationship between management and labor and eliminated labor's long-standing work rules that prevented one unionized tradesman from doing the work of another. In exchange for job flexibility, the company promised no layoffs for three years. The company's ability to convert from manufacturing destroyers for the U.S. Navy to building commercial vessels hinged on the union workers agreeing to flexible job duties. Reorganized into balanced union–management teams, Bath Iron Works considers flexibility essential to compete with top rivals in Europe, Korea, and Japan.

Job hunters who have experience working in collaborative teams will have an advantage in the market. Make sure you can communicate using the skills involved in working with a team. See Behavioral Interviewing in Chapter Eleven for more discussion of this topic.

Employers are using every means possible to attract and keep good people.

In 1997 alone, employment grew by 3.2 million. The unemployment rate hovered around 4.5 percent nationally as of September 1998, the lowest rate in 30 years. Labor market statisticians view this figure as virtually full employment. In a tight labor market, laid-off workers usually find new jobs quickly. Discouraged workers are lured back into the labor force. New and less experienced workers find jobs more easily, and employed workers take advantage of opportunities to get ahead either with their current employer or by changing jobs. With shortages in the labor supply, employers are striving to attract workers away from other organizations and to meet the needs and demands of their own workers in order to retain them.

The labor market of the late 1990s is entirely different from that of the early years of the decade, when employers were radically reducing overhead costs, largely by downsizing their workforce. This egregious solution occurred in every sector of employment and created a crisis characterized by high and long-lasting unemployment. The unwritten contract that had existed between employers and employees ended forever. Implicit in the old employment contract was guaranteed employment in exchange for loyalty to the company. The lesson in this painful history for all American workers was "there are no guarantees." We will examine how this has changed employees in a subsequent trend. For now, let's look at how this trend affected employers.

No longer able to offer long-term security, employers lost some of their power and hold over workers. Employees began to see themselves as free agents. The tremendous growth in the economy in the past several years resulted from many factors, including innovation in products and services and the redesign in organizational processes. Most organizations have reengineered themselves in the past decade. In addition, huge technological changes have occurred in all aspects of most organizations. And, finally, there was the blood, sweat, and tears of an overburdened workforce. As a result of the growth and the corporations' return to prosperity, millions of new jobs have been created and qualified workers are in short supply.

In some ways, it appears to have become an employee's market. Employers have had to create new ways to attract and retain workers. Tactics they use to lure workers away from other organizations and keep the ones they have include: offering lucrative sign-on bonuses, even to entry-level workers, provided they possess the needed "hot" skills (see related trend); offering personal services, from dry cleaning pickup and delivery to on-site gyms and day-care centers; offering sizable "finder's fees" (usually paid if the employee remains for six months) to current employees who bring in new workers who succeed in the organization; offering stock options and bonus incentives tied to the company's performance; making the workplace fun by offering outings, team sports, and other social activities that build (or rebuild) a sense of belonging; creating a team identity by dressing in matching T-shirts and other trendy fashions; and relaxing dress codes to "corporate casual."

When looking below the surface glitter and gold, however, the important long-term benefits may be completely missing or significantly reduced in comparison to former compensation packages. Pension plans and health insurance policies that lock organizations into commitments that must be met during good times and bad have been eroding. Even sign-on bonuses are one-time payments, not annual salary commitments. In essence, the company brings the employee in at a lower salary level disguised by a bonus.

 These changes reflect a shift in values as organizations strive to reduce overhead. At present, the worker has some leverage in negotiating for hire and advancement, but long-term incentives have been compromised. In some ways, employers miss the loyalty they enjoyed for decades, but they simply can't afford to meet their end of the bargain. So they're dancing as fast as they can to attract and keep workers without offering them secure futures.

Hiring decisions are based on demonstrated competency in "hot" skills.

Technical and computer skills are in high demand

Workers in U.S. manufacturing facilities used to say they were hired "from the neck down," meaning they were hired for their physical strength and speed and weren't expected to think. Management did the thinking and made decisions. That has changed. Workers at all levels and in all kinds of organizations are expected to be well educated and able to solve problems, make decisions, and collaborate with other workers. "Knowledge workers" are in demand.

According to economist Lester Thurow, a knowledge gap is growing in the United States. While our postgraduate education system is recognized around the world, our elementary, secondary, and baccalaureate levels of education are considered inferior to those of most industrialized countries. Students from the U.S. system of education are especially weak in math. Without a solid math background, U.S. workers lack the foundation for technical skills needed in the workplace (Thurow, 1992).

While companies and organizations are casting wide nets to find new employees, they may be more particular than ever about the skill sets and competencies of the people they hire. Many positions go unfilled for months because applicants don't have the required skills. Hiring today is skills-driven. There are several categories of skills that employers seek, and in which they refuse to compromise.

The first is general technical skills. Most jobs outside the lowest-level service jobs require general technical skills. In other words, most employees are expected to be computer-literate. An administrative assistant position, for instance, might require proficiency in Microsoft Word, Excel, and Access software. Fortunately, computers have become user-friendly, and learning basic word processing is now simple. Furthermore, training is readily available and cheap, sometimes even free. Job seekers are usually expected to pick up basic computer skills on their own if they don't already possess them. These general technical skills fall in the category of functional skills, discussed in Chapter Five.

The second category of "hot" skills is specific technical skills for particular technical jobs. These skills fall in the category of work content skills, discussed in Chapter Five. This area is often where employers seem to be the least willing to negotiate. A position in computer graphics may require experience with Photoshop and Adobe Illustrator software; a Web developer may be required to know HTML, Java, and CGI. Companies seem less willing than in the past to hire people with analogous but not the exact software skills. Often, they are using expensive placement agencies as recruiters; when a fee is involved, employers want their ideal candidate.

The third category of skills of concern to hiring managers are soft skills. Like the general technical skills discussed above, these are functional skills in areas such as leadership, problem solving, team collaboration, and interpersonal communication. Employers are looking for competent, capable workers who can make a significant contribution, starting on the first day, and who can handle themselves well in stressful and challenging situations. In Chapter Eleven, we will discuss behavioral interviewing techniques, which are used to assess the "soft" functional skills of applicants.

Employers are now less interested in "old" credentials. They like evidence of new learning, such as a certificate in a specialized area. Here's where those "hot" technical credentials are so important. You must be marketing current technical skills that match the needs of the employer. Anyone who avoided college for many years has a chance to upskill quickly with a "hot" credential and skip the traditional bachelor's degree. While this may not ensure long-term job security, it can provide fast access to good jobs now. If employers can't find qualified applicants, they may hire international applicants or send the work overseas before hiring someone they would have to train.

The use of the Internet for the purpose of commerce is exploding.

Enormous growth in computers and telecommunications has dominated the market. Perhaps the most notable recent expansion has occurred in the overall use of the Internet. Once the bastion of computer geeks from around the world, the Web has become a global resource and linking mechanism used extensively by all sectors of the economy and by individuals everywhere. Open access to information has changed everything from job hunting to presidential impeachment proceedings.

With more information available to consumers, from comparison pricing to locating hard-to-find products, Internet commerce provides both consumer protection and convenience. Government has so far resisted the temptation to regulate the Internet or to tax its commercial transactions. That may change as increasing business is conducted through this medium.

Electronic commerce (known in the biz as "ecommerce") is booming. Sites like amazon.com, the online bookstore, and llbean.com, the outdoor equipment and apparel store, paved the way for mass consumerism via the Internet. Airline ticket and stock purchases are commonly transacted on the Internet. Now that security problems have been resolved with encryption software, the possibilities are limitless. The medium is being used by small, independent niche marketers as well as large, established mail-order companies. We can now shop 'til we drop in front of our home computers 24 hours a day. The Internet offers a great opportunity for small entrepreneurial ventures to bring their products to the global marketplace at very low cost.

Quality customer service has expanded into the realm of customer relationship management and customization of products and services.

Organizations have moved from being customer-focused to customer-driven as they learned how to better serve and retain existing customers and acquire new ones. Companies are applying advances in information technology to bring the right product to the right customer, through the right channel at the right time. Customization of products and services was a natural next step to quality customer service.

You may have discovered that mail-order companies will hem your pants to the length you specify. Or a local store may send advertisements about its line of toddler clothing and toys just as your child turns two. In addition, grocery stores have established Internet sites where you can place an order; the company will then deliver your groceries to your home by appointment or store them in a refrigerator that they provide in your garage.

On a larger scale, retailers electronically monitor the sales patterns of their individual stores and restock fast-moving products within 24 to 48 hours. They are also able to analyze buying patterns in different locations to provide merchandise appealing to local culture; Sears and many other chain stores practice "mass customization." Data inform the production process as well as the distribution process. A product that is selling well may continue in production while one that is not moving comes out of production before too much excess is produced.

These innovations are the result of data warehousing, data mining, and meaningful and timely data analysis using specialized software. Sales, marketing, and customer service departments access the same relational databases to analyze customers' individual buying habits, predict future needs, and conduct "one-to-one marketing"—all for the purpose of getting more of your business. This knowledge-based strategy has potential for long-term customer relationship management. Business will develop products and services as fast as your needs change.

Meanwhile, the American consumer is spending as never before. According to Juliet B. Schor, author of *The Overspent American,* consumers no longer compare themselves to the Joneses next door, but to exorbitantly paid professional athletes, performers, and others whom they see on television. Their reference group also includes fellow workers in much higher income brackets. The new consumerism is fueled by the accelerated pace of product innovation and a continuous ratcheting up of standards. Television advertising exposes middle- and working-class people to buying pressures never intended for them. Most income groups report feeling that it's a struggle to meet basic necessities. Needless to say, households are taking on credit-card debt at record levels as the new consumerism has led to mass overspending.

Work/life balance issues have finally made it onto the radar screen of corporate America.

It may be too soon to tell whether we have real progress or merely lip service, but some employers are beginning to respond to the struggles many workers report in balancing multiple demands of work and life outside of work. Labor shortages have no doubt contributed to employers' loosening the reins. Flexible work schedules, one of the most requested concessions of working parents, are more common. The option to work from home has been aided by technical advances, such as computers, fax machines, cell phones, and pagers.

Companies can also save on the bottom line when they don't have to provide an office for each employee. Some companies now provide generic work stations to those who show up on a particular day. MCI (now MCI-WorldCom) has perfected this model for flexible work arrangements.

The Family and Medical Leave Act was passed by the legislature in 1993 to help workers manage family crises without jeopardizing their jobs. The Health Care Portability and Accountability Act of 1996 allows workers to keep their health insurance benefits when they change jobs or suffer a family emergency. Additional initiatives have been raised by labor unions as part of collective bargaining efforts. For example, the UPS strike in 1997 challenged the company's practice of heavily using contract workers, and the General Motors strike of 1998 challenged the practice of forced overtime.

Most workers report working longer and harder than ever. Telecommuting technology exacerbates the problem. Employees can log on any time of the day or night, thus blurring the boundaries between work and the rest of life.

Savvy employees today actively manage their work lives and learning.

The recession of the early 1990s was a terrible blow to American workers. Whether personally laid off or not, everyone was impacted by widespread downsizing and long-lasting unemployment. We learned from this experience that there are no guarantees. In the intervening years, it has become evident that many workers have internalized this lesson and recalibrated their sense of ownership of their work life.

Successful workers assume responsibility for their careers. They choose their jobs carefully and for reasons that advance their own career agenda. At the same time, they make sure the work they do adds value to the organization; they are learning to document and quantify the value they add.

Those on the cutting edge are also learning to benchmark their skills against those of other professionals in their field. They take responsibility for their continuing education and upskilling to remain technically current and employable. They anticipate the changing needs of their employer and the marketplace and acquire relevant skills to stay ahead of the curve. They are primarily loyal to their profession and to their projects; they are loyal to their employer as long as the arrangement is mutually beneficial. In addition, they are well connected both inside their organization and outside the organization within their profession. They are likely to be active in professional organizations.

Some enlightened corporations, such as Sun Microsystems and Raychem, have fostered career self-reliance by providing their valued workers with the information and resources they need to actively manage their careers. When employers and employees work together to prepare for the future, they have a chance to arrive at the same place with the needed human resources. Unlike the old contract where the employer was expected to take care of you just because of your loyalty and hard work, the new partnership values human resources, recognizes changing needs, and empowers workers to prepare for the future.

Where the Opportunities Are

The marketplace is continually evolving, and often the change is tumultuous. The 1998 third-quarter slowdown in U.S. business abroad triggered dozens of large-scale layoff announcements from major corporations, including Gillette, Compaq Computers, Travelers-Citicorp, Boeing, Lucent Technologies, Hewlitt Packard, and Raytheon. Fluctuations in the market are part of the information you need when planning career moves.

The best way to assess the market when considering a change is to collect current information from the Department of Labor and the local and national business press. Figure 7.2 contains listings of the fastest-growing occupations and the occupations projected to have the largest numerical increase in employment between 1996 and 2006. These are long-range projections. The information is organized by level of education and training. Consult the Department of Labor Web site at http://stats.bls.gov/ for updated information.

Combining the long-range projections with current, actual business and market events will give you the best information available. Career decisions should not be based on short-term market behavior. For example, huge layoffs in high tech in the early 1990s discouraged many from applying to computer science programs; four years later when the industry was booming, there were far more jobs than graduates. We will look at some patterns and projections in hiring and job creation.

Long-range projections indicate strong growth in jobs in computer systems, health care, and education.

Jobs in the computer field and positions requiring strong technical/computer skills in all fields will remain in high demand through the year 2006, according to the Bureau of Labor Statistics. Looking closely at Figure 7.2, in the categories "Work experience plus bachelor's or higher degree" and "Bachelor's degree," you can see the demand for computer and technical personnel. Systems analysts, computer engineers, database administrators, and computer support specialists will have the largest numerical increases in

employment, while computer systems managers will have one of the largest percent increases. This information reinforces the tremendous need for high-technology training.

A second theme in the data, especially at the associate's degree level and below, is positions in health care. Registered nurses, licensed practical nurses, radiologic technologists and technicians, dental hygienists, and emergency medical technicians are among the fields predicted to add personnel.

Positions in education, from the doctoral level on down, reflect the aging population of teachers and professors and, within the public education arena, the emphasis on educational reform, including new mandates to reduce class size.

FIGURE 7.2

Fastest-growing occupations	Education/training category	Occupations having the largest numerical increase in employment
	FIRST PROFESSIONAL DEGREE	
Chiropractors Veterinarians and veterinary inspectors Physicians Lawyers Clergy		Lawyers Physicians Clergy Veterinarians and veterinary inspectors Dentists
	DOCTORAL DEGREE	

Biological scientists
Medical scientists
College and university faculty
Mathematicians and all other mathematical
  scientists
		College and university faculty
		Biological scientists
		Medical scientists
		Mathematicians and all other mathematical
		  scientists

	MASTER'S DEGREE	
Speech-language pathologists & audiologists Counselors Curators, archivists, museum technicians Psychologists Operations research analysts		Speech-language pathologists & audiologists Counselors Psychologists Librarians, professional Operations research analysts
	WORK EXPERIENCE PLUS BACHELOR'S OR HIGHER DEGREE	

Engineering, science, and computer systems
  managers
Marketing, advertising, and public relations
  managers
Artists and commercial artists
Management analysts
Financial managers
		General managers and top executives
		Engineering, science, and computer systems
		  managers
		Financial managers
		Marketing, advertising, and public relations
		  managers
		Artists and commercial artists

	BACHELOR'S DEGREE	

Database administrators and computer
  support specialists
Computer engineers
Systems analysts
Physical therapists
Occupational therapists
		Systems analysts
		Teachers, secondary school
		Database administrators and computer
		  support specialists
		Teachers, special education
		Computer engineers

	ASSOCIATE'S DEGREE	
Paralegals Health information technician Dental hygienists Respiratory therapists Cardiology technologists		Registered nurses Paralegals Dental hygienists Radiologic technologists and technicians Health information technicians
	POSTSECONDARY VOCATIONAL TRAINING	
Data processing equipment repairers Emergency medical technicians Manicurists Surgical technologists Medical secretaries		Licensed practical nurses Automotive mechanics Medical secretaries Emergency medical technicians Hairdressers, hairstylists, and cosmetologists

(continued)

FIGURE 7.2 Fastest-growing occupations and occupations having the largest numerical increase in employment, projected 1996–2006, by level of education and training.

Fastest-growing occupations	Education/training category	Occupations having the largest numerical increase in employment
	WORK EXPERIENCE	
Food service and lodging managers Teachers and instructors, vocational education and training Lawn service managers Instructors, adult education Nursery and greenhouse managers		Clerical supervisors and managers Marketing and sales worker supervisors Food service and lodging managers Teachers and instructors, vocational education and training Instructors, adult (nonvocational) education
	LONG-TERM TRAINING AND EXPERIENCE (more than 12 months on-the-job training)	
Desktop publishing specialists Flight attendants Musicians Correction officers Producers, directors, actors, entertainers		Maintenance repairers, general utility Cooks, restaurant Correction officers Musicians Police patrol officers
	MODERATE-TERM TRAINING AND EXPERIENCE (1 to 12 months on-the-job experience and informal training)	
Physical and corrective therapy assistants and aides Medical assistants Occupational therapy assistants and aides Social and human services assistants Instructors and coaches, sports and physical training		Medical assistants Instructors and coaches, sports and physical training Social and human services assistants Dental assistants Physical and corrective therapy assistants
	SHORT-TERM TRAINING AND EXPERIENCE (up to 1 month on-the-job experience)	
Personal and home care aides Home health aides Amusement and recreation attendants Adjustment clerks Bill and account collectors		Cashiers Salespersons, retail Truck drivers, light and heavy Home health aides Teacher's aides and educational assistants

Source: Bureau of Labor Statistics Online at http://stats.bls.gov/oco/ocotjtl.htm.

Organizations are hiring temporary and contractual workers, which creates opportunities for self-employment.

Layoffs also mean increased self-employment opportunities

In the past, it was not unusual for employers to have surplus workers. This practice was especially common in defense industries, where government contracts created boom times and where there could be lags between projects. Employers were reluctant to lay off good employees when they knew they would need them again in a matter of weeks or months. Such practices are no longer affordable. Companies are eliminating those positions and, in their place, hiring workers on a temporary or project basis.

Many terms are used to identify temporary workers, including contingency workers, contractual workers, and "temps." There are several advantages to this solution for companies. First, the companies pay only for work completed. This permits them to keep a tight rein on their head counts and production costs. Second, when using temps, companies don't incur the expense of fringe benefits, such as medical insurance, tuition reimbursement, and vacations. Third, companies can make rapid changes in personnel in response to advancements in technology, shifts in the market, or changes in their needs. These advantages allow companies to remain flexible and competitive.

Career changers who want to start their own businesses have a ready market for their hot skills. They can market themselves to companies or use agencies that place contract workers. While the disadvantage of temporary work is the uncertainty of long-term employment, the advantages include the ability to set your own schedule, the opportunity to run your own small business, and the chance to work in many different settings. As this form of employment has grown, many temporary employment agencies offer health insurance and other benefits to their regular clientele. Incidentally, Manpower is the largest employer in the United States today. Contracting will be discussed in more detail in Chapter Thirteen.

Organizations have outsourced many functions, which has created new business opportunities.

Organizations are outsourcing, or subcontracting, many of their functions rather than employing permanent personnel. For example, some companies outsource their MIS (management information systems) functions. Instead of employing an MIS manager, project leaders, and programmers, these companies contract with an outside company that provides all of their MIS services. In this way, they pay only for the exact services they need. If new software becomes available, the contracted firm makes the conversion; the original company will not have to buy new software and retrain or replace workers. Companies may do the same with their marketing, accounting, field service, or human resources departments. In 1998, Rockwell International spun off its semiconductor business. In this way, the original company becomes smaller and more focused on its core business. At the same time, it spurs the creation of other small companies to provide needed products and services.

As a career changer, consider the possibility of working for a firm that provides services to large corporations. Often, former employees of a large company start their own firm by selling their services back to the firm that once employed them. Other firms are popping up in response to gaps being created by corporate streamlining.

There is good growth potential for businesses handling functions for bigger businesses

Job opportunities are expanding in small- and medium-size companies.

Job growth is occurring primarily in small- and medium-size companies. Many enterprising individuals and groups have split off from large companies or started companies on their own, having identified niches in software development, biotechnology, and telecommunications, to name a few. Smaller companies have the advantage of being able to target specific markets, respond to customers' increasing requests for customized products and services, and to rapidly adapt to shifting market demands.

Searching for employment opportunities in small companies presents a challenge to job hunters and career changers. Most major urban newspapers have historically written about the *Fortune 500* companies on their business pages. More recently, the press has reported stories coming from emerging companies producing innovative products or offering creative new services. The Internet may be your best source of both information and job leads. Business directories are also available. For example, *Hoover's Directory of Emerging Companies* is an excellent resource. Others are listed in Chapter Ten.

Job opportunities have shifted from the manufacturing sector to the service sector.

The service industry currently accounts for three-quarters of the U. S. gross domestic product; the figure was close to 60 percent in 1950, so we see tremendous growth in this sector. The opposite is true of the manufacturing sector. In 1950, 34 percent of employment was in manufacturing jobs in the United States. Today, manufacturing jobs account for 17 percent of employment (U.S. Department of Labor et al.). There are several explanations for these shifts. The first is the global competition discussed earlier; the United States has lost market share because of intense competition. Some manufacturing companies have closed down or moved production facilities offshore, where they can pay workers lower salaries.

Second, automation has streamlined production and eliminated many manufacturing jobs; robots have replaced workers. This phenomenon is not as significant as originally predicted both because robots need monitoring and because the more sophisticated products being made today require skilled workers at all steps in the production process.

Third, the U.S. manufacturing industries focused largely on defense for most of the last 50 years. Consequently, they missed the huge boom in consumer product development, especially in the electronics industry. We make *none* of the video cameras and recorders, fax machines, or CD players consumed by millions of Americans and others worldwide. Sadly, Americans invented both camcorders and the fax. It is no longer enough to invent a great new product; you also have to be able to manufacture it more cheaply than anyone else (Thurow, 1992).

Defense conversion is well underway, and industries are recognizing the importance of manufacturing and exporting superior products globally. While they have a great deal of catching up to do, they have the determination. The signing of the North American Free Trade Agreement (NAFTA) and the Uruguay Round of the General Agreement of Tariffs and Trade (GATT) were steps intended to put U.S. products back in the ballgame.

Of concern are statistics revealing that many people who have lost manufacturing jobs have migrated to lower-paying service sector jobs. There has been a monumental shift of workers from manufacturing to the service industry. However, don't confuse the service industry with service jobs. *Service jobs* include retail salespeople, cooks and waitpeople, delivery people, and maintenance workers. The *service industry* includes financial services (banking, investing, and insurance), legal services, health-care services, design and engineering services, and computer services. These are not low-level positions!

Well-conceived and professionally run training programs are needed for workers who have gone from well-paying manufacturing jobs to lower-paying service jobs. The service sector is expected to continue growing rapidly. A strong background in technical skills will make career changers competitive for the better paid positions in the service sector.

Entrepreneurship is on the rise.

Dissatisfaction with organizations and the resulting stress have inspired many individuals to start their own businesses. Owning a business, a dream of many Americans, can have enormous risks—and payoffs. Starting a business can take many forms. Perhaps the most common is becoming a consultant. Consultants typically have 15 or more years of experience in their field and specific expertise (such as ISO 9000 regulations for quality standards in international trade). They often market their services to their former employer and to other companies with which they have developed professional relationships throughout their careers.

Other entrepreneurs turn a hobby into a business, buy a franchise, or purchase a business started by someone else. They may identify a need in their community and start a business to meet that need, or start a company that spins off from their former job. Chapter Thirteen is devoted to starting your own business.

Opportunities for part-time employment have increased dramatically.

People laid off or prematurely retired have difficulty finding comparable new jobs when the overall unemployment rate is high. Preferring work to unemployment, or forced to take something in order to survive, many workers discover an abundance of part-time jobs. Unfortunately, the jobs are often seasonal, with low pay and no fringe benefits. They also require fewer hours, which may be very appealing to workers able to easily shift priorities to family or other areas.

Some part-time workers, however, must take a second or even a third part-time job to make ends meet. Soon these individuals are working long hours, commuting many miles, and paying for health insurance. These part-time workers would be happier and more productive in a full-time job. We need to find better employment and hiring practices where individuals are in the situations they prefer.

Changes in public policy, especially deregulation of some industries, have created opportunity.

Deregulation of the electric power utilities is creating new jobs and business opportunities nationwide and globally. Timetables vary from state to state, but the overall intention is to dismantle public utilities and permit private companies to compete for the business of providing electric power to industry and eventually to the domestic market. Individuals with strong business and entrepreneurial expertise are needed to create profitable businesses in electric power delivery.

Banking is another area where deregulation has changed the rules of the game. This industry is undergoing major shifts. The merger of Bank America and Nation Bank creates the largest banking institution in the U. S. Many more large mergers are anticipated. While significant downsizing is also anticipated, having the "hot" skills needed for this industry will mean opportunity for job seekers and career changers.

The telephone and cable television industries were deregulated awhile ago, and growth has been explosive ever since. Some of the massive changes in health care are also attributable to alterations in public policy. Knowledge of public policy initiatives will help you to identify new opportunities and emerging markets. Changes in tariff laws, discussed earlier, are still another example. Government may deregulate some industries and create regulations in other areas, such as environmental protection. The changes will stimulate growth and opportunity.

Despite low unemployment and overall economic growth, the job market remains a mixed bag.

There are hot spots and cold spots in the marketplace. To be successful changing jobs or careers, you must be offering skills, abilities, creative ideas, and solutions to problems that match the needs of the marketplace and specific employers. That is, of course, if you want to be hired by someone. If you intend to start your own business, your success will be a measure of your ability to identify and fill a need in the market for a product or service.

We have discussed several major forces that influence markets, creating growth, decline, or, as we've seen most recently, turbulence. Additional factors to be aware of include local and regional issues; investments such as those made by venture capitalists, corporations, and the general public; and the performance of individual organizations. Devastation from floods and hurricanes creates jobs in the affected region. Venture capitalists put $5.8 billion into fledgling technology firms in 1997, a fivefold increase in five years (Shaffer, *Fortune*, July 20, 1998). This kind of activity impacts opportunity. Development of an even faster computer chip can change an entire industry.

There is so much to take into account when you are making career decisions. The next chapter will help you put together what you learned about yourself and what you learned about the market in order to make career decisions. In Chapter Ten, we will discuss job-search strategies that are effective in a highly competitive market. Unlike preceding generations, today's workers will have to consciously manage their careers over their life span. Periodically, they will have to review their present situation, assess their satisfaction level, and make adjustments.

WORK IN PROGRESS

The Business Press Revisited

Purpose: In Work in Progress 2.4, you were asked to browse the business press. Now it's time to take a more in-depth look at these publications. This assignment is intended to help you feel more informed about the changing work world. With an understanding of what is happening, you can feel more a part of that world.

Directions: Select one of the economic trends presented in this chapter, and research the topic using sources such as *Business Week*, *Fortune*, and the *Wall Street Journal*. Read some articles that have appeared in these publications in the last two years. Write a two-page summary of your findings and prepare to share them in class.

Reflections: What have you learned from your research and from the reports shared by your classmates? How is the world of work changing? How can you use this information to reinvent your own career?

CHAPTER EIGHT

MAKING TOUGH DECISIONS

We make decisions every day of our lives, some more important than others. In this chapter, you will look at your decision-making behavior and develop a reliable tool to help you with the significant decisions you will face in your life.

KNOW YOUR DECISION-MAKING STYLE

Some people make decisions fairly easily while others agonize over their options. Some base their decisions on logical analysis, and others rely on their intuition or gut feeling. Still others postpone making decisions until circumstances force an outcome or until someone else makes it for them. You can see that certain ways of making decisions work better than others. How do you make decisions? How well does your method work for you? Complete the following activity to learn more about your personal decision-making style.

Decision-Making Timeline

Purpose: This exercise will give you a view of how you make decisions and how well your method is working for you. See Figure 8.1 for a sample timeline.

Directions: On a blank piece of paper, draw a horizontal line. The line represents your life. Place a dot at the left end and label it with your birth date. Place a second dot on the line to represent today and label it with today's date. Where you place the second dot depends on how far into your life you think you are. Now think of the three most important decisions you have made in your life. Many people find that a major turning point occurred in

Example of a
decision-making
timeline.

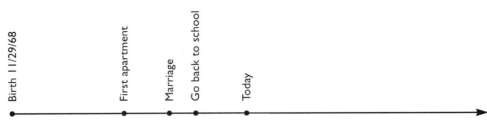

their lives without their having consciously made a decision. Carl, for example, discovered that his marriage to Sally had not involved making a major decision. They married because Sally was pregnant and they had not considered other alternatives. Carl's subsequent decision to end that marriage was major and involved a great deal of thought and feeling.

Major turning points sometimes occur in our lives without our making conscious decisions

After you have selected your three biggest decisions, place dots on your timeline to represent their occurrence and label them. Next, answer each of the following questions three times, once for each major decision:

What alternatives did you consider? What were the primary issues involved? How did you make the decision? (Did you identify options and apply logical analysis? Did you decide based on a hunch? Did you make a random choice? Did you yield to someone else's wishes?) Who, if anyone, helped or influenced you? How did things turn out?

Reflections: What patterns do you find in your decision making? Are you satisfied with the results? Are there things you want to change about how you make decisions? If your decisions have led to unsatisfying outcomes, you may need to develop new methods.

Directions: Return to the timeline. What is the next major decision you anticipate? Place a dot on the line to the right of the dot representing today, and label it with the upcoming decision and give it an approximate date (see Figure 8.2 for an example). Later in this chapter, you can try using a different decision-making style for that decision, applying a specific model to be discussed.

ASSESS YOUR TOLERANCE FOR RISK

Change inevitably involves risk

Change inevitably involves risk. Your level of comfort in taking risks influences the choices you make. What underlies risk? Fear of change. Fear of the unknown. Fear of loss. Fear of failure. Fear of success. Fear of rejection. As unappealing as these fears are, you will need to address them if you are going to be free of their potentially limiting hold on you.

When people consider career alternatives, they usually think of possibilities closest to their work experiences because that feels safest. They can predict the job requirements and feel confident about performance. As you ponder your choices, remember that the cost of selecting the safe route is that you may miss an opportunity to grow. Taking the less familiar path may be scary because you are less confident of your ability to perform the required tasks and, therefore, to be successful. However, look at the potential gain! If you succeed, you may gain a much greater payoff than you would have gained with the safe choice. You may have the opportunity to learn, to advance, and

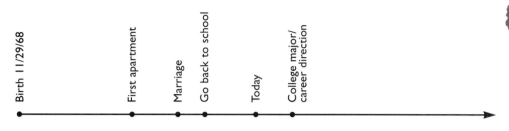

FIGURE 8.2

Example of a decision-making timeline, including next major decision to be made.

to earn more money. As you can see, you need to weigh risk against opportunity and decide for yourself where to draw the line between tolerating risk and needing comfort and safety.

Taking risks involves moving outside of your comfort zone. When you take risks, you have to be willing to feel the fear and still act. Remember the first time you jumped off a diving board as a kid? No one could really tell you how it would feel. If you were going to be "one of the gang," you had to take a chance. You may have wanted to change your mind when you looked down over the edge of the board. Perhaps you did change your mind and didn't jump the first time. When you finally took the leap, you were probably surprised by how deeply you plunged before you bobbed up to the surface. Do you remember feeling exhilarated? That energy is empowering. It makes you feel you can do anything. People who take a lot of risks thrive on that energy. Those who prefer a safer approach to life miss out on much of it.

You have to be willing to feel the fear and still act.

When you are making changes in your life, take a close look at the risks involved. Ask yourself, "What is the worst thing that can happen?" Then ask, "Can I live with that?"

WORK IN PROGRESS

Don

Don had been working as a proofreader at a publishing house for two years. He was brilliant at his work but had grown bored. Although Don applied for several in-house promotions, he was never selected for the more challenging, higher-level copyediting jobs.

Don also disliked the internal office politics. Ideally, he wanted to work as a freelancer. But what if no one hired him? He stayed, feeling stuck, for several months and then, unexpectedly, was laid off in a downsizing. Don was not ready to hang out his shingle as a freelancer so he started applying for jobs with other publishers. At the same time, he began contacting specific people in his network who either had been published or had expressed an interest in writing, offering them his editorial services. He got an excellent response from reaching out to people he knew and little response from his job applications to publishing houses.

For many months, Don lived with uncertainty. He was never sure if he could make the next month's rent. Sometimes he took odd jobs to cover his bills. Slowly, ever so slowly, Don started to get freelance work. Although at first the projects still involved proofreading, he gradually obtained a number of jobs providing copyediting and manuscript consultation services to authors.

Three years later, Don still isn't sure where next month's rent will come from, but he hasn't been late once! He now has a long and impressive list of completed projects, and he has the luxury of being more selective about the projects he accepts. At least for now and the foreseeable future, Don is comfortable living on the edge. He loves what he's doing and delights in the flexibility of his schedule.

Responsibilities can become excuses to stay within your comfort zone

Not everyone could take the risks that Don took. Family obligations, mortgage payments, and multiple responsibilities often limit people's freedom to choose. However, it is important for you to be certain that you aren't limiting yourself on the pretext of the family or the mortgage payment. Those are necessary responsibilities, but often they become excuses to play it safe, stick within your comfort zone, and remain unsatisfied with your life.

USE A DECISION-MAKING MODEL

When you need to make major life decisions, it helps to have a model as a guide. Then you can feel confident that you have done all you could to arrive at the best possible decision for yourself. The model presented here has nine steps, as shown in Figure 8.3.

Step One: Identify the Decision

When you have to make major decisions, there are often extraneous matters that distract your focus from the core decision. Individual, family, and career issues are usually interconnected in our complex lives. Take time for yourself—to isolate and identify *your* specific decision or decisions.

Step Two: Generate Alternatives

The more ideas you generate, the better your decision will be

People often feel backed against the wall by decisions. "I had no alternative" is a common refrain. Rarely is there only one alternative. Look at your situation carefully, and identify as many alternative solutions as you can. The more ideas you can generate, the better your decision will be. Use your creative talents, and ask for help if you need it.

Step Three: Assess Related Experience and Knowledge and Identify Gaps

In this thoughtful step, you apply your previous experience and knowledge to the problem. Think about what you already know that could shed light on the current situation; then identify the gaps in your knowledge. What additional information do you need to make a good decision?

Step Four: Gather Information

Gather the information you need to make a decision

Now that you know what you don't know, begin to research the information you need. Sometimes, this entails going to a library or getting on the Internet to do some reading. When you lack information, you can't distinguish among your alternatives in a productive way. If you are planning to buy a new car, for example, you need to gather enough information to feel comfortable making one choice from any number of alternatives. The same applies to choosing career alternatives.

Step Five: Weigh the Pros and Cons

There are pros and cons to consider for each alternative that you have identified in step 2 and analyzed and researched in steps 3 and 4. What do you stand to gain from each alternative, and what must you give up? In other words, what are the costs and benefits of each? Write them down and review them. Your decisions may take awhile, especially life-altering decisions. That's okay.

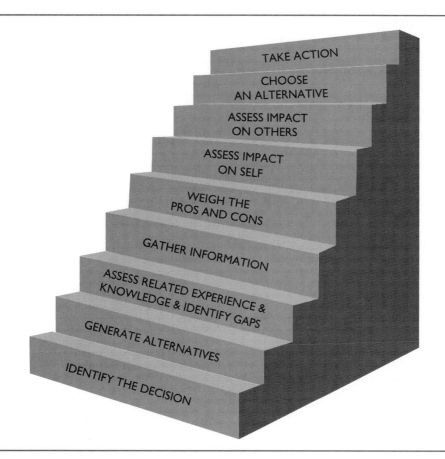

FIGURE 8.3

Nine-step decision-making model.

Step Six: Assess Impact on Self

Each alternative you consider has the potential for a different impact on you and your present lifestyle. You will need to weigh these, too. You may want to review your values to see if your alternatives support or compromise your values. You might also look at your personality and lifestyle preferences to evaluate their compatibility with each of the alternatives.

Step Seven: Assess Impact on Others

Our lives are intricately connected with others. Decisions we make will impact loved ones, friends, and colleagues. For each alternative you are considering, assess the impact your choice may have on those close to you. You may want to involve those who will be affected by your decision. Sound them out. Hear their viewpoints. You may find that people are more inclined to support you when they have been able to give their input.

Step Eight: Choose an Alternative

This is it! You can consider and ponder and weigh for only so long. Eventually, you have to make a decision. You might already have a feeling about the best path to take. For some, this is an intuitive inner knowing. For others, the process remains objective and analytical: they decide on the basis of facts, not feelings. Neither approach is right or wrong, but knowing your preferred style is essential.

Remember, few decisions in life are irreversible. If you make the "wrong" decision, you can change your mind later. It is not productive to agonize over or postpone a decision indefinitely. Make your decision by choosing one of the alternatives you identified.

Step Nine: Take Action

Your final step is to take action. Until then, nothing has changed. In the next chapter, which discusses goal setting, you will develop a specific action plan for carrying out a decision.

WORK IN PROGRESS

Marilyn

Marilyn came to a career management course in a rather frazzled state. She was 40 and married, with three children under the age of 5, and had an associate's degree in business from a community college. She and her husband had run a small business out of their home for several years, but in the last year, they had closed the business; her husband had gone to work for a former competitor. Marilyn described herself as "trapped at home with the kids all day." She had a part-time job working nights and weekends in a convenience store to help make ends meet. She said she was miserable.

During the course, Marilyn assessed her skills, interests, and talents; explored career alternatives; and decided on a management career in high-end retail, a competitive and demanding field. She felt enormously enthusiastic about her choice and began to grapple with how to make it happen. Her next major decision involved child care for her children. In her decision-making exercise, she identified two alternatives: hiring someone to care for her children at home or taking the children to her mother's home. Both she and her husband were opposed to putting the children in day care.

Marilyn asked the class for help because she was not comfortable with either of her alternatives. Her fellow students made suggestions such as hire a live-in nanny, reconsider day care, and postpone your career move until your youngest child is in school. Her classmates gave her the names of organizations to call and shared their experiences with different child-care arrangements. Marilyn realized that she was feeling guilty about choosing to return to work full-time; with the support of her classmates, Marilyn was able to consider all of their suggestions.

Ultimately, Marilyn found a highly professional day-care program in her community that satisfied her needs. The cost was high for three children, but she also found a higher-paying job in a prestigious retail environment, and the extra money helped to pay for day care. Marilyn did not qualify for the management training program with her new employer because she didn't have a bachelor's degree. After a few months, when her family had adjusted to their new lifestyle, Marilyn enrolled in an evening course to continue her education. She has a long way to go toward her long-term goal, but she has made tremendous progress.

Marilyn's story shows how making a change begins with a single step. Her willingness to confront barriers she had imposed on herself allowed her to move forward. She was able to set aside her preconceived notions of day care and investigate the realities. To her surprise, she found an excellent day-care program just four miles from home. This resource gave Marilyn the freedom to open up still other options for her life. She didn't have to stay "trapped at home"; she had alternatives.

MAKE MAJOR LIFE DECISIONS WITH HEAD AND HEART

At the beginning of this chapter, we discussed different styles of decision making and compared logical and intuitive decision-making styles. In the previous section, you worked on a logical decision-making model in detail to help you organize the issues and gather the information you need to make a sound decision. The intellectual parts of the process should not be a substitute for your intuitive process. For that reason, let's examine more closely the eighth step of the model, in which we refer to attending to your "intuitive inner knowing."

It is important to listen to your own "inner knowing" when you make life-altering decisions. Students have spoken about going through with marriage plans that they knew were wrong or taking a job they knew wasn't right for them. If you ignore important inner knowledge, you risk making serious errors or diverting your life from a satisfying path to one less satisfying. Learn to trust your intuitive sense of what is best for you.

Your best decisions will be those that stand the test of logical analysis and, simultaneously, are supported by a personal conviction. If you were buying a new home, for example, it would be important that the house you select meet your objective criteria. Those might include the house being structurally sound, having the right number and configuration of rooms, being affordable with reasonable taxes, and offering good schools and an attractive neighborhood. You would define all of the subjective terms like "affordable," "attractive," and "good." When the objective information you have supports your decision, then you need to look at broader, subjective issues. Some of the questions you might ask yourself are: Does it feel like *home* to me? Do I want to return here at the end of every day? Can I envision celebrating family holidays here? This is where intuitive, gut-level knowing comes into play.

Learn to trust your intuitive sense of what's best for you

To find out what your inner knowing can contribute to a decision, find quiet time for deep reflection. Relaxation techniques, such as listening to a meditation tape, can help to calm your mind and soothe anxieties you may have about your decision. Some people find it helpful to connect with a higher power; others relate to a higher self. The purpose may be simply to ask for guidance. A member of the clergy or a spiritual advisor can help you develop these higher or inner resources, or you can develop your own through prayer and meditation.

SYNTHESIZE YOUR SELF-KNOWLEDGE, CAREER ALTERNATIVES, AND MARKET INFORMATION

In Chapters Three, Four, and Five, you spent a great deal of time looking at yourself, identifying skills and interests, clarifying values, and learning about your personality and lifestyle preferences. In Chapter Six, you explored career options and researched alternatives that were particularly appealing. You looked at the current market's needs and how the workplace is changing in Chapter Seven. In the following activity, you will put all of this information together to come up with a career decision that satisfies both your needs and those of the market. In Chapter Nine, you will set specific goals and complete your action plan for implementing your decision.

WORK IN PROGRESS

Career Assessment

Purpose: This exercise gives you a chance to put together in one place and reflect on the results of several self-assessment activities from earlier chapters. The activity structures the decision-making process for your next career decision.

Directions: Answer the questions to the best of your ability. Refer back to previous activities where indicated. There are also new questions here to round out your assessment and move you toward a career decision.

MISSION: What do you see as the overarching mission or purpose for your life? Why are you here? What makes life meaningful to you?

....

....

....

....

....

SUCCESS: What is your personal definition of success? (See Success Chart, Work in Progress 5.5.) How will you know when you are successful?

....

....

....

....

....

....

....

....

....

VISION: What kind of life do you want to create for yourself? What is your lifestyle preference? (See discussion of lifestyle alternatives at end of Chapter Three.) With whom do you expect to share your life? How do you plan to share responsibilities?

....

....

....

....

....

....

....

....

CAREER: What do you hope to gain from your career over your life span? What does your work life mean to you? What do you hope to achieve?

....

....

....

....

....

....

....

....

....

....

VALUES: What are your top five work values? (See Work in Progress 3.5 in Chapter Three.) Are these values compatible with your comments about your career in the previous item? If not, how do you intend to resolve the conflict?

....

....

....

....

....

....

....

....

....

....

SKILLS: What are your five most marketable functional skills? (See Your Functional Skills, Work in Progress 5.2.)

1. ....

2. ....

3. ....

4. ....

5. ....

What are your five most marketable adaptive skills? (See Identifying Adaptive Skills, Work in Progress 5.3.)

1. ....

2. ....

3. ....

4. ....

5. ....

What three knowledge areas do you most want to apply in your next career move? (Refer to Work Content Skills, Work in Progress 5.4.)

1. ....

2. ....

3. ....

PERSONALITY: List your four preference indicators from Work in Progress 4.1:

1. ....

2. ....

3. ....

4. ....

What clues did you gain from this personality exercise that inform your choice of career? How would you describe your preferred style of working?

....

....

....

....

....

....

INTERESTS: What was your "type," as indicated in the Interests Survey, Work in Progress 4.2? What was your second-highest choice?

....

....

How does this activity influence your self-understanding and choice of career?

....

....

....

....

....

ENVIRONMENT: In what kind of setting do you prefer to work (e.g., small business, hospital, university, large corporation)?

....

....

....

What is your geographic preference? What is your second choice?

1. ....

2. ....

What kind of organization would you like to work for? What is its size? What are the people like? What is the atmosphere like?

....

....

....

....

....

ROLE: What role do you see yourself playing in an organization (e.g., leader, follow-through person, change agent, peacemaker)? Work in Progress 3.2, The Me Everyone Knows, may provide insight.

....

....

SYNTHESIS: Based on the above information and the exploratory research you've been doing, what kind of work would you most like to do? Why?

....

....

....

....

In what kind of environment would you most like to do it?

....

....

....

....

....

What is your current or most recent position? For whom do/did you work?

....

....

....

How does that position relate to your career goals? If there is a strong connection, how can you make the most of it? If there is little connection, what can you do about this?

....

....

....

....

....

What decisions do you need to make about your career? List them in order of priority.

....

....

....

....

....

What conflicts do you need to resolve?

....

....

....

....

....

APPLYING THE DECISION-MAKING MODEL

LIST CAREER DECISION: What is the next career decision you need to make?

....

....

....

....

GENERATE ALTERNATIVES: What specific career alternatives are you considering at this time?

....

....

....

....

ASSESS EXPERIENCE AND KNOWLEDGE: What do you already know about the alternatives you are considering? What additional information do you need to choose an alternative?

....

....

....

....

....

....

....

....

GATHER INFORMATION: Record new information collected through research that will help you make your decision.

....
....
....
....
....
....
....
....
....
....

WEIGH PROS AND CONS: For each alternative you are considering, list the costs and benefits.

....
....
....
....
....
....
....
....
....
....

ASSESS IMPACT ON YOURSELF: How would each of the career alternatives affect you? Would you have to move, change work patterns, go back to school, compromise values, give up something important to you?

....
....
....
....
....
....
....
....
....

ASSESS IMPACT ON OTHERS: How would each career alternative affect others close to you? Will they have to move, assume responsibilities you once assumed, change their lifestyle or routines? How do they feel about possible changes?

....

....

....

....

....

....

....

....

CHOOSE AN ALTERNATIVE: Which alternative have you decided to pursue at this time? Congratulations on making a decision!

....

....

....

Reflections: The first part of this exercise involved reviewing your self-assessment. When you gathered the various "pieces of the puzzle," did you feel you got a useful and accurate picture of who you are today? What patterns and themes emerged?

Next, you used the decision-making model. How do you feel about the decision you have made? Does it feel right to you? Do you feel enthusiastic about your choice? Did the process you followed give you an opportunity to examine all of the issues completely? Are there issues related to making this decision that you have not addressed? If so, what are they? How can you address them?

In Chapter Nine, you will work on developing an action plan to realize this decision. You are now ready to develop both long-term and short-term goals. You will also find additional exercises at the end of this chapter to further help you with your decision-making process. Remember, our lives don't unfold in a linear pattern; the process of goal setting may create the need to make further decisions. You may find yourself moving back and forth between decision making and goal setting.

WORK IN PROGRESS

Risk Taking

Purpose: This activity will give you a look at your behavior in relation to risk taking. The first part reviews risks you've taken in the past; the second part addresses risks you chose not to take.

Directions: The activities listed below involve some type of risk. Some involve physical risk; others involve personal risk. Place a check mark to the left of activities that you have done in the past. On the line to the right of each activity you check, write a phrase that describes the result. Was it a risk for you? What was the result? For example, "got great job" or "lost my shirt." The list is intended to stimulate your thinking about past risks; feel free to add and comment on any other activities you've done that involved risk:

_____ entered a new relationship	....
_____ invested in a stock	....
_____ bought a house	....
_____ raised a tough question	....
_____ learned to ski	....
_____ drove car in unfamiliar city	....
_____ climbed a mountain	....
_____ quit my job	....
_____ told someone negative feelings	....
_____ said no	....
_____ talked to a total stranger	....
_____ climbed a tree	....
_____ ended a relationship	....
_____ answered a personal ad	....
_____ answered a job ad	....
_____ acknowledged my mistake	....
_____ conquered a fear	....
_____ tried something new	....
_____ expressed unpopular view	....
_____ blew the whistle	....
_____	....
_____	....
_____	....

Directions: Below are some examples of behavior that represent risks not taken. Which of these can you relate to? What kept you from taking decisive action?

_____ stayed in a job I hated	....
_____ stayed in an unhealthy relationship	....
_____ turned down an opportunity	....
_____ missed the writing on the wall	....
_____	....
_____	....

Reflections: In general, how do you deal with risk? Do you avoid it, embrace it, minimize it? How satisfied are you with your level of risk taking? Have you made any surprising discoveries about your risk-taking behavior? What do you need to do to become more comfortable with risk taking?

....

....

....

What are the lessons to be learned from taking risks? When do you risk, and when do you take the easy way out?

What part does risk taking play in your growth? Do you feel you can move forward in your life without taking risks? If not, how can you minimize risk?

In the decision-making timeline Work In Progress 8.1, you were asked to identify the next major decision you need to make in your life. Discuss the risks involved in this decision. What do you stand to gain? What could you potentially lose? How can you make this decision less risky?

Experimental Risk Taking

Purpose: This activity is designed to give members of a group a supportive climate in which to experiment with taking a desired risk.

Directions: In groups of four, discuss your answers to the questions in the last exercise. Share your experiences with risk taking. When you are finished, have each group member identify a risk that he or she will take by the next class meeting. The risks you select should be meaningful and appropriate for each individual. Share the risks within your group so you can support one another.

If one of you chooses a risk that seems too big for this exercise, help that person to identify a more limited risk. Examples of appropriate risks might include:

I will make a cold call to a potential employer/customer.

I will express my opinions in the staff meeting at work.

I will sign up for a computer literacy course.

Think of an area in which you have been immobilized. Make a commitment to change your behavior in this area at least temporarily. This will involve taking a risk. Note what fears come up for you. Share both your commitment and your fears with your group. Find ways to help one another minimize risks. For example, if someone has committed to expressing opinions in a staff meeting and is nervous about it, suggest that the individual make a brief outline of comments to say. Or have the person schedule a dry run with a group member or a "safe" colleague prior to the meeting. Use the group's support. When everyone in the group has refined the risk they will take, record the risks on paper for reference in class next week.

Reflections: In class the following week, return to your groups to share your risk-taking experiences. How did it go? Did you take the risks you agreed to take? If yes, how did it go? If no, how do you feel about not taking the action? What do you need to do to be ready? Is there a smaller step you can take? How can the group support you?

Meeting of the Board

Purpose: In Work in Progress 8.1, you were asked to identify the next major decision you would be making in your life and date it approximately. In Work in Progress 8.2, you used the decision-making model to start working on that decision. In the next activity, you are given a board of directors to assist you with your decision. After all, not even corporate presidents make decisions independently. Boards of directors are created to bring to bear the best thinking available on proposed decisions. You can have your own board.

Directions: First identify the decision you want to make.

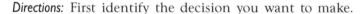

Now think about who can help you with this decision. Some of the people might be family members, a counselor, or friends. Other possible members of your board can be experts in the area of your particular decision. If you are making a career decision, you may want to have on your board your partner or spouse, your parents, your instructor or career counselor, the U.S. Secretary of Labor, a financial advisor, and experts from the career fields you are considering. If this sounds intimidating, fear not. This board will be meeting only in fantasy.

Draw an imaginary table at which the board will sit to discuss your career. It can be any shape you like: round, oval, rectangular, or whatever. When you've designed the table, place yourself there. Then mark where the other key people will sit, with your comfort as the primary concern. You may, for example, want your father opposite or farther away from you, if he has been obstructing your career planning, and a close friend next to you for support. Perhaps the field experts should flank your father. See Figure 8.4 for an example.

When the seating is arranged, imagine the meeting. Think about how you, as chair of the board, would conduct the meeting. What questions would you ask? What would the participants say? What would they bring to the table, so to speak? Jot down some brief notes about their contributions.

Reflections: What insights did you gain from imagining a meeting of your board? Were you open to different points of view? Did you confirm your own preference for the decision? Can you use your board members for help in making your decision? What do you need to do next?

Playing It Out

Purpose: This activity is a role play for the class. It is intended to provide a demonstration for scripting a meeting of a board of directors from the previous activity.

Directions: Your instructor will ask for a volunteer from the class to stage a meeting of his or her board of directors. Arrange chairs in the shape of the volunteer's boardroom table. The volunteer assigns roles to selected class members, giving each person one brief instruction about that role. For example, "Pat, you play my wife. She's very anxious about my deciding to be an engineer because I will be going back to school."

The chair (volunteer) then calls the meeting to order and asks the board for help with the stated decision. Board members may then comment, based on their assigned roles. Discussion is limited to 10 or 15 minutes.

Reflections: At the end of the role play, the participants debrief. Board members, how did it feel to play your role? Chair, how helpful was the input from your board? What happened here? Was it helpful? Do you know what you need to do next?

This activity can often be amazingly powerful for the individual role-playing the chair of the board. While it is unlikely to yield a major life decision, the role play demystifies the decision and makes it more tangible and manageable. The person who is the chair is usually energized by the result and able to see what needs to be done to arrive at a decision.

Adapted from Sidney B. Simon, *Meeting Yourself Halfway*, Sunderland, MA: Values Press, 1991.

Sample board table.

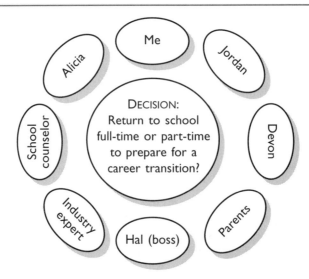

SETTING AND ACHIEVING GOALS

Now that you have made a decision about your next career move, it is time to set goals and develop an action plan for achieving those goals. You will first view your life in its entirety and decide what you hope to accomplish and experience in the future. With the big picture in mind, you will then create specific plans for making those wishes, dreams, and goals become reality.

START WITH A VISION

Draw another line to represent your life, place a dot at the far left side, and label it with your birth date. Place a second dot on the line to represent today and date it. Now move your eyes to the far right end of the line to the point representing your death. Don't try to date the point, but think about what it might be like to be at or near the end of your life. Think about the world you hope to leave behind to your children and your children's children. How might the world be different from today's? Take a few minutes to visualize a better world, one in which the problems that plague us today have been resolved. Dare to hope for a better world tomorrow, and then think about how you might contribute to improving the world today. Of all the challenges our society faces, is there one area in which you might like to make a positive difference?

When you decide on and commit to a goal, an inexplicable force often seems to take over

For example, your concern for the elderly could lead you to regularly visit a senior citizen in your community, providing companionship and doing occasional errands. Perhaps the AIDS epidemic has touched your life. You might contribute to finding a cure for this disease by participating in the Walk for Life fund-raiser or by training to become a medical laboratory researcher. If you are concerned about disadvantaged children, you could choose a career in teaching or counseling. Sometimes social concerns influence our choice of career, and sometimes we help society outside of our work lives.

HARNESS THE POWER OF GOAL SETTING

Goal setting is the first step in creating what you want in your life. Learn to use this powerful tool wisely and effectively. When you decide on a goal and commit to it, an inexplicable force often seems to take over to guide you. Some think of that source as divine or spiritual intervention. Others say the force exists within us. In any case, when you set clear goals, you will probably discover that many new and unexpected resources and opportunities emerge. This doesn't mean that you can kick back and wait for what you want to come to you. What it does mean is that, as you do your part, you will be supported and assisted.

WORK IN PROGRESS

Kit

Kit discovered this phenomenon in the early 1980s after participating in a week-long leadership training workshop in Hawaii. In one session, the group wrote numerous endings to the sentence, "Someday I'll . . ." Kit wrote: "Someday I'll visit Ireland," "Someday I'll train new career counselors," "Someday I'll write a book," "Someday I'll go to Mexico," "Someday I'll own my own home," "Someday I'll own a golden retriever," and almost 100 other statements. She remembers imagining her whole life in front of her and all the possibilities that appealed to her.

On her flight back to Boston, Kit reread her "Someday I'll . . ." statements. When she arrived home, she put the folder into a file drawer. Two years later, as she was rummaging through her files to prepare to teach a career development course, Kit came across the exercise. When she read the statements again, she was shocked to discover how many of them she had already done. Of those not completed, Kit had taken a step of some kind. For instance, she had not (and still hasn't) bought a golden retriever, but she had obtained the names of two breeders whose dogs were particularly appealing to her. It was then that Kit came to respect the power of goal setting. Information and opportunities had come to her and, because she had identified goals, she recognized and took advantage of those opportunities.

You may already be setting goals for yourself. Many people write or mentally create New Year's resolutions each January. Others use their birthday as a time to evaluate where they are and where they want to go. In addition, many employees, as part of their job duties, establish objectives for the year or the quarter that are related to the overall mission of the organization and the specific charge of the department.

Defining a larger personal purpose gives you forward momentum

Even if you haven't done this type of long-range goal setting, you might be someone who makes a long list of things "to do" when Saturday morning arrives. This is a version of short-term goal setting. One of the purposes of long-term goal setting is to create a broader perspective, so that as you move through your daily life, you can also head in a specific direction rather than repeatedly get caught up in each hour's most pressing crisis. When you define a larger personal purpose, you inevitably gain forward momentum.

No doubt you have had one of those days when you wake up with a toothache, get a flat tire on the way to work, arrive late, and discover that the project you turned in yesterday needs to be reworked. Meanwhile, your room-mate calls to say the air conditioner is broken and the temperature is 95 degrees. There are countless versions of this "day from hell"; we have all experienced them. When you are goal-directed, however, you move through the bombardment and still make it to class that night because you know that your life has a higher purpose than handling daily frustrations.

In this chapter, you will find several activities to help you practice and use goal setting as a tool. You may want to do them all or choose a few to experiment with. Your instructor will most likely make suggestions. There are numerous ways to identify and develop goals, and a variety of useful techniques to ensure that you achieve them. Discover what works best for you.

SET LIFETIME GOALS FIRST

Before you begin setting goals, you may want to try a relaxation exercise to relax your mind and body. If you have a relaxation tape, play it while you sit or lie down. Breathe slowly and deeply. If you don't have a relaxation tape, try listening to soothing music or sitting quietly in a private place. Concentrate for several minutes on your breathing. Take in long, slow, deep breaths and let them out slowly. Breathe in the life-sustaining energy of the universe. Breathe out the tensions and clutter of the day. Repeat this until you feel fully relaxed. Then complete the following exercise.

Ninety Years Young

WORK IN PROGRESS

Purpose: This is a goal-setting activity. In completing this exercise, you have the opportunity to begin to create the life you want to live.

Directions: Visualize yourself moving along your timeline to your 90th birthday. See yourself dressing for your birthday party. You hear the first guests arriving. Take a few minutes to reflect back on the life you have enjoyed for the past 90 years. What has your life been like? What have you accomplished? Look at your family life and the career or careers you've pursued. Consider your friendships, your interests, your travels, and the material possessions you've acquired. Note the contributions you've made to your community. Recall the leisure activities in which you've engaged. Now record some brief, general observations below.

....

....

....

....

....

When you are ready to attend your imagined party, enter the room where your guests have gathered. They are seated at four large round tables, and they applaud when you enter. After you are seated, some of your guests recite testimonials in your honor. The first speaks about your family life. The second talks about your career. The third talks about you as a friend. The last one speaks about your interests and community involvement. In the space provided below, write down what you imagine each guest said about you. (Feel free to alter the topics of the testimonials to fit your personal life journey.) If you enjoy writing, you may want to actually write the fictional speeches. If so, use your own paper so you aren't confined by space.

Family life testimonial:

....
....
....
....
....

Career testimonial:

....
....
....
....
....

Friendship testimonial:

....
....
....
....
....

Interests and community involvement testimonial:

....
....
....
....
....

When the speeches are over, a fifth guest sings a song dedicated to you. Can you think of a song that expresses who you are and what your life has meant?

....

Reflections: This exercise allowed you to visualize a major portion of your life that you have not yet lived. You also reflected on the years you have already experienced. How do you feel about your imagined life? Is this a life you would like to experience on a daily basis? Are you pleased with the people you've brought into your life? Are you happy with the way you allocated time, money, and energy? As you refine and improve the picture, you have the opportunity to design your future.

After you have worked with the birthday party reflections, translate the images that emerged into a list of goals. All of the items should represent real goals that you wish to achieve in your life. They can relate to your family life, work life, spiritual life, recreation, travel, political activities, physical well-being, and so on. Consider what is meaningful to you. Some examples might be:

- Maintain my commitment to my spouse, with whom I share values, goals, and dreams.
- Raise our three children to become happy, productive individuals.
- Provide a good education for my children.
- Spend quality time with my family.
- Have a successful career in biotechnology.
- Become a consultant in my field with an international client base.
- Maintain a healthy, fit body.
- Donate clothing and food to a shelter for battered women and children.

Someone else's goals might be:

- Find and commit to a partner who shares my hopes and dreams.
- Complete a bachelor's degree.
- Have a good job that I look forward to when I wake up in the morning.
- Make enough money to own a small home and a reliable car, have some money left over for travel and entertainment, and be able to buy a new CD when I want to.
- Create a nice home and grow my own vegetables.
- Have good friends.
- Take care of Mom and Dad when they get older.

Record your goals in the space provided. Consider these goals to be in draft form at this point. Next, we will discuss reworking goals to make them even more helpful.

....
....
....
....
....
....
....
....

OPERATIONALIZE YOUR GOALS

There are a few tricks to making your goals even more effective tools for you. Use the following suggestions to operationalize your goals:

1. *Make your goal statements clear and specific.* Vague goals are hard to achieve because you aren't sure what you are going for. "Look into going back to school" is vague. "Make an appointment with the Plymouth State admissions counselor to find out about transferring credits from Berlin Tech" is clear and specific.

2. *Make your goal statements realistic and achievable.* If you set goals that are totally unrealistic, you set yourself up for failure and disappointment. Think carefully and set goals that you can reasonably expect to achieve while meeting your other responsibilities. For instance, if you have work and family obligations, it may be unrealistic to set a goal of quitting your job and starting over. Make incremental changes; take it step-by-step. Take one or two courses, or do a part-time internship to gain new skills; then look for a more satisfying job.

3. *Establish a time frame for your goal.* For each goal you set, establish a structured time limit for achieving it. Be realistic: "By June 2002, complete associate's program in early childhood education"; "By October 30, complete paper for Sociology I"; "Write new chronological-style resume by February 1."

4. *Specify the costs.* Goals are achieved at the cost of other things. Be sure you know what you are giving up when you set goals and work toward their completion. When you decide to go back to school, you may give up financial freedom you have enjoyed. What will those tuition bills cost? In addition, your free time may become scarce. Time with family or friends and time for recreation will be precious. When you decide to change jobs, your life may become more stressful while you are job hunting.

5. *Make your goals measurable.* The goal of losing weight is a cloud hanging over many of us. Yet how useful is this goal? How do we know when we have achieved it? If this is one of your goals, it will be more helpful if you state it as, "I will lose 20 pounds by Easter." It will be even more helpful if you say, "I will weigh 140 pounds by Easter and maintain that weight." With this last statement, you can always step on a scale and determine where you are in relation to your goal. You should also state in specific terms your goals related to income or net worth. "I want to be making $40,000 by my 40th birthday" is specific and measurable; "I want a 5 percent raise at my next annual review" is also a measurable goal.

6. *Break goals down into achievable steps.* "Complete a telecommunications certificate by June 2000" is a clear goal. To help you achieve it, specify what course or courses you will take each term. For example, the goal, "Start a new job as an oncology nurse by November 1" can be broken into:

- Graduate in June.
- Study for boards (licensing examination) in July.
- Take and pass licensing exam July 28–30.
- Start job hunting in August, with first interviews lined up by the end of the month.
- Get an offer by mid-October.

Even these steps can be further broken down. For instance, you could specify what subjects you will review each week in July as you prepare for exams. Dividing up goals into small steps will help yield success.

State the small, achievable tasks as "next actions." Next actions are the specific things you need to do to move forward toward your goal. You could have "Get the car serviced" on your "to do" list for weeks and not complete it because it is not stated as a next action. The next action is "*make an appointment* to get the car serviced." Try fine-tuning your short-term goals by using next actions.

Applying all or some of these methods can help you to achieve your goals. You become more focused and productive. If you find that some of your goals aren't working out, do some renegotiating with yourself. After all, a list of goals is similar to a contract, one that you have negotiated with yourself. If you have set goals that turn out to be unattainable, rewrite them to reflect what you can reasonably achieve. Or, if your life circumstances change, you may need to change or alter your goals. Remember, goal setting is intended to *help you get what you want.* It is not meant to create undue stress, disappointment, or feelings of failure. Review your goals regularly and assess your progress.

DESIGN REALISTIC EDUCATION AND CAREER GOALS

Now that you have a sense of "the big picture," you will want to develop specific shorter-range goals that will help you to move incrementally toward your long-term goals. After you have decided on a long-range career goal, you are better able to assess your qualifications in your field of choice. Do you have training and experience that have prepared you for this career? Do you need further credentials? The research and informational interviewing you completed in Chapter Six may have provided the answers to these questions. You may have enough training and experience to enter the field, or at least to work in a relevant setting, but you may need further education to advance or move laterally in the field. If you need further education, continue your research by exploring academic and professional training programs that are either geographically convenient for you or available through distance learning.

Your education goals might include acquiring a certificate within a year and completing an associate's degree within three years. Or perhaps you have a bachelor's degree and you want to complete a master's by attending school part-time for two years. These are major decisions, so you may want to refer back to the decision-making model in Chapter Eight. Remember to involve in your decisions those people in your life who will be affected by them.

You have identified the field and general path you plan to pursue. The next step is to develop a plan for moving within the field and for advancing or evolving in ways that continue to broaden your experience and increase your satisfaction.

For example, Keith had worked in construction for many years when he injured his back on the job and suddenly needed to consider alternatives. He enjoyed working with building materials and decided to explore a new career that involved producing or selling these products. He eventually got a job selling construction materials. Keith might also have considered a career transition into project planning and estimating or construction management.

In another instance, Claire decided to become a computer professional. She first spent four years as a software programmer, during which she learned the ins and outs of two languages and several systems. Next, she applied to become a project leader, which she hoped would eventually lead to becoming a manager of management information systems (MIS). Claire could also have chosen to become a systems analyst, a technical trainer, or a relational database specialist. Each of these options had the potential to take Claire's career in widely different directions. But Claire had researched and defined her area, and she chose the job that best suited her interests and talents.

Can you begin to see a variety of career possibilities emerging? What path will you choose? What will you select for "Plan B" in case your chosen field changes along the way and once-appealing options become less desirable?

Many fields interconnect. You could start in the computer field and eventually move into a specialty or related career path. For example, you could start with business applications programming and shift to information management in a hospital setting. Here, you might specialize in medical records administration or billing and budgeting systems. An opportunity in budgeting could lead you back to school for more accounting courses and ultimately into an auditor's position with a regulatory agency.

Peter spent several years as a high school science teacher. After being RIFed (RIF stands for reduction in force) due to declining enrollments, he made a transition into the field of environmental research; then he moved to a writing position with an environmental publication. After three years at the writing job, Peter took a position as a science writer for a large urban newspaper. Perhaps the frustrated novelist or science fiction writer in him will appear in his next career transition.

As organizations move away from hierarchical structures, they offer career options that are more complex than simple career ladders to climb. Instead, you have a myriad of possibilities to consider, each of which can take your career in different directions. Instead of a ladder, picture a lattice of interconnecting opportunities (see Figure 9.1).

LOCATE EDUCATION RESOURCES

The Internet is an excellent source of information about education options, both local and long-distance. If you are unsure about using the Internet, your school advisor or local library staff can help you to identify the best education resources for your particular objectives. As part of informational interviewing, ask people in the field you intend to pursue what they think of the available education and training programs. If possible, speak directly to program directors and to graduates of the programs to get their opinions and recommendations. Some credentials are offered by government-funded

FIGURE 9.1

Career lattices are replacing career ladders in organizations.

training programs, especially for workers who have been laid off. Your local department of employment and training can refer you to these programs. Professional organizations and schools also offer training programs.

Shop around! Compare distance learning modalities with traditional classroom instruction. Also look at programs that combine the two. Compare program content, convenience, and costs. Be a wise consumer when choosing a program and making the financial investment. Further education is likely to be part of everyone's goals because of the continually changing needs of the workplace.

RESOLVE FINANCIAL CONSIDERATIONS

Deciding to further your education represents an investment in your future. Review employment trends to be sure you are "up-skilling" in an area where demand is predicted to grow. U.S. government publications, such as the *Occupational Outlook Handbook*, provide useful information about projected employment trends. The Department of Labor, Bureau of Labor Statistics, provides information, including employment projections, online at www.stats. bls.gov.

A number of financial issues must be considered when you are thinking of returning to school. First of all, can you afford to attend school full-time? Can you survive for weeks, months, or years without an income? Few of us can. Are you able to live on part-time income while attending school full-time? Or do you need to maintain a steady income in order to survive? Exactly what are your non-negotiable financial obligations?

Some adult students qualify for government grants to fund part of their education. Many also qualify for low-interest government loans. Schools offer scholarships, some of which may be specifically earmarked for adult returning students. College financial aid offices offer detailed information about sources of funds for adult students. Information is also available on the Web. See the resources listed at the end of Chapter Ten.

Returning students often make an agreement with a spouse or partner to be supported financially for a period of time. They may later reverse roles so the other partner can go back to school. If you are employed, your company may grant educational benefits. The human resources office where you work can provide information about educational benefits.

One ingenious way to fund your education is to get a job at the institution where you want to study. Most colleges and universities provide educational benefits to their employees, and often for their families as well. The school may allow you to take one or more courses each term for free. Look at these benefits carefully, as some might not become available until you have worked there for a designated period of time.

Adult students are incredibly resourceful when it comes to funding further education: They'll work nights or days, weekends, and vacations; they'll sell their house or their van; they'll take a job with the school; they'll teach themselves a subject and then take a CLEP (college-level examination program) exam to earn college credit for their learning. First, identify what it is you want to study; then figure out how to get the education you want. Get help from school instructors and advisors as well as from friends who are already enrolled.

One difficult financial issue for many career changers involves having to take a pay cut in order to move into a new field. You may have worked for

Changing careers might require a pay cut, at least temporarily

many years in a field and reached the high end of the salary and advancement scale. Most likely, you have developed a lifestyle that is comfortable at your present earning capacity. Changing fields could mean that you'll have to enter the new field at a lower salary than you now make. No one makes this decision lightly. If income is one of your core driving values, be sure that the potential for financial growth in the new field exceeds your current earning potential.

Throughout the 1980s and 1990s, computer-related industries have been growing wildly, and many people have moved from other fields into this one. They often took pay cuts, knowing that with the right technical credentials they could earn more money within a year or two and continue to grow from there. You have to look realistically at your current situation and the fields you are considering. No one can promise you a job and a future; it is always a risk, but some choices are less risky than others. Career literature that includes employment and salary projections for the future provides valuable information, and informational interviews will give you the current perspective of professionals in the field in your geographic area.

Deciding to return to school usually involves changing your lifestyle. Classes and homework take time. Anticipate as accurately as possible how your lifestyle will change, and prepare for those changes. You may have less time for family or friends, or for yourself. The house may not get painted this year, and sometimes the dishes may pile up in the kitchen sink. If you are a single mother, you may need to arrange child care and contingency plans. You may have less money, even for the essentials. There is tremendous sacrifice involved in going back to school; there's no doubt about it. Given today's market, it may be fair to say that you have to do it anyway if you hope to obtain a good position and stay gainfully employed.

DEVELOP AN ACTION PLAN

The next step is to develop an action plan. An action plan identifies the incremental steps you plan to take toward completing your goals and the dates by which you intend to take these steps.

WORK IN PROGRESS

Action Plan

Purpose: We will focus on the career decision you made at the end of Chapter Eight for the purpose of learning how to make an action plan. Some of you will be developing an action plan that involves making a job change within a short period of time; others will be making plans for further education that will lead to a job or career change at some point in the future. The model presented below can be used in either circumstance.

Directions: At the end of Chapter Eight, you completed an exercise in which you synthesized information from self-assessment and career exploration and made a decision about your career. The questions that follow ask you to continue planning the necessary steps to accomplish your career decision.

TAKE ACTION: In the space on the following page, list the incremental steps you will take toward implementing your decision. List each step and the dates by which you plan to complete them.

TASK   DATE

....
....
....
....
....
....
....
....
....

NEEDS: What information and resources do you need to achieve this goal?

....
....
....
....

SUPPORTS: Who can help you carry out your plan? What do you need from them? How can they help you? When will you ask them?

....
....
....
....

OBSTACLES: What could get in the way of your plans? Who or what is imposing the obstacles? What can you do about them?

....
....
....
....

COMMITMENT: How committed are you to your decision? Are you ready to roll up your sleeves and begin? Are you excited about your plan?

....
....
....
....

Reflections: This activity has helped you to break your goal into incremental steps and set specific dates for completion of these steps. Does your goal feel achievable to you now? Does your plan seem realistic? Are there any obstacles still stopping you from moving ahead?

CONFRONT OBSTACLES

Explore potential constraints, separating fact from fiction

At this point, you may notice a little voice beginning to chatter away in your mind about why the goals you've selected can't possibly be achieved. Review all of your goals, and consider what constraints could prevent you from actualizing them. For instance, if one of your goals is to find a new job in the banking field, you could feel constrained if you are so busy in your present job that you have no time to research the field and develop a network of professional contacts. You may also be worried because local banks are laying off workers or because you assume banks won't talk with you unless you have a degree in finance.

Explore each of these potential constraints. Separate fact from fiction; identify and resolve your fears, if possible. We will look at the constraints one at a time.

It is always hard to conduct a job search when you are simultaneously employed full-time. You will need to do your research and informational interviewing outside of work hours. If this isn't possible, consider using a week of vacation to devote heart and soul to your job-search campaign. Chapters Ten and Eleven expand further on the subject of job-search campaigning. What other obstacles interfere with reaching your goals? Some people are resistant to trying; they may be afraid of rejection. Overcoming fear of rejection involves developing a thick skin and learning not to take rejection personally. When Chase Manhattan Corp. advertises an opening, they may receive hundreds of responses, including yours. If you aren't selected for an interview, it does not mean you are not a good or valuable person; it usually means that other applicants appear better matched to that particular job. The whys and wherefores of how your resume lands in the "yes" pile are not always fair or rational.

If Chase is laying off workers, you can make inquiries about which positions are being eliminated. They may be cutting middle-management positions and hiring in the customer service area. Be sure to get the facts. Don't postpone your job search based on incomplete information or assumptions.

You also need information to resolve the last constraint—your education. Sometimes Chase hires people with financial credentials, but they may also hire people with high school diplomas or with liberal arts backgrounds. You may be far better off getting into the organization now and gaining experience while you are going to school than you would be if you waited to complete your degree. Many companies promote from within and look favorably on employees who continue their education part-time. Don't take yourself out of the running based on your assumptions. Ask questions and get the right information.

When you do your research and find indisputable obstacles to your goals, you have to accept reality and look for alternatives that closely match your original goal. You can't become a brain surgeon without attending medical school and doing residencies in surgery and neurosurgery. If you do not have the money or the years to devote to this profession, you will need to identify a new goal. You could explore becoming a surgical nurse or surgical assistant, for example.

Seek the help of family, friends, teachers, and advisors in identifying obstacles and finding ways to eliminate or sidestep them. Notice that some road blocks are externally imposed, such as entry requirements, while others are self-imposed, such as making false assumptions. When you cannot overcome particular obstacles, find alternatives that capture the essence of your original goal.

Identifying and Resolving Obstacles

Purpose: This exercise will help you to feel empowered. You will be identifying obstacles to your goals and finding ways to deal with them.

Directions: Make a list of the constraints or obstacles that get in the way of achieving your goals and having what you want in your life. Next to each obstacle, identify its source—that is, is this your belief or assumption, or is it a societal, market, or personal reality? Perhaps it is a combination. In the third column, list what you can do to eliminate the obstacle or work around it.

OBSTACLE	SOURCE	RESOLUTION
Examples		
My engineering skills are outdated.	Market reality	Take courses to gain current skills or try another location.
I lack experience.	Market reality	Do volunteer work.
	Personal belief	Sell transferable skills.
....	....	....
....	....	....
....	....	....
....	....	....
....	....	....
....	....	....
....	....	....
....	....	....

Reflections: What is in the way of your goals? What can you do to overcome or resolve these obstacles? Do you see viable alternatives?

USE AFFIRMATIONS

Goal setting is a powerful technique. Its effectiveness can be significantly increased by using affirmations and visualization techniques. Affirmations are statements of belief and purpose that you develop to focus on your goals. They are used to create positive self-talk and to replace negative thinking. Any affirmation statement should be carefully crafted. Once you have the statement just right, repeat it frequently; also write it down many times. Find appropriate places to post your affirmation where it will serve as a reminder. This could be on your computer, in your wallet, or in your datebook. These actions move you to achievement of goals.

In the process of developing your affirmation, you will benefit from looking at how you might be subconsciously sabotaging your goal. Your affirmation can be designed to replace negative thought patterns with positive self-talk.

Danny was a 37-year-old man whose work history was a series of disasters. He had been fired from several jobs. He had sold heating and air-conditioning equipment but had not met his quotas. Then he worked as a laborer in a large construction project but was fired because he had two accidents on the job. He had held clerical office jobs, too, but received consistently negative evaluations. Danny was liked by his coworkers, but he couldn't seem to deliver on the job. He felt like a failure and a loser; his self-esteem was extremely low.

Three years ago, Danny had married a successful businesswoman, and, when he joined the career development class, his wife was expecting a baby. With the prospect of becoming a father, Danny felt newly motivated to succeed in work. He spent many weeks doing self-assessment and exploration exercises, but he especially benefited from creating and using affirmations.

Danny realized that he did not feel *worthy* to hold a job. His father had abandoned his family when Danny was three years old, and this fact had cast a shadow over his self-esteem ever since. When he saw the connection between that event and his work failures, he began to change. With help, he wrote the following affirmation: "I, Danny, am a man *worthy* of a satisfying job. I am ready to succeed in a position where I use my interpersonal skills and improve my clerical skills."

Danny wrote down these sentences hundreds of times, and he said them over and over in his mind, especially when negative thoughts crept in. He worked hard to replace his negative self-image with his new, positive outlook. When he had thoughts like, "I'm a failure," "I don't count," and "I can't do anything right," he learned to replace the thoughts with his affirmation.

Within a few months, Danny got an entry-level job with the Internal Revenue Service. It was a demanding job where, after an initial training program, he was on the telephone all day answering taxpayers' questions. His phone calls were closely monitored. But Danny was relieved to be employed again. After a successful year, he applied for and obtained a new job with the Social Security Administration. The new position was also in customer service, but he felt less pressured.

Danny changed his thinking about himself with his affirmation. Through his use of positive self-talk, he internalized the belief that he was worthy of having work and of being successful, and he changed his behavior accordingly. Danny has no desire to be on the fast track—he just wants a "regular job," what he once called a "C job." He has found work where he feels comfortable and productive, and he is proud of his newfound success.

Work in Progress 3.6 guided you in developing an affirmation. If you have not yet completed that exercise, you may want to do it now. On the other hand, if you completed it earlier and have had success with your first affirmation, you may be ready for a new one related specifically to your latest career goal.

TRY VISUALIZATION TECHNIQUES

Another empowering technique to use with goal setting is visualization. Visualization is creating a vivid mental image of yourself doing or having something you want. It has been used by people to overcome or reverse terminal illnesses, among other purposes. The technique doesn't work for everyone, but medical experts have been amazed by its success with some patients. A number of books have been written about healing and visualization, including Dr. Bernard Siegel's *Love, Medicine, & Miracles* and Louise Hay's *You Can Heal Your Life.*

WORK IN PROGRESS

Donna

Donna is a single mother with two small children. She was having serious money problems because her ex-husband was not keeping up with child-support payments. She had a part-time job in a restaurant, where she earned enough to pay for the rent on her modest apartment; her sister took the kids on those days.

Last fall, Donna enrolled in a career development class at her local community college. It was her first college-level class and, she figured, her last. She would not have the money to continue. Donna was quite taken with the notion of visualization. Her class spent time talking about poverty versus prosperity consciousness and then discussed the technique of visualization. She learned that she had a choice of viewing the world as a place either with scarce resources or with abundant resources. Donna decided to visualize prosperity and abundance. She specifically visualized herself as a college student and also saw herself receiving money in the mail. She kept repeating those images in her mind.

Eager to change her circumstances, Donna also gave serious thought to other possible funding sources. She considered relatives who might pay the tuition for her class, people who owed her money, items she could sell in a yard sale, and so on. She began dealing with her money problems directly. Three weeks later, Donna announced that she was going to be able to continue courses for a couple of terms. She was elated. While she didn't share all the details, she did say that she unexpectedly got a check in the mail from her mother for her birthday. She also had a court date for a hearing on her ex-husband's nonpayment, and she had seen the financial aid officer at school.

Visualization is most effective when you combine it with deep, meditative relaxation. The technique itself is simple. Think of something you want, and visualize yourself having it. If you want a job as a flight attendant, visualize yourself in the uniform: the suit, the tie or scarf, and the white shirt or blouse. See the wings on your lapel. Picture yourself standing at the entrance to the plane greeting passengers. Imagine yourself demonstrating safety precautions, serving meals, distributing magazines and blankets. Make the picture as detailed as possible and keep visualizing it. Return to the meditative state several times a day to visualize yourself having achieved your goal.

Try the visualization technique; if it works for you, you may want to use it often. It is one more tool to help you create the life and career you desire. If you use visualization in a job search, be sure that your images of having the job don't cause you to sound overconfident in the job interview. There is a balance needed here; convey genuine interest and enthusiasm but not an assumption that the job belongs to you.

GET THE SUPPORT YOU NEED

Career transitions can be difficult to achieve; this is true for many of our goals in life. We all need help to achieve our goals. Family and friends may be sources of support. Your classmates are also a source of support. As you hear their stories and learn about their goals, you no doubt feel excited for them; they feel that way about your ambitions, too. A career class is an ideal laboratory for offering and accepting support. Your instructor has probably worked with many people going through the transition process and can offer guidance and encouragement. The more you put into the class, the more you will gain from it.

When the class ends, you and your classmates may decide to continue meeting informally as a support group. Or you may decide to stay in touch via e-mail and to have a reunion in six months. A career class provides many tools; participants often need additional time after the class is over to carry out all the changes they desire.

If your classmates aren't interested in further meetings, find out what groups are available in your community. Support groups help participants stay on target. They may be coordinated by a church or civic organization or by the unemployment office. Your instructor may be able to give you contacts. Job hunters' support groups are ideal for those who are out of work and looking for new positions. Group members understand one another's feelings of identity loss, frustration, anger, and powerlessness because they are in similar situations. Support groups provide a safe place to share feelings and get recharged for your search. When job hunters express their darkest fears and doubts in support groups, they are easier to live with at home. Family members can become alarmed by these feelings.

Overcome reversals, hold on to your vision, and keep moving forward

When you have been forced into a career transition by a plant closing or by downsizing, your employer may provide outplacement services. The scope of the services varies but often includes job-hunting seminars and help with resume writing and interviewing. Take advantage of whatever services are offered even if you feel too angry to do so. You may learn about job opportunities or resources that can prove invaluable. Spending time with other laid-off employees can also be a healing experience.

In this chapter, we have presented numerous goal-setting and achievement techniques. We challenge you to go after what you want in life. Make your hopes and dreams reality. Life has many obstacles and disappointments. Learn to overcome reversals, hold on to your vision, and keep your life moving forward. In the next chapter, we will help you to make your next career move. You have made a career decision and developed an action plan; now you are ready to undertake a job search that will lead you to a satisfying position. Chapters Ten and Eleven address finding a job in an organization, while Chapter Twelve examines ways to make a good start on the new job. Chapter Thirteen looks at starting your own business or private practice or becoming an independent contractor.

WORK IN PROGRESS

Goal-Setting Brainstorm . . . By the Clock

If you do the exercise in class, your instructor will pace you. If you are doing it on your own, you will need a timer. You will also need five separate sheets of paper.

Purpose: The intent of this activity is to identify goals in your life and to integrate them into your present life to help you achieve your goals.

Directions: Label your first sheet of paper "Lifetime Goals," set the timer for three minutes, and write down as fast as you can all the goals you would like to achieve in your lifetime. Think about all aspects of your life: family, work, education, recreation, spirituality, friends, travel, material possessions, and so on. List whatever you want to do or have.

At the end of three minutes, reset the timer for one minute. Review your lifetime goals. You have one minute to add, delete, edit, or change your goals.

When the buzzer rings again, set aside your long-term goals. Take a second sheet of paper and label it "Ten-Year Goals." Set the timer for three minutes and begin writing everything you can think of that you would like to have or do in the next 10 years. Again, think of all aspects of your life: career, family, social, spirituality, and the like.

At the end of three minutes, reset the timer to one minute and review your 10-year goals. You may add to, delete, or change your goals at this time.

At the end of the minute, set aside the "Ten-Year Goals" and take another sheet of paper. Label this page "One-Year Goals" and set the timer for another three minutes. Write as fast as you can. Where do you want to be in your life one year from now? What do you want to have achieved by then?

When the three minutes are up, reset the timer for your one-minute rethink. Is this what you really want within the next year? Make your changes and additions quickly.

Take your fourth sheet of paper and label it "Three-Month Goals." Set the timer for three minutes and begin writing. What do you want to do in the next three months? What do you want to complete? What do you want to learn? What do you want to acquire?

After the beep, reset the timer for one minute; edit and review your three-month goals. Make any necessary changes or additions.

Label your last sheet of paper "Two Weeks to Live." For this activity, imagine that you just learned that all the lights are going out forever on planet Earth two weeks from now. No one will suffer, but all life will end instantaneously. You are the only one who has advance information about this phenomenon, and there is nothing you can do to change it. Knowing this, what do you want to do during the next two weeks? How will you spend your time and with whom? What will you do? What is important to you under the circumstances? Set the timer for three minutes and begin writing.

You now have one last editing to do. Set the timer for one minute and review the goals for "Two Weeks to Live." What needs to be changed, deleted, or added?

Reflections: How did your outlook change when you got to the last writing assignment? What was most important to you? Did you find it easier to identify long-term goals (Lifetime, Ten-Year) or short-term goals? Your answer can be helpful information to have. Did the long-term goals provide a framework for your short-term goals? Was organizing the brainstorm in this way helpful?

You can do this exercise every year. It is a great way to keep moving forward in your life. You may want to review your goals again in a week or two, after you've gotten some distance from the writing. See if your goals still fit and excite you. If not, make the necessary changes, and then start creating what you want. Remember, you're the artist and it's your canvas.

Adapted from Alan Lakein, *How to Get Control of Your Time and Your Life* (Phyden, 1973).

Goals Collage

Purpose: Not everyone is a writer. Many people do their dreaming and future planning visually. This exercise provides another medium for setting goals.

Directions: Buy a large piece of poster board, at least 13" x 17", and a glue stick. Go through old magazines and cut out pictures that symbolize things you want in your life. Maybe you've always wanted a pair of cowboy boots or a motorcycle. Your heart's desire could be a computer, a home, a trip to Peru. If a serene lifestyle is important to you, find a picture that represents serenity (perhaps a sunset or an ocean view). Select pictures that remind you of your specific goals. Collect dozens of colorful images of things you want to do or have. After you have collected 30 or more pictures, arrange them attractively on the poster board. When you are pleased with the arrangement, glue the pictures in place. Hang your collage in a prominent place, where it will inspire you.

Reflections: Does your collage warm and inspire you? Select a trusted friend and share your collage with him or her. Explain the symbols you have selected to represent your hopes and dreams.

CHAPTER TEN

NETWORKING AND JOB CAMPAIGNING

Conducting a job search is challenging and time-consuming. This chapter will address the preparation phase of looking for a new position. If you have been working your way through this book as part of a career development course, you are prepared to acquire additional skills for your search. If you have just opened the book to this chapter because you find yourself in the job market, you would benefit from doing the preliminary work outlined below. To complete the steps, please see the earlier chapters and Figure 10.1 (also found in Chapter 2).

REVIEW THE CAREER DEVELOPMENT PROCESS

Assess Yourself First

Chapters Three, Four, and Five introduced the process of self-assessment, a critical aspect of career decision making. When you are ready to engage in a job search, it is a good idea to revisit your self-assessment. Regardless of whether you're job hunting by choice or by chance, review your interests, work values, and personality traits, zeroing in on the needs that you most want to satisfy in your next position. Reexamine your abilities, paying particular attention to your strongest and most marketable skills. Throughout your job search, you will be asked to justify your candidacy. Once you have assessed yourself and your strengths, you will be confidently and comfortably able to market yourself in person, on paper, and online.

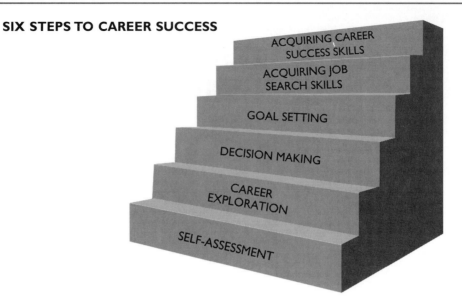

FIGURE 10.1

Career development model.

SIX STEPS TO CAREER SUCCESS

ACQUIRING CAREER SUCCESS SKILLS

ACQUIRING JOB SEARCH SKILLS

GOAL SETTING

DECISION MAKING

CAREER EXPLORATION

SELF-ASSESSMENT

Do Research Second

When you have established what you have to offer, it's time to examine the marketplace to learn who is hiring. Find out what kinds of positions are open now or are likely to become available in the near future. Use the Internet, newspapers, and library resources. Explore what fields are "hot." Suppose you have gained strong skills in office management from years of experience in the insurance field. If insurance companies are downsizing in your area, but health care is booming, look for an office management position in a hospital or health maintenance organization. Identify and target the organizations that need your skills. Once you have the job, you can work on plans for advancing your career or developing a specialty.

In Chapter Six, you used informational interviewing to gather information necessary to make a career decision. When you are entering a job search, you will need to make other career and life decisions to further focus your search. Another round of informational interviewing could help you to clarify your immediate career goals. Be clear that you are seeking people out for *information*—then you are likely to glean valuable insights and inside information about what is occurring in your field and where opportunities may be materializing.

Informational interviewing may help you to identify a dilemma that you hope to resolve. Here is an example of a request for an informational interview for the purpose of deciding a next step: "I have three years of experience in retail sales, and I'm considering alternative paths. One area that I find appealing is becoming a manufacturer's representative, selling equipment or parts to other large companies. High-tech sales also interests me. I'd like to talk with you about your sales experience to help me fully understand the realities of these alternatives." This approach allows you to explore a variety of career choices by asking questions of people who are doing the kind of work you think you'd like to do.

If you are out of work and confronting survival issues, such as feeding and housing your family, self-assessment and informational interviewing can seem like luxuries you can't afford. In reality, these steps are crucial to a successful search in a competitive market. Take the time. Otherwise, you may find yourself desperately applying for positions that have little to do with your interests, talents, or career goals. Be both as clear as possible about your strengths and certain of who needs what you offer; this is a good use of your valuable time and energy. Enter the market confident of your abilities and focused on your goals.

Make Preliminary Decisions Third

Having looked at yourself and the marketplace, you are now ready to make preliminary decisions about what you would most like to do or, when options are limited, what kind of position you have the best chance of getting. You also need to know in what kind of organization you would like to work. Using the decision-making model presented in Chapter Eight, determine the parameters of your search. Identify the geographic area you will target. Select the occupation you will pursue and the pay range you expect, given your background and market realities.

Develop an Action Plan Fourth

Next, identify the companies or organizations you plan to target. These initial choices will help you conduct a focused campaign. Using the action plan presented in Chapter Nine, make a plan for developing job leads and contacts.

WORK IN PROGRESS

Louise

Louise recently earned a paralegal certificate and wants a full-time paralegal position within a 30-minute drive of her home. As a result of her research, she has learned that there are seven law firms in her area. In addition, one of Louise's instructors gave her the names of two insurance companies and a government agency that have hired graduates of the program in the past. Through the local chamber of commerce, she learned of three local companies that have small legal departments. Also within her 30-minute radius are three town governments and a county courthouse. Louise can target these organizations as well.

If you aren't sure how to go about targeting organizations, visit your school or local library to become familiar with the many print and online directories that list and cross-reference companies. Some directories are very large and list national and international corporations. Others are local or regional and field-specific. Many directories use standard industrial classification (SIC) codes that can help you to pinpoint organizations that hire workers in your field. A partial list of directories appears at the end of the chapter. Note that many of these directories are available on CD-ROM and are thus accessible by computer.

Newspaper articles and information that you gather from individuals can also help you decide what organizations to target. Even the yellow pages telephone directory is a valuable source of company names. If you are planning to relocate, you can purchase a phone book from your new town and subscribe to the local newspaper long before you start packing.

Later in this chapter, we will provide additional information about conducting a thorough job-search campaign. The next order of business is creating dynamic resumes and cover letters to support your campaign.

WRITE A WINNING RESUME

The primary objective of a resume is to get you selected for an interview

Your resume is a skillfully designed advertisement, or marketing piece, that provides information about your education, work experience, and other qualifications pertinent to prospective employers. Your resume must reflect who you are and showcase your qualifications in the best possible light. It should also make you feel proud. Resumes are not meant to be all-inclusive biographies, listing every position you've held and every course you've studied. Instead, include in your resume a *selection* of achievements and *highlights* of your background that will pique the reader's interest and that relate to the job you are seeking. The primary objective of a resume is to get you selected for a job interview.

Employers usually respond positively to two resume styles: the *chronological* and the *functional/combination*. We will first look at the chronological resume, since it is most commonly used by job hunters and most readily accepted by employers. It also happens to be easier to write. For those readers who have not written a resume for quite some time, we will review the typical parts of a chronological resume. We will then examine ways to vary the format to highlight your particular strengths. Later in the chapter, we examine the functional/combination resume, often the best style for career changers.

Chronological Resume

A chronological resume always contains the following parts:

Heading: Your name, complete mailing address, and a telephone number where you can be reached during the day. If you are presently employed and don't want other employers to call you at work, use an answering machine at home. If you have a computer and modem, you may want to include your e-mail address in the heading. Include your fax number if you are applying for a position by fax.

Experience: Your work history, presented in *reverse* chronological order, with your *most recent* position first. Include position titles, names of your employers, city and state, dates of employment, and brief action statements describing what you did. Start your action statements with verbs, preferably phrased in the past tense. Whenever possible, quantify and qualify accomplishments. For example, "Surpassed sales quota by 10 percent," "Recruited and trained five new employees," and "Streamlined order-processing system, saving the company $7,000 annually."

Usually it is sufficient to go back 10 years, but there are exceptions to this guideline. If you have been with the same employer for 10 or more years, you may want to go back further in order to include another employer. When you include "ancient history," summarize it. For example, you could say, "Earlier experience included seven years teaching high school mathematics."

Education: Your education background that qualifies you for the position. Starting with the *most recent*, name the schools and locations; list programs, certificates, or degrees. Add other information that supports your candidacy, such as a good grade point average, specific courses related to your career objective, related activities, and awards. Once you're in college, you do not need to include high school education. You may also include in this section, or a separate section called "Training," any in-depth training programs you have completed through employers while on the job. Include only those that relate to your current career goal.

Other parts of a chronological resume that are considered optional but may be included if they advance your candidacy include:

Objective: A brief statement of your present career goal. Objectives should be specific. When you include an objective on your resume, you give a focus to the entire document. State what you want to do; then use the remainder of the resume to substantiate that statement.

Summary of achievements: Often a series of statements highlighting past accomplishments. Especially handy for people with several years of work experience, this section allows you to summarize your qualifications. It can also be titled, "Accomplishments," "Achievements," "Summary of Accomplishments," or "Experience Highlights." The section normally appears between the Objective and the Professional Experience sections.

Skills: A bulleted list or a series of brief statements. This category can be used to highlight specific skills related to the position you are seeking. You can name it "Computer Skills," "Technical Skills," or "Business Skills" to call attention to your specific credentials for the position you seek. You can also highlight "soft" skills, such as interpersonal and communications skills, on a resume that is otherwise dominated by technical qualifications. In that instance, the section could be titled, "Personal and Professional Strengths." List the most marketable skills first, followed by the skills in less demand.

Affiliations: A list of organizations and your role, such as "Society for Technical Communication: Chair, Program Committee." If you are active in professional associations in your field, include them. You can list membership in civic organizations, too, but don't overload your resume with activities unrelated to your career objective.

Interests: A brief list of interests is sufficient. This optional section gives employers material for informal conversation during the rapport-building phase of an interview. Interests also convey a picture of a well-rounded candidate. Include only interests that you actively pursue and can speak about credibly in an interview. Some interests could be considered controversial, such as political activities or religious affiliation. You will have to decide if it is more important to you to reveal yourself and attract (and risk losing some) interest versus presenting a more neutral image that offends no one and may appear bland.

Military experience and volunteer experience: Either integrated into the "Experience" section or given separate sections. Try it both ways and decide which results in a stronger resume. Translate military jargon into language that is meaningful in civilian settings.

Training, licenses, and/or certifications: Used for credentials that don't fit into the other categories. It is not necessary to include your real estate license if you are looking for a quality assurance position in manufacturing. Include only relevant information.

Writing and editing your resume will take time. Your first draft will undoubtedly not be your last. Several rewrites and thorough editing will produce a strong, focused, and polished final version. If you have never written a resume, start by filling out the following form. You will then have all the necessary content for a first-draft resume.

WORK IN PROGRESS

Resume Worksheet

Purpose: This worksheet, when completed, may serve as a first draft for your chronological resume. It will also serve as a summary of information for the other types of resumes discussed below.

Directions: Complete the following worksheet by filling in the information required in each section. You may leave a section blank if it doesn't pertain to your background. Give careful thought when selecting your words, especially those describing your previous jobs. If you need inspiration for the wording, review the skills activities in Chapter Five. When you have completed the form, copy the information onto blank paper and include the section heads that are typed in capital letters. The result is the first draft of your chronological resume.

First name   Middle name   Last name

Street and number

City   State   Zip code

Area code/phone number   (Home and work if preferred; e-mail address)

OBJECTIVE

EXPERIENCE

Company/organization   City   State

Job title   Dates of employment

Brief job description emphasizing skills, accomplishments, results:

● Company/organization   City   State

Job title   Dates of employment

Brief job description emphasizing skills, accomplishments, results:

....

....

....

....

....

Company/organization   City   State

Job title   Dates of employment

Brief job description emphasizing skills, accomplishments, results:

....

....

● ....

....

....

EDUCATION

College   City   State

Degree (or degree expected)

Major   (Minor/concentration, if applicable)   (Expected) Date of graduation

Coursework included:

....

....

....

....

● ....

Activities   Honors

College   City   State

Degree (or degree expected)

Major   (Minor/concentration, if applicable)   (Expected) Date of graduation

Coursework included:

Activities   Honors

INTERESTS

Activities, hobbies, interests

SPECIAL SKILLS

Languages (computer or foreign), skills, abilities

AFFILIATIONS

Memberships in professional and community organizations

References furnished on request

Reflections: How does your resume sound? Does it accurately and strongly present your background? What aspects of your experience are not reflected? Do they need to be added? What aspects of your background can be eliminated from the resume or stated more succinctly? How does your resume look? How can you improve the graphic design?

Carefully Craft Your "Hot Zone"

Once you have gathered the information you need for your resume and written a rough draft of the content, you can begin to play with the order and the amount of detail. The top third of your resume is the "hot zone," the area most likely to be read and, therefore, the place where your strongest credentials belong. You will have to decide whether your experience section or your education section should appear in the hot zone. If you have broad experience related to your career objective, put that first in the resume. If, on the other hand, you are making a career change with a new educational credential that qualifies you for the position, put your education in the hot zone.

Figure 10.2 shows a job listing and two sample chronological resumes, one emphasizing educational credentials and one featuring related experience. In your opinion, are both candidates qualified for the position?

If you are a midcareer individual with both substantial experience and education, you run the risk of losing your reader if you stick strictly to chronology. There is a solution that keeps only the most relevant information in your hot zone. This format also works well for people whose chronology works against them. For instance, if you are looking for a position as a purchasing agent and you did that work until three years ago but now are in another field, you could use this structure to organize your resume. The order of the resume sections would look like this:

Heading

Objective

Related experience: Include only experience that directly relates to your objective, in reverse chronological order. Be detailed here because this is your best credential to qualify you for the position. In other words, this is your hot zone.

Related education: Include only degrees, certificates, or courses that directly relate to your objective; if there is more than one education item, put them in reverse chronological order. Again, detail is appropriate here.

Additional experience: List remaining experience in reverse chronological order; use far less detail. Whenever possible, describe past experience using action verbs and skills that are relevant to the new direction you are pursuing.

Additional education: Briefly list other educational credentials, including other degrees and certifications. You do not have to include all of your educational background; if something could be a distraction, leave it out.

Interests, etc.: Include this and any other resume categories only if they strengthen your candidacy. Be selective; information overload can work against you.

See Figure 10.3 for a sample resume using the altered format for a chronological resume as described above.

Parexel International Corporation, headquartered in Waltham, Massachusetts, recently advertised for an Applications Support Programmer:

> We require an entry-level applications support programmer in our Information Systems Department. You will provide support to users of Parexel's information systems and will participate in the design, development, and implementation of system improvements. You must have a bachelor's degree in an appropriate field or equivalent experience and be proficient in at least one computer language.

(continued)

FIGURE 10.2

Employment ad and two chronological resumes of applicants

FIGURE 10.2
Continued.

JOHN F. HARRISON
106 Indian Hill Road
Newington, Connecticut 06111
860-665-9074
JFH BAND@aol.com

OBJECTIVE:
A programmer/analyst position

TECHNICAL SKILLS:
Languages: C, C++, and COBOL
Hardware: IBM PC and Apple Mac
Software: Windows 98 and NT, Excel, and PowerPoint

EDUCATION:
COMPUTER SYSTEMS SPECIALIST PROGRAM, Certificate, June 1999
Northeastern University, Boston, Massachusetts

- An eight-month intensive program providing 45 credit hours in Electronic Data Processing, Systems Analysis and Design, Database Management, Operating Systems, UNIX, and Communications and Networking.
- More than 450 hours coding, debugging, and maintaining business applications. Experience in inventory control, payroll, accounts payable and accounts receivable, table handling, sorting, report generation, and random and sequential processing.
- Computer languages: C, C++, and COBOL.

EXPERIENCE:
Office Manager, Pharmacy Department
Hartford Hospital, Hartford, Connecticut, 1994–Present

- Scheduled staff and maintained personnel records.
- Generated intravenous medication usage reports.
- Forecasted, scheduled, and ordered inventory deliveries based on usage reports.
- Resolved billing discrepancies with accounting department.
- Trained new staff.

Professional Musician and Music Director for Band,
The Touchstones, Waterbury, Connecticut, 1985–94

- Managed business transactions with agents and club owners.
- Composed original music.
- Organized and coordinated rehearsals.
- Arranged and performed music with five-piece band.

INTERESTS:
Championship chess, mountain climbing, and traveling the electronic super-highway.

AFFILIATIONS:
Appalachian Mountain Club Web Site Committee

References available on request

FIGURE 10.2

Continued.

Ilene Rudman
6550 Woodland Avenue
Lynnfield, Massachusetts 02488
978-432-7654
irudman@whitney.com

OBJECTIVE:

A software programmer position

TECHNICAL QUALIFICATIONS:

Hardware: IBM-compatibles, MAC, and VAX-11/785
Software: MRP, MS Word, Access, Excel, PowerPoint, and Lotus 1-2-3
Operating systems: Windows 95, Windows NT, UNIX, MAC OS, and VAX/VMS
Languages: C++, C, and COBOL

PROFESSIONAL EXPERIENCE:

Database Administrator, 1995–present

Whitney Manufacturing Corporation, Harbordale, Massachusetts

Maintain computerized on-line receiving and order entry system for material. Process purchases of raw materials totaling over $1 million annually. Assist in scheduling, using MRP system to track inventory. Prepare documentation regarding finished products for both domestic and foreign deliveries totaling $2 million annually. Provide information to shop personnel on technical matters relating to bills of material, inventory status, and computer operations. Supervise one part-time clerical assistant.

Department Manager, 1989–1994

Lechmere, Burlington, Massachusetts

Scheduled 12 employees in small appliance department. Verified daily sales reconciliations. Analyzed departmental reports to maximize sales. Oversaw merchandise planning and presentation. Implemented computerized inventory-tracking system. Promoted from sales associate to manager after 18 months.

EDUCATION:

Northeastern University, Boston, Massachusetts
Certificate, Computer Systems Specialist Program, 1995

Coursework included:
- C++
- Systems Analysis & Design
- Data Base Management

Bachelor of Science in Business Administration (candidate),
Management Information Systems Major

AFFILIATIONS:

Women in Computing

FIGURE 10.3 Chronological resume with altered format

DAYLANA M. RODRIGUEZ

954 Blue Hill Avenue, #5
Boston, Massachusetts 02117
617-375-8812

Objective   Probation Officer

Related Experience

Child Care Worker, St. Germaine's Youth Home: Pre-Independent Living Unit
Atlanta, Georgia, 1988–1992

- Supervised the daily living activities of eight behaviorally disturbed adolescent girls.
- Enforced house rules (i.e., curfews, school attendance, and chores).
- Taught socially acceptable behavior and independent living skills.
- Provided counseling and crisis intervention.
- Observed and documented behavior and daily activities of clients.
- Participated as a team member in monthly case plan meetings along with therapists, teachers, and department heads.
- Maintained the security and safety of the facility.

Education

Bachelor of Science in Criminal Justice, 1988,
University of South Carolina, Columbia, South Carolina

Additional Experience

Employment Coordinator, Jobs for Youth Atlanta, Inc.
Atlanta, Georgia, 1996–present

- Reviewed applications and matched candidates to employers.
- Referred qualified applicants to government offices, retail stores, hotels and restaurants, and hospitals.
- Canvassed organizations to establish employment listings.
- Completed telephone reference checks.
- Supervised two part-time employees and three volunteers.

Wait Staff, Chart House
Miami, Florida, 1992–1996

- Served busiest section of restaurant.
- Supervised setup of formal dining area.
- Attended to customer needs.
- Used computerized system for placement and billing of orders.
- Promoted from hostess.

Sales person/Cashier, The Bookstore Cafe
Fort Myers, Florida, 1988–1992

- Assisted customers with selections.
- Operated computerized cash register.
- Designed book displays highlighting new arrivals and seasonal favorites.

References on Request

Functional/Combination Resume

The functional/combination resume is designed to highlight your overall qualifications and skills, with less emphasis on specific work titles, employers, and dates of employment. This style is most useful for career changers and applicants who have gaps in their employment or a diverse work history. The parts of a functional/combination resume are:

Heading: (See discussion on p. 156)

Objective: (Optional but strongly recommended for this style; see discussion on p. 157)

Professional experience: Can also be called "Achievements," "Selected Accomplishments," or "Highlights of Experience." This section contains descriptions of your experience, usually organized into skill clusters containing action statements that describe your skills. The skill clusters should directly relate to the position you are seeking. For instance, if you are looking for a management position, you might use the skill clusters *Supervising, Strategic Planning, and Communicating.* Here is part of an early resume draft in which the applicant has done volunteer work with Campfire Girls, worked as an assistant manager in a retail store, and managed a home and family. The experiences are blended to emphasize the applicant's relevant skills:

Objective: Management Position in Nonprofit Organization

Supervising

- Recruited and selected volunteers for youth organization.
- Trained and evaluated staff of retail store.
- Assigned major projects and delegated tasks.

Strategic Planning

- Identified medium- and short-term goals and objectives for youth organization.
- Used management by objectives to achieve goals in retail setting.
- Developed long-range goals for family unit.

Communicating

- Worked effectively with upper management, peers, and staff.
- Addressed large audience at town meeting and led small-group discussions.
- Wrote business letters.

This bare-bones sketch needs to be fleshed out with details and examples, but it's a start. The writer has described experiences that relate to the management position for which she is applying. Do you think she sounds like a credible candidate so far?

Work history: Can also be called "Professional Experience," "Experience," or "Work Chronology." Here is where you list your chronological work history. Include the names of employers, locations, titles of positions, and inclusive dates of employment. This list is brief and factual, with only one or two lines for each position.

Education: (Same as for chronological resume on page 156)

Affiliations: Memberships in associations can be important credentials for career changers. They demonstrate strong interest and involvement in your new field. Local as well as national affiliation may be appropriate, and committee work may be helpful.

Interests (optional): Can be a handy place for a career changer to include information that relates to the objective but might not fit into other categories. Someone making a transition into the computer field may mention that he or she is a chess player or musician, as abilities in these areas are known to correlate with computer aptitude. A candidate moving into field service could mention putting together a stereo or computer kit, and someone switching into health care may include an interest in nutrition or physical exercise. These items add punch to the resume.

To write a successful functional/combination resume, know the skills required in the field you plan to enter. In the resume, emphasize skills you have developed that relate specifically to the position you seek. If you are unsure of the most critical skills, look at advertisements for the position in the newspaper or on the Web. Also, check the *Dictionary of Occupational Titles* for a description of the functions. Figure 10.4 contains three sample resumes using the functional/combination style.

Keep in mind the hot zone when laying out your functional/combination resume. Give top billing to the skill cluster that most directly relates to the position you seek. For a sales position, emphasize skills in selling, marketing, or promoting; for an engineering position, designing or developing; for a counseling position, counseling or advising; for a training position, teaching or leading or delivering; for a nursing position, treating or managing; for a purchasing position, buying or negotiating, and so on.

Preparing a Scannable Resume

Many organizations today are tracking applicants by scanning their resumes into computer databases. The resumes are retrieved through keyword searches when openings occur. What gets the attention of a computer is different from what gets the attention of a hiring manager. The rules for writing a scannable resume, therefore, differ significantly from the previous discussion and samples of resumes. Scannable resumes are not attractive to look at because they are devoid of graphic enhancements such as boldface print. They must be written using a plain font because that is the type of characters scanners will recognize.

The other major change is that the programs used for scanning and retrieving resumes are set up to recognize nouns, not action verbs. This means that the content of the resume must be written in noun form, with phrases such as management experience, platform skills, supervisory training, and data analysis. It is even recommended that you repeat keywords because if they appear often, your resume has a better chance of being recognized by the computer when it searches the database for qualified candidates.

Some key points to consider when preparing a scannable resume include the following:

- Use industry jargon. A computer search will target keywords specific to your profession.
- Use nouns rather than verbs.
- Use keywords throughout your resume; for scanning purposes, repetition works in your favor.
- Use 12-point type; using smaller type may confuse the scanner.
- Avoid graphic enhancers, such as boldface, bullets, italics, underlining, and fancy fonts, because they do not scan well.

Examples of a functional/combination resume.    FIGURE 10.4

JOANNE SUTTON-DRESYICH

793 Illinois Avenue
Washington, D.C. 20904

202-623-4384 (h)
202-667-3867 (w)

OBJECTIVE: Management position in social service agency

PROFESSIONAL EXPERIENCE

Managerial and Organizational Skills

- Managed a caseload of 32 families, assessing need for public assistance and making appropriate referrals.
- Coordinated student fund-raising activities for senior trips.
- Planned all aspects of air and ground travel of 14,000 Americans touring in Europe.
- Negotiated $1.5 million in European hotel contracts.

Communication Skills

- Wrote federal and corporate grant proposals for arts programs.
- Taught high school English and served as advisor to performing arts group.
- Tutored students with special needs.
- Delivered training programs to new travel industry personnel.
- Briefed American travelers about foreign travel, local customs; recommended attending special exhibits, sites, and/or performances.

Program Development Skills

- Established enrichment program in fine arts for public school, working with area museums and state arts council.
- Participated in curriculum development project that produced language arts instruction manual.
- Designed and implemented training programs for travel industry personnel.
- Developed training manuals used by major charter tour operator.
- Assisted in planning European tour packages and led group tours in Asia.

Computer Skills

- Microsoft Word, Excel, Internet

EMPLOYMENT HISTORY

Manager, Corporate Travel, Carson Travel Agency, Washington, DC; 1997–present
Tour Planner, International Weekends, Inc., Kansas City, MO; 1994–1997
Teacher, John F. Kennedy High School, Midland, DE; 1990–1994
Social Worker, Department of Welfare, Baltimore, MD; 1985–1990

EDUCATION

- University of Maryland, College Park, MD
- Certificate in Teaching, 1990
- Bachelor of Arts in English, 1985
- Minor in Social Work

AFFILIATIONS/INTERESTS

International Association of Meeting Planners, Friends of the Smithsonian
Worldwide travel, silversmithing, community theater

FIGURE 10.4
Continued.

William Andrew Maher
9824 Main Street
Sweetwater, Texas 78678
915-776-0906

OBJECTIVE   Retail Management/Buyer Position

PROFESSIONAL
EXPERIENCE
- Managed all aspects of sales, buying, inventory control, and policy making for two stores, each grossing over $2 million annually.
- Utilized inventory control software and customer information database.
- Analyzed market and developed merchandise plans and sales forecasts: formulated strategies to increase sales volume by targeting additional market segments and broadening product lines.
- Forecast sales and inventory levels based on market and competitive analysis: succeeded in meeting and increasing sales plan by approximately 50%.
- Planned advertising budgets and directed advertising campaigns: achieved dominant position in the marketplace.
- Recruited and trained retail sales staff: designed and implemented commission sales program; emphasized product knowledge, customer service, and satisfaction.
- Initiated program for inventory control and developed loss prevention procedures: achieved inventory shrinkage significantly below industry average.
- Made purchasing decisions and bought directly from vendors: worked with open-to-buy budget in excess of $1 million.

EMPLOYMENT
HISTORY
General Manager, CHARLES SAUNDERS, COUTURE, Austin, Texas; 1996–present

Sales Manager, NORDSTROM, Fort Lauderdale, Florida; 1991–1996

Department Manager, NEIMAN MARCUS, Dallas, Texas; 1987–1991

Assistant Buyer, Sales Associate, LORD AND TAYLOR, Fort Worth, Texas; 1983–1987

EDUCATION   Associate Degree in Business, Major in Retail Merchandising, Amarillo College, Amarillo, Texas, 1992

AFFILIATIONS   Chamber of Commerce, Program Committee
                 International Mass Retail Association

References Available on Request

FIGURE 10.4
Continued.

SANDRA L. KARDARIAN
354 Bedford Road, Salt Lake City, Utah 84124
808-785-5112

OBJECTIVE: Leadership position in health maintenance organization

SUMMARY OF QUALIFICATIONS

- Highly developed skills in organizing personnel and streamlining operations in business and medical settings.
- Computer proficiency in Windows 95, Excel, Medical Systems Management, SQL.
- Proven communications skills in areas of patient care, office operations, and customer service.
- Ability to function both independently and as part of a team.
- Over ten years of experience in nursing, providing direct patient care.

EXPERIENCE

Leadership

- Managed clerical staff of 14 for health insurance provider.
- Hired, trained, supervised, and evaluated staff.
- Initiated and developed reward system to motivate staff; improved attendance by 20% and productivity by 30%.
- Supervised night nursing staff in critical care hospital.
- Elected treasurer of local chapter of nursing association; served two-year term.
- Represented union in collective bargaining negotiations with hospital.

Office Operations

- Designed and conducted study to determine problem areas in existing operations of underwriting department of insurance company.
- Interpreted and summarized findings.
- Formulated work plans and assignments.
- Developed and implemented methods for improving office operations.
- Organized the physical move of the office to new building.

Patient Communications and Services

- Coordinated nursing team members in providing patient care.
- Established short- and long-term goals for patient management.
- Documented daily observations and made recommendations for patient care.
- Taught patients preventive and maintenance care and explained technical information.
- Advocated for patients and acted as mediator between patient and physician.
- Interviewed and evaluated suitability of blood donors, performed phlebotomies, and provided postdonation care.

CHRONOLOGY OF WORK

- Office Manager, Blue Cross Blue Shield of Utah, Salt Lake City, Utah; 1995–present
- Charge Nurse, Mayo Clinic, Rochester, Minnesota; 1990–1995
- Nurse, American Red Cross, Denver, Colorado; 1985–1990

EDUCATION

St. Mary's Hospital School of Nursing, Denver, Colorado; Registered Nurse, 1985

- Avoid columns because scanners read from left to right.
- Use white or off-white paper; avoid blues and grays as they minimize the contrast with letters and may be unreadable to the scanner.
- Use standard $8\,^1/_2$" x 11" paper; send unfolded resumes because creased lettering is not recognizable by scanners. Multiple pages are not a problem.
- Send original printed resumes because photocopies do not scan clearly.

Portions of a scannable resume are provided in Figure 10.5.

A scannable resume can be used to transmit your resume electronically either for a position for which you are applying or to a resume listing service on the Internet. There are four ways to prepare your resume to be sent electronically. The first is to prepare the resume in word processing software, such as Microsoft Word, and paste it into an e-mail. Here's how it's done. When you have written the resume, hit "select all" and then "copy." Now open e-mail, and indicate that you are going to prepare a document to send. Enter the address and subject as prompted. When you get the screen for your message, click "paste"; your resume is now in the e-mail document and ready to send.

The next is to store the resume in a document file and attach it to an e-mail. This method is less desirable as employers don't always open attachments. Further, attachments are often unreadable because of computer incompatibilities. Always send a cover letter with your resume.

Third, you can prepare your resume in an ASCII (text-only) file. The ASCII file is what you submit to job-related Web sites.

Finally, for technical professionals, you can prepare an HTML-coded resume either to post on your own Web page or to submit to job boards.

When sending a resume and cover letter by regular mail, send two versions of the resume—one that is graphically enhanced and printed on quality bond paper matching the cover letter and a second that is scannable and printed on plain white copy paper. That way, when the resume is being handled by people, they can have the attractive version; when they are storing resumes, they can use the scannable version. Label the resume "scannable" either in pencil or using a post-it note.

Have Your Resume Critiqued

Show your resume to others for feedback, content editing, and, finally, proofreading

When you have reworked your resume to the best of your ability, it is time to show it to others for content feedback and editing. The content feedback will tell you if you have written a resume that successfully communicates your qualifications for the position you desire. Would the person reviewing your resume select you for an interview? If not, what could be done to improve the resume? Ideally, content feedback should come from someone in the field.

Once you have made these changes and the final content is decided, have someone with strong editing ability review the resume to ensure consistency in construction and to eliminate typographical errors. You should have no spelling or punctuation errors in your resume either. After working long and hard on the document, it will be almost impossible for you to spot errors. Career development instructors and career counselors often have a trained eye in this regard.

Following the section on cover letters, we will discuss the mechanics of job-search correspondence, which will address preparation of resumes and cover letters on a word processor, and selection of paper. Additional job-search correspondence will be discussed in Chapter 11.

Mark Peterson
Marketing Manager
858 Lombard Drive
Boston, MA 02117
617-936-1234
mpeterson@evernet.com

FIGURE 10.5

A sample scannable resume.

MARKETING MANAGER, PRODUCT MANAGER, PRODUCT DEVELOPMENT

Summary: Results-oriented professional with management, marketing, and product development experience in small and midsize companies.

Supervising, budgeting, and forecasting; marketing and product positioning; advertising; employee development; public relations; customer support; total quality management; troubleshooting; strategic planning merchandising.

Team player with strong interpersonal skills and the ability to work well with all levels of an organization; well-developed organizational, product development, and market research abilities.

Computer skills: Macintosh, IBM; PageMaker, Word, Windows, Excel, FoxPro (PMI), SPSS, Now Contact.

Bachelor's degree in Business Administration (concentration Marketing), University of Chicago, IL, 1997.

Career History 1995–Present:

Marketing Manager, Brand Names, Chicago, IL.
International show company with revenues in excess of $30 million; over 500 employees in Ireland, Canada, and the United States.

Supervision of 22 employees in marketing, market research, product development, account supervision, advertising, and total quality management.

Coordination of daily operations for worldwide marketing efforts. In 1997, introduced two new products that made up 20 percent of market share for that year. Realized 33 percent increase in sales over previous year.

[This is only a portion of entire resume]

CREATE COVER LETTERS THAT GET ATTENTION

When you have perfected your resume, turn your attention to the next piece of job-search correspondence: your cover letter. You use a cover letter to introduce yourself to a prospective employer and to call attention to your enclosed resume. For experienced workers, this section will serve as a quick review of the basics.

One of the best payoffs of circulating your resume through networking encounters is that you write fewer cover letters! Networking is discussed later in this chapter. A cover letter is used primarily when you are sending your resume to an organization to apply for a specific position, usually in response to a newspaper ad. The well-written cover letter highlights selective aspects of your background that best suit the employer's needs. The cover letter bridges the gap between your skills and experience and the qualifications of the position. A well-written cover letter commands the reader's attention. It stimulates interest in you and the background described in your resume, and it conveys your interest in the position and the organization.

Always try to obtain the name of the person to whom the letter should be addressed. If a name does not appear in an advertisement, call the organization to get the name. When you are addressing an individual, your letter will flow more smoothly, and you will also have someone with whom you can follow up later on.

Blind ads with box numbers make life difficult for job seekers. Alternative salutations when you are unable to identify the organization and the individual include "Dear Sir or Madam," "To Whom It May Concern," and "Dear People." Make sure you do not use a gender-biased salutation such as "Dear Sir."

Content of a Cover Letter

Cover letters bridge gaps between your skills/experience and position qualifications

A cover letter usually includes a minimum of three paragraphs; each paragraph has a different goal:

First paragraph: The opening paragraph explains why you are writing the letter. State your purpose, identifying the position you are applying for and how you learned about the opening. If you are responding to an advertisement, state the name and date of the publication where you saw the ad. If a well-respected person referred you to the organization, mention the person's name and briefly explain your connection.

Second paragraph: Here is where you tailor your cover letter to a particular job. Tell the employer why you are a strong candidate for this position. Highlight relevant achievements, skills, and/or experience, mentioning the most interesting points on your resume. Demonstrate an understanding of the employer's needs. Explain how you intend to contribute to the organization.

If you are changing careers, mention this in your letter and emphasize your transferable skills. Show how your past experience has contributed to making you a strong contender in your new field.

Third paragraph (optional): This paragraph can be included if there is additional information that either adds strength to your qualifications and hasn't been mentioned on your resume or needs to be described in more detail (for example, a special project you undertook in a previous job or in your community).

Closing paragraph: The final paragraph should be action-oriented. State when and how you will contact the individual to arrange a mutually convenient time to interview. Employers will not automatically contact you once you've sent your cover letter and resume, but be sure to state how and when they may contact you. Finally, thank the person for considering your candidacy and mention that you are looking forward to meeting him or her. Figures 10.6 and 10.7 provide sample cover letters.

MAKE GOOD USE OF TODAY'S TOOLS

Resumes and cover letters are usually prepared on computers, using word processing software. This makes it fairly easy for you to revise your resume frequently and to tailor cover letters. If you don't have your own personal computer, you no doubt can use one at work or school. *One word of caution:* Refrain from overusing boldface and italic in designing the resume. They are eye-catching devices for creating an attractive document, but too many font

---

8678 Euclid Avenue
Bloomington, Indiana 47405
July 14, 1999

FIGURE 10.6

Sample cover letter.

Ms. Mary Jean Lavinski, President
Nearing Environmental Association
Indianapolis, Indiana 46354

Dear Ms. Lavinski:

Your advertisement in the *Indianapolis Journal Inquirer* on July 12 indicated the need for an Assistant Director of Development for your association. My current position in public relations has prepared me for this role. In addition, I have been active in environmental organizations for many years.

As my resume indicates, my two years of experience working in public relations for Hammersmith Hospital involved planning fund-raising events, editing a monthly newsletter, and writing press releases. An active member of and trip leader for the Sierra Club, I have also helped with its annual membership drive.

In addition to my job and my volunteer work, I am presently pursuing a bachelor's degree in business administration at the University of Indiana. I am the first part-time student to volunteer for the university's annual alumni telethon.

I would very much like to put my skills to work for your organization. I will call you within the next two weeks to discuss the possibility of an interview, or you can reach me at 321-8765 during normal business hours. Thank you for your consideration; I look forward to talking with you.

Very truly yours,

Eliot Darveau

FIGURE 10.7

Sample cover letter.

Mayfield Road
Auburn, OR 97090

September 4, 1999

Mr. David Madison
Manager of Human Resources
Leader Federal Savings Bank
2468 Beacon Street
Portland, OR 97040

Dear Mr. Madison:

Thank you for taking a moment yesterday to confirm the posting of the Financial Analyst position within the bank. With over ten years of extensive and practical experience, I believe I am well qualified for the position.

As Accountant at Cummings Property Management Co. for three years, Receivable Coordinator for five years at Los Angeles County Hospital, and an appointed member of the Town of Auburn's Finance Committee, I have been exposed to a wide range of financial audits and reporting. Furthermore, I have acquired excellent interpersonal, communication, presentation, and customer service skills as a result of participating in special projects and task-oriented groups.

I am accustomed to environments where deadlines are a priority, handling multiple jobs simultaneously is the norm, and teamwork is essential. My ability to plan, organize, and document the details through accurate record keeping enables me to solve problems and be successful in my career.

I would welcome the opportunity to discuss my experience and abilities in more depth, as well as explore my potential value to Leader Federal Savings Bank. I will give you a call next week to follow up.

Most sincerely,

Ellen Casey

---

sizes and too much italic and boldface can detract from the content. Keep your formatting simple. Additionally, many employers are scanning resumes into computerized applicant-tracking systems. Simpler formats scan in more successfully.

If you have a laser printer, you can print out copies of your correspondence yourself. If you do not have a laser printer, you may want to use a printing service to have copies made from your disk. Use good-quality bond paper in a white or off-white tone such as ivory. Matching stationery for letters, resumes, and envelopes conveys a professional image. Remember, all job-search correspondence should be free of typographical and grammatical errors.

Keep detailed records of your job search

Having your own computer can streamline your job search considerably. Letter writing can be a snap when you have a ready-made file of cover letters to adapt and send. If you are connected to the Internet, you can transmit resumes and cover letters directly to organizations whose listings you found online. You can also create and maintain a database of your job leads and a calendar for tracking your search.

If you don't have a computer, keep detailed records of all aspects of your search. Every time you apply for a job, make a copy of the listing or job description, your cover letter, and the resume you sent (if you are using more than one version). If you have researched the organization, keep your notes with the other material. When you follow up, make notes of telephone conversations and any actions you've agreed to take. After interviews, record your impressions, the names of the people you met, and all factual information you learned. Keep track of follow-up plans, and save copies of additional correspondence such as thank-you letters, offer letters, and acceptance or rejection letters.

Using a three-ring binder with tabbed dividers, you can develop a system for organizing your search. At the front of the notebook, keep a chart that lists each position and its status. Make notations here to remind you to make follow-up calls. Enter all interview appointments and other pertinent dates on a calendar. Figure 10.8 offers a sample chart for organizing your campaign.

BUILD A NETWORK OF PROFESSIONAL CONTACTS

Maintaining a network of professional contacts is essential in today's work world. Surely you've heard the term, "the old boys' network," and perhaps you never felt part of it. We can learn a lot from that practice. Given the changes occurring in the workplace, a network is more important than ever before. Unfortunately, when a word such as "network" is overused, many people simply tune it out. You can't afford to do that!

The people in your network can assist you in several ways. They can give you timely information, refer you to others who may be able to add to that information, and share their points of view. Occasionally, they also provide job leads.

A network is made up of relationships developed over time. On paper, it looks like a list of people's names, their addresses and phone numbers, and their job titles and organizations. Some people keep business cards of associates they meet through their work. Others keep a database. How you store information is entirely up to you. The important things are to keep it simple and keep it current. When you join a professional organization, you are usually given a directory of the members; that too can serve as the basis for your network. E-mail is an ideal way to stay in touch with your network. It is fast and informal and avoids telephone tag.

Developing a network when you are out of work poses problems. First of all, your self-esteem may be shaky, so contacting people may feel uncomfortable. Second, you may feel needy or that you have little to offer contacts in return. To avoid these discomforts, it is best to build your network when you are employed. However, if you are unemployed and without a network, start building a network immediately, even if doing so is uncomfortable. Contact friends and former colleagues, look for support groups, and visit your local employment office.

One way to approach a contact would be, "I'm considering a career shift from technical writing to Web site development. I've done some coursework that I believe gives me credibility. I would be very interested in your assessment of the market."

Another example: "I'm interested in entering the environmental field. I learned about your organization through my research, and I'm interested in

FIGURE 10.8 Job-search position status chart.

CONTACT	METHOD OF CONTACT	PURPOSE	CONTACT DATE	FOLLOW-UP DATE	OUTCOME
Examples:					
Harry Smith at Digital	resume/cover letter	exploratory letter	7/30/99	8/20/99	not hiring at present time
Julie Reed at IBM	phone call	informational interview	7/31/99	8/12/99	informational interview 8/12/99
Jeffrey Hanlon at Microsoft	resume/cover letter	response to ad	8/1/99	8/15/99	job interview 8/22/99
Bev Zhang at Silicon Tech	professional association meeting	networking	8/1/99		job lead
Kevin Shields at Silicon	phone call	information on opening	8/1/99	8/2/99	fax resume
Jeffrey Hanlon at Microsoft	meeting	job interview	8/22/99	8/29/99	still interviewing—call 9/9
Kevin Shields at Silicon	phone	screening interview	9/3/99	9/4/99	full day of interviews
Kevin Shields & team	meetings	interview	9/6/99	9/9/99	Great group! I want the offer.
Jeffrey Hanlon at Microsoft	phone call	follow-up	9/9/99		still interviewing
Kevin Shields	phone call	follow-up	9/9/99	"Call in January!"	position frozen
Jeff Hanlon	phone call	follow-up	9/12/99		second interview! 9/15/99
Jeff Hanlon	e-mail	thank-you	9/15/99		
Jeff Hanlon	phone call	third interview	9/21/99		got the offer!

- Be on time for networking appointments.
- Be prepared. Do your homework first.
- Be clear on what you want from the person you are meeting.
- Be trustworthy. Do not share confidential information.
- Be positive and receptive. Accept opinions or advice openly.
- At professional gatherings, act as a greeter rather than as a guest. Help others to feel welcome and included.
- Take responsibility for yourself and respect the boundaries of others.
- Follow up with people. Let them know when their suggestions have paid off.
- Nourish your network. Find ways to stay connected with your contacts. Refer business to them, send them information, or informally check in from time to time. Watch for them at association meetings.

FIGURE 10.9

Develop and maintain professional connections.

talking with you to learn more about the kinds of projects you take on and the results you've had."

Building a network when you're employed may start with meeting someone for an informational interview. You could also contact a colleague in your field who works for another employer. Perhaps you want to compare notes over the phone or meet for lunch to talk shop. When you attend professional meetings or conferences, you will be surrounded by potential members of your network. You can collect business cards from people at your table or pick out one person to talk with in depth and follow up the conversation with a phone call or an e-mail, expressing appreciation for the time you shared.

A network must be nurtured. If you forget the people as quickly as you meet them, you will find it hard to build and maintain your network successfully. It is important that you recognize these people when you see them again at other conferences or meetings. You might telephone once or twice a year to see how things are going for them or to find out what they know about the market, new developments in your field, or changes in their organization. You can also use your network to obtain advice on handling a delicate problem. A nice way to make a nonintrusive connection with people in your network is to send a clipping you think they'd be interested in, with a brief message on an attached note.

A network must be nurtured

Remember, professional relationships must be reciprocal. You and your network contacts have information and contacts that are useful to one another. Always be mindful of what you can share with members of your network and make "goodwill deposits." If you function in this way, you won't feel guilty when you have to ask for something, such as a job lead or a recommendation. You will be drawing on your "goodwill reserve." Figure 10.9 contains some hints about successful networking.

Having a healthy, active network is a valuable resource should you find yourself looking for work or, for that matter, looking for someone to hire.

USE MANY SOURCES TO FIND JOB LEADS

When most people think about looking for a new job, they automatically go to the Help Wanted advertisements in their local newspaper. The most complete listing usually appears on Sundays. For the next several weeks, job seekers pore over the ads, agonize over the lack of fit between the opportunities listed and their particular qualifications, and painstakingly compose and send cover letters and resumes for jobs that seem only marginally interesting or appropriate.

A successful job-search campaign is multifaceted; it will involve many sources of job leads, contacts, information, and support. Leave no stone unturned in the process of finding the best position for you.

The most successful job-search campaigns draw job leads from a wide range of sources. The following list is intended to inspire you but not limit you. Be creative as you consider where you could learn about opportunities. An estimated 80 percent of job opportunities never go public. These openings are referred to as the *hidden job market*, and they are the positions that are filled by insiders and others who find themselves in the right place at the right time. You could attribute that to luck, but it is likely that those individuals worked very hard to position themselves. They probably talked to a lot of people and read widely to become experts on what was happening in their field. They may also have attended professional meetings to meet people and learn about new developments in their area. In addition, they may have done an internship or taken a course to acquire the skills or experience that set them apart from other applicants.

An estimated 80% of job opportunities never go public

SOURCES OF JOB LEADS AND PROFESSIONAL CONTACTS

- Colleagues in your present organization and field
- Professional association members
- Family members and their friends
- Friends and *their* friends and relatives
- Faculty and classmates where you attend school
- Online job listing services accessible through the Internet
- Home pages of hiring organizations
- College/university career services department
- Alumni network from your school
- Job fairs and career expos at your school or in your community
- Public and private placement agencies
- Job postings at local companies and organizations
- Newspaper ads in local as well as major urban areas
- Online newspaper advertisements
- Libraries, both public and private
- Trade journals and newsletters
- Directories

WORK IN PROGRESS

Chris

Chris worked for seven years as a stock clerk for a defense contractor. The last year was gloomy as employees watched colleagues receive pink slips and waited for the ax to fall on them. Chris updated his resume but found himself immobilized until he received his walking papers.

Once out of work, Chris contacted several employment agencies, answered newspaper ads, networked with students in his night classes, and registered with two or three temporary agencies. To his surprise, each avenue he pursued yielded a return. He had two or three interviews a week during the five months he was out of work.

Eventually he was offered a temporary assignment as a call director supporting the customer service department of a company that provides remote access services for computer users. Chris took calls from customers having difficulty using the company's product. Chris listened empathetically to sometimes irate customers, took notes, and then usually had to refer customers to the product support engineers. After a few weeks, Chris decided that he would add much more value to the company if he could resolve some of the questions customers had, especially those that came up over and over.

Chris came in on weekends and taught himself how to use the product and how to solve basic problems. Now he handles about 50 percent of the inquiries he receives. He is thrilled to be giving good customer service. He has also been empowered to take action independently to resolve customer complaints. He can offer customers a month of free telephone support or a free product upgrade. In one case, Chris sent a customer a free replacement unit and was praised by his boss.

After three months as a temp, Chris was offered a permanent position. Coincidentally, he received another offer from a competing company during the same week. As a result, he was able to negotiate a respectable salary while staying with the company that is committed to delivering "knock-your-socks-off" customer service.

THE INTERNET AND JOB SEARCH

The Internet has become an incredible resource for job hunters and career changers. For those of you already familiar with the Internet, you have probably discovered the vast array of sites related to job search and career development. For those new to the Internet, you will be amazed to discover the information available. Getting started can be a challenge; the second hurdle is dealing with the vast amounts of information. First, you need access to a computer that is connected to the Internet. At a library or computer lab, you would most likely use a Web browser such as NetScape. From home, connect through a service provider such as AOL or PRODIGY.

If you are brand-new to the Web, take an introductory seminar on using the Internet, buy a book that takes you step-by-step through the process (such as *The Internet for Dummies* or *The Complete Idiot's Guide to the Internet*) or find a patient, computer-savvy friend to get you started. The Internet contains over 300 million sites; it is easy to become overwhelmed, lost, or frustrated. However, your initial investment will be well worth it.

Excellent career-related sites exist that provide an overview of what's available online. These sites offer information, describe the benefits of using other sites, and link directly to those sites. So you can check out one site to find out about another site of specific interest. Then use your mouse to "click" on and go directly to the new site. The new site will offer information and additional connections to other linked sites. You'll very quickly find yourself "surfing" the Internet. While it will be tempting to take off in many directions, thoroughly exploring one of the following sites will familiarize you with the way sites are structured. Develop the habit of bookmarking sites you find useful so you can return to them without linking through other sites. In no time, you will have your own list of favorite sites. Directions for bookmarking can be found on the help menu of your Web browser.

The following sites are ideal starting points.

http://www.tenspeed.com/parachute

To get to this site, open your browser (e.g., NetScape) and enter the Web address into the appropriate window. With NetScape, the window is labeled "go to." Then watch the gyrations on the screen as the site downloads onto your computer. The length of time it takes to download will vary, depending largely on how complex the graphics are. Other factors include the speed of your computer and modem and the time of day. When the Internet is jammed with users, everything slows down and sometimes access to sites is blocked.

Hassles aside, let's proceed to the rich career resources available at this gateway site. The author of this site is career development guru Richard Bolles, whose well-known *What Color Is Your Parachute?* has 6 million copies in print. His site is informative and friendly, and he will gently walk you through the process of orienting to the Internet online.

Bolles explains that the Internet can assist the job seeker in five ways: searching for *job listings* by employer; posting *resumes*; acquiring *career counseling* advice; making *contacts* with people; and doing *research* into fields, occupations, companies, and so on. His site is organized into those five categories. The first time you visit the site, peruse other "gateway sites," paying particular attention to the "Parachute Picks," where he identifies his favorites. Bolles annotates several sites in each of the five categories. You can visit them later by clicking on their highlighted names. Upon returning to this site, you can go directly to "just the sites" and skip the descriptive annotations.

http://www.dbm.com/jobguide

Another well-established career site that is great for getting started is called the Riley Guide. It too provides lots of useful information, including annotations of linked sites. Margaret Dikel (formerly Riley) spends all of her work time surfing the Net to stay on top of the continuous changes. One frustration of the Internet is that Web addresses change. And since there is no quality control on the Internet, Dikel reviews the content of sites and recommends the ones that have been most reliable over time.

Once you've been introduced to the Internet and feel ready to explore further, the following sites are worth checking out. Before you go there, form a question or goal in your mind so you can search for information relevant to your current needs. *Note:* All addresses start with http://www. Type that in front of the Web addresses listed below.

ajb.com

The U.S. Department of Labor and the state-operated public employment services have partnered to create one of the largest job-listing sites, containing over 900,000 jobs nationwide, representing all types of work (mostly in the private sector). A number of options exist for searching this database, which has links to many state employment services. A free registration service is available, allowing you to create and store custom searches for future use as well as create individual cover letters for each job to which you are applying. Registration also allows you to create an electronic resume via a "fill-in-the-blanks" form. Your resume will exist in its database to be searched by potential employers.

careermosaic.com/cm/home.html

This site is one of the oldest online recruiting sites, having been created in 1994. It is one of the easiest to use, as well as one of the largest, offering more than 70,000 current jobs in a variety of industries from around the world. You can search by description, title, company, and location. An extremely useful zip-code tool allows you to view all job openings within a given distance from any zip code in the country. CareerMosaic indexes postings from more than 20 job-related newsgroups in addition to its own postings. You may post your resume at this site for free, to be searched by job recruiters; however, be aware that there is no option to block private information on your resume from potential viewers. The site offers a comprehensive Career Resource Center with information on job hunting, resume and cover letter writing, relocation resources, wage and salary information, and other research tools.

careerpath.com

Cofounded in October 1995 by six major newspapers (*Boston Globe, Chicago Tribune, Los Angeles Times, New York Times, San Jose Mercury-News*, and *Washington Post*), CareerPath.com offers listings both from Help Wanted ads of the nation's leading newspapers and from Web sites of leading employers. The listings at this site are particularly current as no listing remains in the database for more than two weeks. The newspaper jobs database is searchable by geography, newspaper, job type, and keyword. The employers' listing database is searchable by geography, employer, job type, and keyword. Notable features include a "saved job search" function, which allows you to specify your search criteria once and store it at the site for future use, and a resume posting feature, which allows you to create a complete career profile to be searched by potential employers. Use of these features requires registration, which is free.

careers.org

The Career Resource Center, one of the largest collections of career-related links on the Internet, boasts of having over 7,500 links to jobs with major employers. It offers links to its selection of the 100 most useful and creative career Web sites, as well as links to numerous job-listing sites that have been nicely categorized. The Regional Pages are especially useful for locating job-listing sites by state, although they do not contain complete listings for every category. The site offers numerous links to education-related sites, including colleges and libraries. Useful links also exist for the small or home office.

careers.wsj.com

The *Wall Street Journal* site is exclusively geared toward executive, managerial, and professional job seekers. It is a well-maintained site, which is updated on a daily basis. The site contains articles by *Wall Street Journal's* career columnists, job-hunting advice, industry salary data and trends, human resources issues, and tips for new college graduates, as well as entrepreneurial/franchising and venture capital information. The site features a vast database of jobs that is easily searched by industry, job function, location, academic degree, salary level, experience, and keyword. The jobs featured include senior and general management, sales, marketing, finance, technology, and a range of related fields.

espan.com

One of the original recruiting sites on the Internet, E-Span offers a daily updated database of thousands of jobs geared toward professionals. The site is extremely user-friendly, offering a variety of simple, interchangeable options for creating online resumes as well as simple steps for searching its job listings. Numerous career tools are offered, including writing resumes/cover letters, salary information, and industry and business information, as well as interactive practice interviews. After preparing your online resume at this site, you can forward your resume to specific companies with one mouse click. You can easily elect to keep your resume "private," which offers a blind profile of you on demand from potential employers. E-Span offers a personal job-search agent, which will regularly search the database and e-mail you new jobs that match your criteria.

headhunter.net

This site is one of the easiest to use, with the most complete options for searching its job-listing database. Particularly valuable is their wide range of salary levels from which to choose. The jobs that meet your criteria are displayed in a consistent format, allowing you to easily see a job description, compensation information, and specific contact information. This listing of over 150,000 jobs in all fields is continually updated, and jobs are never over 45 days old. Upon free registration, you may also post your resume in its database.

job-hunt.org

This site provides a listing of numerous useful job-search resources and services that historically have been stable and are relevant to a broad range of job types and geographic locations. With its beginnings in 1993, it is one of the oldest job-related sites on the Internet. It is updated regularly, with 5 to 10 new links added per week to the already existing 700 links. Job-listing sites are categorized by academia; general; science, engineering, and medicine; classified ads; recruiting agencies; companies; and newsgroup searches. Collections of other job resources include resume banks, reference materials, commercial services, university career resource centers, and other meta-lists. A particularly useful feature of this site is the flagging of both new and outstanding sites.

jobfind.com

This site is geared toward employment in the New England area and was launched in 1996 by the publisher of the *Boston Herald*. This site allows you to search for jobs by state, area, job category, and job title. You also may submit your resume to its database online, to be searched by potential employers. Corporate profiles exist for a number of companies in the Boston area; each has a direct link to the employment openings. News services are available through links to sites geared toward national and international employment news, human resources, and Boston business news.

jobtrak.com

This unique site is the result of over 750 college and university career centers nationwide contracting with JOBTRAK to make their job-listing services available to students and alumni via the Internet. Employers are able to target their job opportunities to students and alumni from their choice of campuses. To access this site, check to see whether the college or university you graduated from is listed; then call and request the password. You may search the jobs database, post your resume online, and access a wealth of other career resources, including Career Forums, a Job Search Manual, and the Guide to Graduate Schools. This is a very active site, which claims the addition of 3,000 new job openings daily.

monster.com

Established in 1994, the Monster Board offers more than 30,000 job postings, ranging from entry-level to chief executive officers across all industries. You can create an electronic resume online, to be searched by potential employers, or apply for jobs listed in the database. You have the option of blocking your private information from viewers if you choose. You may also create a simple profile indicating your desired industry, location, and job-specific keywords. A Personal Job Search Agent at this site continually scans the entire job database for opportunities that match the requirements stated in your profile. The results are delivered to your Monster Board account, which is simple to establish and access on a regular basis.

nationjobs.com

This site has a large collection of job openings as well as company information. You may search the database by industry, location, education, salary level, and keywords. Many of the menu items have multiple levels so searching may take more time than at other sites. You can target a certain group of companies by entering criteria and then looking at the current job openings at those companies. This site also offers a personal job-search agent called P.J. Scout, which searches the database for new jobs that match your criteria and automatically e-mails them to you on an ongoing basis.

occ.com

Continually labeled the "granddaddy of career resources" on the Internet, the Online Career Center is perhaps the most mature and best-known career site. There are a vast number of jobs available at this site, including many international opportunities. You can search by title, keyword, company name, or geographic region. You may easily utilize the site's Job Seeker Agent by setting up an account specifying job-search criteria. Each day, you will be notified via e-mail as to how many jobs have been entered into the database that match your criteria. You can then access those jobs directly in your account at the Web site. There also is a resume bank where you can submit your resume to be searched by potential employers.

Eventually, you will discover search engines on the Web. These sites find resources by searching the entire Internet. Every search engine works a little differently; start by reading their instructions on narrowing a search. There are also meta-sites that simultaneously search several search engines for you. Search engines give you Web addresses related to your topic or question. You will need to visit each one separately to check out its usefulness. The first time you enter a request, you may get a response listing several thousand sites.

Refining your search will help you to narrow the list of sites to a manageable number. Here are two search engines to help you get started.

Yahoo.com

Yahoo! is a Web directory containing links to over half a million sites divided into more than 25,000 categories. In essence, it is a virtual library of sites organized into broad, hierarchical categories of information. You can use the site to both browse and search for information. You can browse by simply clicking on the various categories listed on each page. You can search by simply entering a word or phrase into the search box. With both these options, you can browse categories of indexed information and then search within the categories, or you can perform a search and then browse through the search results.

altavista.com

AltaVista is a search engine designed to track down information based on keywords you type in. Simply type a few words into the search box and click search. AltaVista will search through its entire Web index in less than a second. You will receive results ranked so that the best matches appear at the top of the list. A more advanced search service also exists, which allows a more targeted search by use of Boolean expressions or dates.

CONSIDER THE EMPLOYER'S PERSPECTIVE

Put on the employer's hat when planning your job search

Taking a look at how employers fill vacancies in their organizations may offer additional clues about conducting a successful job-search campaign. When openings occur, managers have a problem to solve. This problem is added to their many other responsibilities.

Managers will usually look in-house first, with the hope of filling the position quickly. Is there anyone who is ready to be promoted? Is there someone who would consider a lateral move? These solutions are appealing because the candidates are known quantities who are familiar to the hiring manager. They also know the organization and how to get things done there. Start-up time for someone already inside the organization would be minimal.

If a viable candidate does not emerge from within the organization, managers will likely look at their network of professional and personal contacts. They may also enlist their staff to contact people in their networks. In this way, the circle is expanded somewhat, but the search remains contained. Only a selective pool of potential candidates is being considered at this stage. All are known to the managers or their staff members. They could include friends working for vendors or competitors or contacts known through community or professional affiliations.

If these steps fail to yield a viable candidate, managers may then need to broaden the scope of their search. At this point, they are likely to involve the human resources area for assistance with a more formal search both inside and outside the organization. They may decide to engage an employment agency to recruit and screen candidates. This alternative is expensive but efficient. They may also use electronic media to publicize the opening to specific audiences. If the position is entry-level or requires specific skills or experience, the organization may contact appropriate local schools. These outreach efforts will generate many more applicants. However, depending on the resources used, the vacancy may still become known only to targeted groups of people.

Deciding to run an advertisement in a major newspaper or to use multiple online resources is often a last resort if no other avenues have yielded a winning candidate. As long as the search stays small and contained, the focus remains positive: attracting and assessing promising prospective candidates. Once the search is opened to the public domain, hundreds of candidates may apply, and the process of selection shifts to a process of elimination. If 140 or 1,400 people apply, approximately 130 or 1,390 of them will have to be turned down right away. Typically, no more than 10 candidates will be interviewed and seriously considered for a position. As you can see, the manager's task of filling the position shifts from positive to negative as most of the applicants must be eliminated. Landing a job that has been listed in the newspaper is extremely difficult. Competition is fierce, and the vast majority of applicants are going to be rejected.

Try to land the job before it is advertised

If you agree that this is a fair representation of how an employer goes about filling a vacancy, how can you use this information to refine your job-search strategies? Can you see that it will be to your advantage if you have been interviewing for information, attending professional meetings, and building a network of contacts? These activities expose you to job opportunities long before newspaper ads and online listings appear. In most cases, vacancies are filled before it becomes necessary to advertise.

In this chapter, we have addressed the major ingredients of an effective job-search campaign for the late 1990s and beyond. We have discussed building a professional network, writing winning resumes and cover letters, strategizing your search, and keeping a record of your progress. We have looked at the hiring process from the employer's perspective in order to reinforce the importance of becoming an "insider." In the next chapter, we will take a close look at the interviewing process and suggest ways you can improve your technique and, consequently, your competitive advantage.

Kodaroid

WORK IN PROGRESS

Purpose: This group activity is intended to give you practice thinking like a hiring manager.

Directions: Get into groups of approximately six students. This exercise involves a role play. Here is the scenario you will address:

Imagine that you are the district salespeople for the northeast region of Kodaroid, an international manufacturer of cameras, film, and photographic supplies. You are here on a beautiful, sunny Saturday morning in late June for a monthly sales meeting.

As you arrived, you learned that your colleague Pat, who covers the state of Maine, resigned yesterday, giving two weeks' notice. Pat is not coming to the meeting today.

Your charge, as a group, is to decide how you are going to go about replacing Pat. Your primary sales season, the period that makes or breaks your entire year, begins September 1 and goes through Christmas. Your goal for that time frame is to fill every department store, discount house, camera store, and pharmacy with as many cameras and accessories and as much film as possible. You have to find someone who will land on his or her feet running by the first of September. And, by the way, you haven't taken your summer vacation yet.

Take the next 15 minutes to make a list of the sources you will use to find Pat's replacement. Prioritize your list to reflect the order you will follow. Select a recorder who will report your results.

Instructor: When the groups are ready, have them report to the larger group. Record each group's list. Lead a discussion of how employers go about filling positions in their organizations.

Reflections: What does this exercise tell you about how hiring is conducted? Given the realities you have identified, how do you plan to alter or expand your job search?

10.3 Heading To Maine

Purpose: This activity is intended to give you practice in varying your image for different kinds of jobs. You will also get practice in assessing and communicating your transferable skills.

Directions: Think about selling yourself to Kodaroid for the district sales position in Maine (or substitute your favorite state). Start with your resume. What would you put in the hot zone to appear credible for this sales position? Consider all your previous experience and education. Develop a rough outline of your resume targeted to the Kodaroid position. Do not invent experience. Consider how experience and skills *you have* can be transferred to this position. If you need more information about what people do in sales, consult the *Dictionary of Occupational Titles* or the *Occupational Outlook Handbook.*

Reflections: Can you begin to see yourself in a sales position for Kodaroid? How can you transfer this learning experience to your real job search? Can you see ways to improve your presentation? Shape your image? Sharpen your candidacy?

10.4 Updating Your Resume

Purpose: By completing this activity, you will have a current resume that incorporates recommendations from the chapter. Your final document will be usable in your next job search.

Directions: Select the resume style that seems most appropriate for your career goal, and draft a resume highlighting your previous experience. Refer to the chapter for complete guidelines on what to include in each section. Pay particular attention to the information you include in the hot zone. Are you supporting your objective? Do you appear to be a credible candidate? What will strengthen the resume? When you have a rough draft, edit it yourself and do some fine-tuning. Then show it to two or three people you trust and ask for their comments. Revise your resume again, and print a copy to be reviewed by your instructor.

Reflections: Are you pleased with your resume? How can it be further improved or strengthened? Will you feel confident about sending this document when applying for positions?

RESOURCES FOR THE JOB SEARCH

Kennedy, Joyce Lain, and Thomas J. Morrow. *Electronic Job Search Revolution,* 2nd ed. New York: John Wiley & Sons, Inc., 1995.

The Internet contains numerous job-listing services; some are free and others are accessible for a fee. There are also services for posting your resume so employers may discover you. Kennedy and Morrow's book describes many of these listing services and other ways that the job-search process is changing as a result of new technology. While it is great to have these new resources, they do not substitute for the person-to-person activities that were discussed in this chapter. Effective job hunting still requires that you go out and talk to people. You are not likely to get a job simply by sitting at your computer surfing the Internet.

Company Directories

Company directories are sources of basic information (i.e., name, address, telephone and fax numbers; year founded; whether public or private; stock exchange and symbol if applicable; annual sales volume; number of employees; names of officers; principal business; standard industrial code (SIC); and sometimes principal banks, law firms and auditors, assets, liabilities, net worth, and subsidiaries/parents, if any). The amount of information varies with the individual directory and type of business. All of these directories are available in print form. Some are also available on computer using CD-ROM. Check with your reference librarian about on-line resources.

Some important directories are listed below.

America's Corporate Families and *America's Corporate Families & International Affiliates.* Dun's Marketing Services. Annual. 3 vols.

Links parent companies with subsidiaries; criteria for inclusion: two or more locations; 250 or more employees or $25 million sales volume or tangible net worth greater than $500,000; controlling interest in one or more subsidiaries.

Vols. 1 & 2: 11,000 U.S. parent companies and their 11,000 U.S. subsidiaries.

Vol. 3: 2,400 U.S. parent companies and their 19,000 foreign subsidiaries; 3,000 foreign parent companies and their 11,000 U.S. subsidiaries.

Entries are arranged alphabetically by parent company, followed by subsidiaries arranged hierarchically; cross-referenced by company name, geographic location, and SIC code.

Directory of Corporate Affiliations. National Register Publishing. Annual. 5 vols.

116,000 entries include the most influential U.S. and foreign parent companies, public and private, and all subsidiaries.

Vols. I & II: U.S. public companies and their subsidiaries wherever located.

Vol. III: U.S. private companies and their subsidiaries wherever located.

Vol. IV: non–U.S.-based companies and their subsidiaries wherever located.

Vol. V: master indexes, including company name, geographic region, and Standard Industrial Classification (SIC.)

Subsidiaries are listed in order of reporting hierarchy.

Dun's Directory of Service Companies. Dun's Marketing Services. Annual.

50,000 largest U.S. public and private companies in the service sector, listed alphabetically, geographically, and by industry (SIC).

Million Dollar Directory. Dun's Marketing Services. Annual. 5 vols.

Top 160,000 U.S. public and private companies; criteria for inclusion: headquarters or single location and 180+ employees or $9 million annual sales volume.

Vols. 1–3: alphabetical listing of companies.

Vol. 4: cross-referenced by industry.

Vol. 5: cross-referenced by geography.

Principal International Business. Dun's Marketing Services. Annual.

55,000 businesses in 143 countries worldwide chosen for size, prominence, and international interest; arranged by country; cross-referenced by company name and by product classification.

Standard & Poor's Register of Corporations, Directors & Executives. Annual. 3 vols.

55,000 public and private companies; U.S., Canadian, and major international.

Vol. 1: company entries listed alphabetically.

Vol. 2: directors and executives.

Vol. 3: companies cross-referenced by SIC and indexes.

Thomas Register. Thomas Publishing Company. Annual. 34 vols.

Guide to who makes what.

Vols. 1–23: alphabetical listing by products/services under 52,000 headings.

Vols. 24 & 26: alphabetical listing of brief profiles of 145,000 companies.

Vols. 27–34: file of catalogs for 2,000 companies.

Partial contents at http://www.thomasregister.com

Ward's Business Directory of U.S. Private and Public Companies. Gale. Annual. 7 vols.

135,000 entries include companies of all sizes.

Vols. 1–3: alphabetical by company name.

Vol. 4: geographic cross-reference.

Vol. 5: rankings within SIC.

Vols. 6–7: rankings in each state by SIC.

Who Owns Whom. Dun & Bradstreet. Annual. 6 vols.

Attempts to cover all corporate groups worldwide, public and private, regardless of size; each volume covers a geographic area of the world; arrangement is alphabetical by parent company, followed by hierarchical listing of subsidiaries, wherever located; includes indexes of subsidiaries, foreign parents, company name, and product classification.

The following directories give company histories and/or narrative profiles in addition to the information typically covered by directories:

Hoover's Handbook of American Business. Reference Press. Annual since 1990.

> Profiles of 750 selected major U.S. companies, public and private; includes a section of lists (i.e., *Fortune 500*, largest employers).

> See also Hoover's on-line at http://www.hoovers.com

Hoover's Handbook of Emerging Companies. Reference Press. Annual since 1993.

> Profiles 250 of America's most exciting growth enterprises with annual revenues between $30 million and $1 billion. Also contains lists of companies featured in other publications, such as *Fortune 100* Fastest Growing Companies, *Business Week's* 100 Best Small Companies, *Inc.* 500 List of Most Rapidly Growing Private Companies, and *Working Woman—* America's Top 50 Women Business Owners.

Hoover's Handbook of World Business. Reference Press. Annual.

> Profiles of 250 non–U.S.-based companies chosen for activity in the United States, global importance, domination of an industry, and other criteria; includes section of lists and selected regional and country profiles.

International Directory of Company Histories. St. James Press. 22 vols.

> Detailed background on 3,200 companies worldwide, most with minimum of U.S. $100 million sales; arrangement by industry; detailed index (vol. 22) includes companies mentioned but not given an individual article.

Moody's Manuals. Moody's Investors Service/Dun & Bradstreet. Annual.

Moody's Bank and Finance Manual

Moody's Industrial Manual

Moody's International Manual

Moody's OTC Industrial Manual

Moody's OTC Unlisted Manual

Moody's Public Utility Manual

Moody's Transportation Manual

> Volumes collectively cover 30,000 public corporations and institutions; entries are alphabetical by company and include company histories, financial data, and subsidiaries.

Journal and newspaper articles are also good sources of information on companies. Check your local or school library for major indexes to business/company literature. This information may be stored in hard copy or on computer.

International Company Directories

Asian Company Handbook. Toyo Kezai, Inc. Annual.

> Current financial data on over 1,000 companies listed on stock exchanges of Hong Kong, Malaysia, Republic of Korea, Singapore, Taiwan, and Thailand; arranged by country.

Canadian Key Business Directory. Dun & Bradstreet. Annual.

> Top 3 percent of Canadian businesses (20,000+ companies); criteria: $20 million sales or 100 employees or $1 million net worth or branches of more than 500 employees; alphabetical arrangement; geographic and SIC code indexes.

Directory of American Firms Operating in Foreign Countries, 13th ed. Uniworld Business Publications. 3 vols. 1994.

> 2,600 U.S. companies with 19,000 subsidiaries and affiliates in 127 countries.

> Vol. 1: alphabetical listing of U.S. firms with operations overseas.

> Vols. 2 & 3: listings by country of American firms' foreign operations, both wholly and partially owned subsidiaries.

Directory of Multinationals. Stockton Press. 2 vols.

> Alphabetical listing of the 450 largest industrial corporations with sales over U.S. $1 billion and significant international investments in 1987. Includes company profile and five years of financial data.

Eastern European Business Directory. Gale.

> Lists 8,000 companies in Eastern Europe, arranged by product/service, then by country. (*Note:* Country configuration as of 1991.)

Japan Company Handbook. Toyo Kezai, Inc. Quarterly. 2 sects.

> Current financial data on 2,067 companies listed on Tokyo, Osaka, and Nagoy stock exchanges; divided according to whether listed in first or second section of exchange.

Japan Trade Directory. Japan External Trade Organization.

> 3,000 companies seeking export, import, or international business opportunities (24,000 products and services); alphabetical by company, with indexes for export, import, service, and trade name; also lists trade and industrial associations; includes guide to prefectures and advertising.

Korea Directory. Korea Directory Company. Annual.

> Lists firms and organizations by category; includes indexes to firms, classified index to commodities, and who's who.

Specialized/Individual Industry Directories: Selected List

Bioscan: Worldwide Biotechnology Industry Reporter. Quarterly.

Biotechnology Directory. Annual.

Computer Industry Almanac. Annual.

Corporate Technology Directory. Annual.

Directory of Supermarket, Grocery and Convenience Stores. Annual.

Editor and Publisher International Year Book. 1995.

Editor and Publisher Market Guide. 1995.

Electronic News Financial Fact Book & Directory. Annual.

Fairchild's Retail Stores Financial Directory. Annual.

Medical and Healthcare Market Guide. Annual.

Sports Marketplace. Annual.

Standard Directory of Advertising Agencies. Quarterly.

Ward's Automotive Yearbook. 1995 (latest).

CHAPTER ELEVEN

PRESENTING YOUR CANDIDACY

By following the many recommendations presented in Chapter Ten, you have put all the pieces into place for conducting a successful job-search campaign. In this chapter, we will focus on job interviewing, the primary vehicle through which hiring occurs. These stressful encounters with potential employers in which a position is at stake frequently determine your future. Highly qualified candidates may be turned down for positions because they failed to communicate their skills and abilities. Similarly, underqualified candidates may be hired for, and ultimately fail in, positions because they successfully oversold themselves.

As we look at the art of interviewing, we will emphasize that the interview should help you *and* the employer make the right match. We will review the basics of interviewing for those who are out of practice and cover some of the thorny issues that experienced workers must contend with in the interviewing process.

SUCCESSFUL INTERVIEWING

A job interview is a meeting between an employer and an applicant to discuss an available position. Job interviewing is stressful for most people, even if you have years of work experience and have made several job changes. Fortunately, you can do a lot in advance to relieve your tension and increase your effectiveness as a candidate. Some individuals believe that just being themselves is sufficient for successful job interviewing. However, you are participating in a highly competitive selection process. You need to know how to sell yourself effectively, communicate your skills and experience, and portray your personality as one that will fit in with the culture of the organization. Being properly prepared and informed about the interviewing process can help you positively focus your energies on what needs to be done and help you find the right job.

Goals of the Interview

In an interview, both the interviewer and candidate have goals

A job interview is more than a conversation. Both the interviewer and the candidate have goals—you might even say hidden agendas—for the meeting. Your goals as a candidate for the position are likely to be the following:

1. To obtain information about the job and the organization
2. To determine whether the job is suitable for you and whether you want the position if it is offered to you
3. To communicate important information about yourself and your qualifications for the position
4. To favorably impress the employer

Meanwhile, the person conducting the interview has another set of goals for the meeting. The interviewer's goals are:

1. To promote the organization and attract the best possible candidate
2. To gather information about the candidate
3. To assess how well the candidate's qualifications match the job requirements
4. To determine whether the candidate will fit in with the organization and the staff

Preparation for the Interview

In order for you to meet your goals for each interview, it is critical that you are well prepared. You can prepare in several ways; each will strengthen your candidacy.

Research the Organization

Find out at least some basic information about the organization and its leaders before you go for the interview. You will be in a better position to ask intelligent questions, and you will impress the interviewer with your initiative and your knowledge of the organization. Find out if the organization has a Web site; if they do, peruse it carefully. Mention the site in the interview. They have probably made a recent and considerable investment here so they will be interested in your response to their home page. If you are interviewing with a publicly held company, you can obtain an annual report by contacting its public relations department; your library may also have the report on file. In addition, you can find out at the library or through an online computer search if the organization is listed in a directory or if it has been featured in newspaper or magazine articles. Familiarity with the organization's recent publicity shows strong interest on your part.

Preparation means research, anticipation, and practice

If you have done your homework at the earlier stages of your career development process, you may have already visited the organization and conducted an informational interview. If so, be sure to review your notes. You may even want to contact your network affiliates on the inside to let them know you are interviewing. They may be able to support your candidacy from the inside. (For more information on how to conduct research, please refer back to Chapter Six.)

Research the Job

Employers often give more qualifications in the employment listing than can realistically be met by most potential candidates. Frequently, this is done as a prescreening device to reduce the number of applicants for the position by setting up artificial barriers. You should not allow this to discourage you or prevent you from pursuing the position. If you are selected to interview, the organization is interested in your candidacy, even if you do not possess all of the qualifications.

Just as you are looking for the ideal job, employers are looking for the ideal employee. Analyze the job description, and match your experience, skills, interests, and abilities to the job. You may find that some of the qualifications are less essential than others. Try to anticipate which of the position's requirements are most critical to the hiring manager, and prepare to promote those aspects of your background. Emphasize your strong points to minimize the effect of possible limitations in your experience.

If you are changing careers, be prepared to explain how you developed the skills for this position through your previous experience. Do not expect the interviewer to translate experience in teaching into skills for human resources management. It is your responsibility to make the bridge between your past experiences and your current aspirations, using the language of transferable skills.

Prior to interviewing, talk with people who have worked in similar positions in that organization or in other companies. Read about the specific job category in the career literature. As a result of your research, you will have gained information about the nature of the job, the skills and content knowledge required, and other pertinent details. There should be no surprises in the interview if you prepare thoroughly.

Prepare and Anticipate Questions

Anticipate questions that you may be asked in an interview. Prepare answers beforehand to some of the more difficult or sensitive questions. (See the discussion on "Handling Difficult Questions" on page 203.) This does not mean memorizing responses or writing a script. It does mean planning the main points you want to make. Decide what you want the employer to know about you when the interview concludes. This might include your achievements, your skills that directly relate to the job, your deep interest in your field, and your great enthusiasm for the position. Those points become your agenda for the interview. You will be able to make many of the points in response to typical interview questions, but you have to remember to make the other points before you leave, even if not asked. Become very familiar with your agenda so you can be sure to make all your points during the interview.

Figure 11.1 contains a sampling of interview questions. As you read the questions, pause to think about possible responses. What is the best response you can give to each of the questions? How can you communicate your agenda while responding to the questions?

Also, prepare questions you would like to ask the employer. For example, "How do you evaluate job performance?" and "How are decisions made in this department?" Toward the end of all interviews, the interviewer asks if you

FIGURE 11.1

FIGURE 11.1

Frequently asked interview questions.

Here are some typical open-ended interview questions. Use them to communicate your interview agenda. Also see the section on behavioral interviews.

- What do you know about this company/organization?
- How would you describe yourself?
- Why did you choose a career in _____?
- What have been your greatest achievements? Why were they satisfying to you?
- What are your long-range and short-term goals? What are you doing to move yourself toward these goals?
- In what kind of work environment would you be most comfortable?
- How would you describe your ideal job?
- How do you handle stress and pressure?
- What criteria are you using to evaluate the organization for which you hope to work?
- What major work problems have you encountered, and how have you dealt with them?
- What have you learned from your mistakes?
- What motivates you to put forth your greatest effort?
- Describe your ideal boss.
- What experience have you had working as a member of a team?
- What do you think it takes to be successful in a company like this one?
- What are your strongest skills for this position?
- What are your strengths and weaknesses?
- What does success mean to you?
- If you were going to run this department, what would your management style be?
- What plans do you have for continuing your education?

have any questions. Be sure to have a few good questions prepared. You may have an opportunity to ask several questions throughout the interview discussion, but save a few for the end. If you have researched the organization, you can ask questions related to an article you read. Or you can ask field-specific questions, product-related questions, customer service questions, and so forth. The possibilities are endless; choose your questions wisely. See Figure 11.2 for many sample questions.

Practice Your Communication Skills

It is important that you use good communication skills during the interview. Practice with a friend, a fellow student, or a career counselor. By far the most productive way to practice interviewing is by videotaping a mock interview. Many career centers offer this service. When you watch yourself on tape, you can quickly see and correct any distracting or inappropriate behaviors. Listen to the content of your responses to the interview questions. Did you answer the questions completely? Did you promote your skills and experience? Did you assert your desire to be offered the position? In other words, did you close the sale? Observe your body language. Do you maintain a comfortable level of eye contact? Do your gestures seem natural?

Here are communication skills you can practice prior to your interviews:

1. *Present yourself in a positive and confident manner.* Some people have no difficulty selling themselves; others find this kind of communicating boastful

The following list is just a sample of the kinds of questions you can ask during an interview. If you have researched the organization, you may have many additional questions based on your reading. See if you can add to this list.

- How is an employee evaluated?
- What are your expectations of the person you hire for this position?
- What qualities are you looking for in your ideal candidate?
- How do you view my qualifications? How do I compare with other applicants?
- Are you comfortable that my technical background satisfies your requirement? Where in particular do you feel my experience is lacking?
- What plans do you have for initial orientation and training?
- What do you see as the organization's strengths and weaknesses?
- Why is this position available?
- Does your organization have plans to develop new products/services?
- Where do you see the organization going in the next five years?
- What would your expectations of me be in the first year?
- What is the reporting structure?
- How are decisions made in this department? How are policy decisions and operations decisions made in this organization?
- How are people kept informed?
- Tell me about your career with this organization.
- What do you like about working here?
- What are the characteristics needed for success in this organization?

FIGURE 11.2

Questions to ask the employer during the interview.

and uncomfortable. In our culture, candidates for employment are expected to make a strong case for why they are an excellent choice for the position. Practice until you are comfortable sharing information about your achievements and abilities.

2. *Offer a firm handshake.* Most men have grown up shaking hands and don't think twice about it. Women, however, often feel uncomfortable with this ritual. Practice until you are at ease introducing yourself, extending your hand, and squeezing another person's hand. Handshakes should be firm, but not bone-crushing. Maintain eye contact during this greeting. Incidentally, both men and women employers expect firm handshakes.

3. *Speak clearly and effectively.* In interview situations, you will be expected to express yourself intelligently. You will be asked questions requiring lengthy responses. Pace yourself. Before you begin your responses, think of the main points you want to make. This will keep you from rambling. Think of each question as a new opportunity to show your best self. Maintain your energy level so your voice doesn't trail off. End your responses deliberately after you have made all your points. Consciously practice this kind of communicating. You can do it while working, while running errands, or while using the telephone. Concentrate on forming complete sentences, communicating complete ideas, and then stopping!

4. *Listen attentively and maintain eye contact.* Actively listening to others is a critically important interviewing skill. This too can be practiced throughout your normal day. When listening attentively, you nod your head, hold eye contact, and show expression in your face. Also ask occasional questions or

make comments. This shows the speaker that you are attentive. You must also concentrate on what the interviewer is saying as he or she is revealing important information about the position and the organization. You will be gaining valuable clues about the employer's specific needs that will help you to promote your candidacy later in the interview.

Not everyone who interviews you will be a competent interviewer. Some will talk far too much. In that situation, be prepared to inoffensively guide the discussion to your qualifications for the position. If you don't take the initiative, the interview could end without the interviewer learning about what you have to offer.

5. *Avoid the use of unnecessary verbal and nonverbal distractions.* If you have any distracting habits, such as repeating "Ya know?" or rolling your eyes or shaking your foot, it's time for some refining. These behaviors will work against you in your job interview. Ask a trusted friend to help you by pointing out when you are doing them. When you see yourself on videotape, you will notice these habits. With effort, you can abolish them. Your goal is to communicate effectively, maintain appropriate eye contact, and appear physically and emotionally composed.

Dress Appropriately

Dress professionally for the interview; you don't get a second chance to make a first impression. Your interviewer will form impressions on the basis of your appearance. You should appear neat and clean, pressed and polished. Conservative business attire is appropriate for most settings. For men, that usually means a suit. Women can wear a business suit, a conservative dress, or a coordinated skirt and blazer.

Within industries and in different geographic regions, there are variations in the appropriate attire for interviews. In large urban banks in the Northeast, men usually wear three-piece suits; in high-tech companies, they may wear slacks and a blazer. *Remember:* Even if you know that a company has a casual dress code (jeans and sweatshirt), this attire is never appropriate for an interview. You are expected to present your best professional image. Assembling your interview attire ahead of time will reduce stress on the day of the interview. Prepare a couple of options in anticipation of multiple interviews.

Be Punctual

Be on time for the interview. Plan to arrive about 15 minutes early. Check in with the interviewer or the secretary 5 to 10 minutes prior to your scheduled appointment. Greet everyone you meet with respect; several people will likely have input on your candidacy.

Use your waiting time to check your appearance, review the points you intend to make, and read any company literature that may be on display. Take advantage of this time to get a feel for the work environment by observing the surroundings and interactions among staff. And relax! Take some long, deep breaths and let them out slowly. Visualize yourself getting the offer!

STAGES OF THE INTERVIEW

Regardless of the style of the interviewer, the interview will progress through four basic stages: the introduction, general information, a narrowed focus, and the closing. The next section covers each of the stages in more detail.

Introduction

The interview begins with small talk initiated by the interviewer. The interviewer may ask a few casual questions or make some general remarks. Typical topics include the weather, the parking situation, and any items from the "Interests" section of your resume. If you don't have an interests section, the interviewer may zero in on your school or the town you live in, but the conversation will be informal. The purpose is to put you at ease, establish rapport, and find a comfortable level of communication. You too have an opportunity to make a meaningful connection at this stage. A picture on the wall or a book on the table may inspire you.

General Information

The interview formally starts when the interviewer shifts from small talk to general information about you, the organization, and the position. You may be asked to review your background, experience, and goals. The interviewer will discuss the organization and its goals as well as the department that is hiring. This will test your listening and speaking skills and will give you additional information about the position on which to base intelligent questions.

Narrowed Focus

This stage is marked by the interviewer beginning to concentrate on the available job and how you might fit in. You will have the opportunity to say more about your skills and to demonstrate how they apply to the job requirements. In addition to detailed questions about the level of your performance in previous jobs, you may be asked to demonstrate that you possess abilities and qualities the interviewer is seeking. See the section on behavioral interviews on page 201.

Interviewers also ask situational questions. These are questions that pose problems similar to what you might encounter in the position should you be hired. You may be asked to describe how you would deal with and resolve the hypothetical problems. These are not questions you can prepare for in advance; they test your ability to think on your feet. However, if you have prepared well for the interview, you will probably sail through this part. If you are poorly prepared, you may find yourself under great stress and unable to think clearly or creatively when situational questions are posed.

Closing

At the closing stage, the interviewer begins summarizing what has been said and clarifying certain aspects of the interview. It is crucial that you express your interest in the position at this time. It is also important that you review your key points, especially how you are uniquely qualified for the position. If you have relevant skills or experience that you have not yet shared, do it now. The employer will probably explain how and when the next contact will be made and may end with, "Do you have any other questions?" Try to save at least one of your questions for the end so that you wrap up the interview on a positive note, leaving an enthusiastic impression. In your closing comment, make your pitch: "I look forward to the next round of interviews"; "The position sounds like a perfect match with my skills. I look forward to getting an offer"; or "This job sounds like just what I'm looking for; when can I start?" are all examples of ways to "close."

TYPES OF INTERVIEWS

Based on Purpose

Screening Interview

This type of interview is used to quickly and efficiently eliminate unqualified or overpriced candidates. These interviews are conducted by professional interviewers, recruiters, or human resources representatives seeking information regarding your educational background and experience using a highly structured question-and-answer format.

Selection Interview

This interview is used after some type of screening process. These interviews are usually conducted by a professional practitioner who will be the candidate's supervisor. There may be additional sessions with other members of the work team, including support staff. They are generally less formal and less structured than the screening interview. Questions tend to be open-ended, with subsequent questions based on the candidate's responses to previous questions.

Based on Format

One-on-One Interview

This is the usual interview procedure. Screening and selection interviews usually include one interviewer and one candidate. At times, a second company representative may join in, or the candidate may have a series of interviews that involves several individual meetings with different people at the organization.

Search Committee Interview

This format consists of many interviewers and one candidate. Search committees are used by business and industry for selection of high-level corporate officers. Nonprofit organizations may use their boards of directors to interview candidates for positions. Search committee interviews are also common for positions in the field of education, including public schools and higher education institutions.

Group Interview

The reverse of the search committee interview, the group interview consists of many candidates and one or more interviewers. Group interviews are sometimes used as a screening procedure by smaller companies. Several candidates may be invited at once to hear a presentation about the organization. The technique is sometimes applied to assess leadership skills and ability to work in groups. Afterwards, candidates may have an opportunity to speak briefly to someone individually.

Based on Style

Question-and-Answer or Directed Interview

This style is highly structured; the interviewer comes prepared with a list of questions. This technique is frequently used by recruiters and professional interviewers to seek facts about your background. The same set of questions is asked of each candidate, and responses are later compared and evaluated. This is the general format for screening interviews.

Building rapport and connecting with the interviewer can be difficult in question-and-answer interviews. Feeling that you may be "striking out," you could become discouraged and lose enthusiasm. Keep in mind that the interviewer is bound by the structure. You may, in fact, be making a positive impression without getting feedback. Continue to promote your experience, skills, and interest to the very end. It could pay off with an invitation to a far warmer second interview.

Open-Ended or Nondirective Interview

This style, generally informal and less structured, is used by professional practitioners to assess candidates' skills, experience, and personality attributes. It is the usual format for selection interviews, which are frequently second-round interviews. The questions in this interview are open-ended, requiring paragraph-long responses from you. Your responses may then prompt a series of follow-up questions to clarify or expand on your answers.

Behavioral Interview

Employers selecting applicants are always looking for better ways to predict the future success of candidates. Recently, behavioral interviewing has become a popular technique used by human resources professionals and hiring managers. Behavioral interviewing is based on the premise that past behavior is an accurate indicator of future behavior. An interviewer identifies particular skills needed to succeed in the job to be filled and then asks applicants to demonstrate their abilities in those areas. Applicants are expected to give concrete examples of their past performance.

Examples of behavioral interview questions include:

- Tell me about a time when you demonstrated leadership.
- Tell me about a difficult problem you solved.
- Give me an example of a time when you calmed an irate customer.
- Would you describe yourself as a self-starter?

Sometimes the questions sound a lot like the open-ended questions discussed earlier. However, the employer is looking for specific content in your responses. To respond effectively to behavioral interview questions, it is necessary to tell a story. There is a formula you can use that will ensure that your response is complete:

THE STAR FORMULA

- Identify the *situation* you were in.
- Tell what the *task* was that needed to be done.
- Describe the specific *action* you took.
- Relate the *result* of your action.

Below is an example of a behavioral question and response. The elements of the STAR formula are indicated in parentheses so you can see how they provide the structure for the candidate's response.

Employer: Tell me about a time when you demonstrated leadership.

Candidate: I'd be happy to. *(Situation)* Last year while I was working for the multimedia department of a large ad agency, we were developing the home page for one of the company's biggest clients. The site was to be interactive and animated so it was pretty cutting-edge. I headed the design team and was coordinating efforts with the programmers, who were supposed to actually write the code that would make our design work. The problem was, they couldn't do it. They tried, but they didn't have the specialized technical knowledge for the project, and there wasn't enough time for them to learn. *(Task)* We were coming close to our design review deadline, and we needed to have a prototype to show the customer. *(Action)* I made the suggestion that we go outside the company and hire someone with the specific technical know-how to bring our design up. When I got the approval, I went looking for the person myself and brought her onboard for the project; *(Result)* we delivered the prototype on time for the design review meeting with the customer. There were some all-nighters involved, but we met the deadline. The customer was pleased, and our VP was elated.

This exchange contains all the elements of the STAR formula, it tells an engaging story, and it gives the employer a vivid snapshot of the applicant's capability. Practice using the formula to answer several behavioral interview questions. You won't necessarily be able to predict the questions you'll be asked, but if the formula has become second nature to you, you'll probably tell great stories when the questions are asked.

Stress Interview

This interview is purposefully staged to determine how a candidate will perform under stress. It may be typified by long periods of silence, challenges to a candidate's opinions or qualifications, or a series of interruptions. While these are extremely uncomfortable interviews, it can be calming to remember at that moment that a technique is being used. The interviewer does not disapprove of you but wants to see how you handle pressure or rejection. In management, sales, and customer service positions, these attributes are essential. Maintain your cool, deal with the negative behavior, and continue answering questions calmly.

If you are repeatedly interrupted and asked new questions, you could say that you would be happy to answer the new question when you finish the previous response. Or ask the interviewer which question to answer, thus calling attention to the interruptions: "Let me clarify—which question would you like me to answer?" If the interviewer minimizes your credentials, restate your qualifications for the position. Remember, they selected you for an interview so they *are* interested.

Technical Interview or Demonstration

This style is used to test your specific knowledge or ability for the position. If you are interviewing for a programming position, you may be given a printout and asked to debug the lines of code. A technician may be asked to repair or diagnose an equipment problem. A sales candidate may be handed an object and asked to sell it to the interviewer. If the position you are applying for involves speaking before groups, you may be asked to prepare and deliver a brief presentation. These opportunities to demonstrate your abilities usually come in the second or third round of interviewing. You may be told in advance that final candidates will be asked back to deliver a brief presentation. Consider all of these as opportunities to compete on the basis of your abilities. If given a chance to prepare in advance, don't decide to "wing it." Your competitors will eat your lunch.

HANDLING DIFFICULT QUESTIONS

What questions do you fear being asked in an interview? Some of the more commonly asked, yet dreaded, questions include: "What are your strengths and weaknesses?"; "Where do you see yourself in five years?"; "Why should I hire you?"; and "Why do you want to work here?" Other troublesome interview questions have a negative cast, such as, "Why did you leave your last job?" or "What did you like least about your last boss or your last position?"

When you think about it, these are all legitimate interview questions. You may not have done sufficient soul-searching or strategizing to handle them well, but each presents you with an opportunity to sell yourself. It is helpful to look first at why interviewers ask these questions and then to strategize responses that work to your advantage.

"What are your strengths and weaknesses?" The employer may be assessing how well you know yourself and how honest and open you are. You have an opportunity to showcase your strengths and also to reveal a not-too-serious weakness. It is best if you demonstrate how you are working to improve your stated weakness. For example, you might say, "My computer experience is somewhat limited. However, I recently took a three-week training program on using Word and Excel, and I'm looking forward to building on those skills."

Difficult questions present opportunities as well as challenges

"Where do you see yourself in five years?" The employer wants to know if you are ambitious and also if you are realistic. If you find it hard to look five years ahead, try this: "Five years seems like a long time. I can see myself as a programmer analyst in two years. Five years from now, I might be a software developer or a systems analyst. I won't know which direction I want to take until I've been in the field for a while."

The response that many people are tempted to give is, "In five years, I hope to have your job." While that might have flown in the fast-track 1980s, it is not a wise response in today's climate. The answer could be perceived as threatening to the interviewer or simply aggressive. In addition, it doesn't fit with today's flatter, less hierarchical organizations. A response that talks about how you intend to add value to the organization by solving problems and continuously learning new skills would be more appropriate.

In general, your future plans should mesh with the position and be realistic given the state of the industry and the economy. If you are planning to work for a few years and then semi-retire with a consulting practice that competes head-on with this company, you may want to keep that information under your hat.

"Why should I hire you?" Here's where they find out how well you understand their needs and how confident you are of your qualifications for the position. Here is a sample response: "I think you should hire me because I have the skills you need in this marketing support position. My technical skills exactly match your requirements, since I've been using the same software in my current job. And my interpersonal skills are strong as a result of my retail experience."

"Why do you want to work here?" This is when the employer finds out how much you know about the organization. Convey your interest in contributing

to its mission or in being part of an important project the organization has been awarded. For example: "I've read about your contract to develop land-use studies for the federal government, and I want to be part of the action."

"Why did you leave your last job?" or *"Why do you want to leave your current job?"* Some candidates may interpret these questions as invitations to unload their frustrations about their job. This would be a big mistake. While the interviewer may bait you for negative information, he or she is also interested in how you handle this situation. It is in your best interests to put a positive spin on your decision to change positions. For example: "I learned a great deal in my last position and advanced quickly to supervisor. I realize that I now need to broaden my industry skills. For that experience, I have to go outside my present company."

"What did you like least about your last boss?" is truly a setup! You can't win by dumping on your last boss. The employer will ask because he or she can learn about your interpersonal skills and your attitude toward authority figures. If you could potentially be a problem employee, the employer wants to weed you out now. One way to respond is to first tell your last boss's strengths. Then suggest one thing your boss did that you might do differently. End your response on a positive note, stating that overall you admired and respected your boss.

There are other questions that you hope no one asks but someone inevitably does, important questions that demand a well-prepared response from you. For example, if your resume doesn't show continuous employment, you should expect to be asked for an explanation. What positive results came out of your decision not to work? An upbeat way to explain might be, "That's correct; I did not work in 1996. I was nearing the end of my degree program at Columbia. I realized that if I attended school full-time, I could complete my bachelor's degree in one year rather than working and taking three years to finish. I feel I made the right decision; when I went back to work, I was offered a salary considerably higher than my previous earnings."

Perhaps you were laid off and dread being asked why you left your last job. Frame your explanation in a way that dispels any shame or guilt you may be harboring. "I was 1 of 180 people laid off last September when XYZ Corporation went through a major downsizing."

What if you were fired for some reason? This can be very worrisome to the job seeker. "To be honest with you, I just didn't fit in with the organization. Finally, my supervisor and I decided it was best for me to leave. While this was a devastating experience, I feel I'm ready to begin again." Or, "I made some serious mistakes in my last position. I found myself overwhelmed with conflicting demands, and I did my best to do what I thought was expected of me. Unfortunately, I failed to talk with my boss about her priorities, and I misjudged some situations. I've done a lot of thinking since then and learned a great deal from my mistakes. In my next job, I plan to communicate regularly with my supervisor, to ask questions, and seek feedback."

Notice in these explanations that the candidate is taking responsibility for past errors and communicating a positive outlook about the future. There is no blaming. These examples show honest, straightforward responses that would be acceptable to an employer. The important thing is for you to come to terms with the issue, accept responsibility for your mistakes, see the positive side, and demonstrate that you are eager to move on in your career.

HANDLING ILLEGAL QUESTIONS

Job seekers find it particularly unnerving when employers ask them illegal questions during an interview. Questions that are illegal refer to personal information, such as your marital status, family situation, age, ethnic or racial identity, sexual preference, or religious affiliation. Although these questions have been made illegal through federal legislation, they still find their way into interviews. When confronted with an illegal question, the candidate cannot be certain as to whether the interviewer is asking out of ignorance of the law or in defiance of the law.

It is necessary to be extremely tactful in these situations. Challenging the interviewer is your legal right, but it may cost you the position for which you are interviewing. Suppose you are asked in an interview if you are married or if you have children. One option is to answer the question, even though you know it should not have been asked. An alternative response that works well is, "I would be happy to discuss my marital status (or family situation) if you can tell me how it applies to the position." Use a friendly tone of voice to avoid possible conflict.

The interviewer may then say, "I need to know if you will be free to travel, including over weekends." Now that you know why the interviewer was asking, you can respond specifically to the concern. "I am available to travel and wouldn't mind if trips occasionally included weekend time. How much travel would you expect me to do in a given month?" Now the discussion is back on the requirements of the position, where it belongs.

The following questions are illegal for employers to ask you during a hiring interview:

- Are you married? Single? Divorced? Engaged? Involved with or living with someone? Straight? Gay?

- Do you have children? Plan to have children? How old are they? What arrangements have you made for their care?

- How much do you weigh? How tall are you? Do you have any physical illnesses or disabilities? Are you on medication?

- Have you ever been hospitalized for emotional problems? Are you or have you been in psychotherapy? Are you on medication for psychological problems?

- How old are you? When did you attend high school?

- What is your nationality? When did you become a U. S. citizen? What is your native language? What church do you attend? What religious holidays do you observe?

- Have you ever been arrested?

Companies may ask you where you live and how long you have lived in this area. They may ask if you are over 18 years of age and if you can provide verification, if hired, that your age meets legal requirements. An employer may also tell you that, if hired, you may be required to show proof that you are authorized to work in the United States.

Employers may inquire about what schools you've attended, what your work experience has been, and what languages you speak, read, and write fluently. They may also ask you if you can perform all the duties outlined in the job description. Employers may offer you a position on the condition that you pass a physical examination. This exam may involve drug screening.

If you think you may be experiencing discrimination in your job search or if you are being asked illegal questions, you may want to contact the Equal Employment Opportunity Commission at 1-800-669-3362 or the Disabled Persons Protection Commission at 1-800-245-0062.

GETTING THE OFFER

Your primary goal in job interviews is to get the offer. Once offered a position, you can evaluate it against other opportunities and decide whether or not to accept it. Ideally, you want several offers so you can choose the best one. This may or may not be realistic, given the market when you are looking for a job. Understanding economic and market realities will help you assess opportunities presented to you.

When you have been searching for a long time with little success, you may feel pressured to take an offer that you intuitively know is beneath your abilities or is a bad personality fit. Pay attention to these intuitive signals. Request another interview to discuss your concerns. If your doubts are confirmed, graciously turn down the offer.

After weeks and months of researching, networking, and interviewing, your hard work will pay off with job offers. When a position is offered to you, express your appreciation for having been selected. Do not feel compelled to accept the offer on the spot. Tell the interviewer that you would like time to consider the offer; you may also want to say, if it's true, that you have other offers pending and that you need to make a careful decision. If you are fortunate enough to find yourself in the situation of having multiple offers, your bargaining power will be greatly enhanced during the final salary negotiations.

Salary is only one of many factors to weigh in comparing offers. Consider all of the self-assessment issues you pondered earlier in this process, especially your current work values, in making the decision about which offer to accept. Which position appears to best meet your present needs? Which offers the most long-term stability and potential for growth? Where will you learn the most? Which organization is most responsive to family issues? Choose carefully. And *congratulations!*

NEGOTIATING THE SALARY

Salary negotiations often make candidates uncomfortable, and rightfully so, as this is one of the trickiest parts of interviewing. A few suggestions on how to manage this topic may eliminate some of the discomfort.

First of all, if the topic comes up too early in the interviewing process, it is advisable to postpone the discussion. For example, you could say, "I would be happy to discuss my salary requirements, but I feel I need to know more about the position first. Could you tell me about . . ." The idea here is to buy time. The more you know about the job, the better you will be able to pinpoint what it is worth in today's market.

Some companies conduct telephone prescreening interviews in which they ask about your previous earnings or present salary expectations. This can put you at a distinct disadvantage because you know little about the scope of the position in question. Your market research will help you to respond appropriately. State a range that is fairly wide and suggest that you can be more specific when you know more about the position. The employer is trying to screen out candidates who have been earning $50,000 for a position that will pay in the $30,000s.

Second, if you are in the final round of interviewing and you are asked about your salary expectations, it is appropriate to clarify why they are asking: "Are you making me an offer?" Try to get the interviewer to commit to you as the preferred candidate. Your negotiating position will be greatly enhanced if you establish that you are the first choice. If they have not yet decided on you for the job, then salary negotiation is premature. Try to get the interviewer to state any concerns he or she may have about your ability to perform the responsibilities in the position.

Finally, there comes a time in the interviewing process when salary negotiation can't be delayed any longer. Ideally, you know a lot about the position and how it compares in the market, and you've established that you are the front-running candidate. You are still likely to do better in the negotiation if you aren't the first one to name a dollar figure. Let's suppose the interviewer says to you, "We'd like to have you come work for us. What will it take to get you here?" You can ask what he or she has in mind or what has been budgeted. If you are told, for example, that the position is rated at $30,000 to $34,000, you can then say why you think you deserve to receive the higher end of the scale, based on your knowledge and previous experience.

When you can't get the interviewer to state a range, you may be forced to state yours first. Your response might be, "Based on my understanding of the position and my knowledge of the market, I would expect an offer in the high-thirties." Or, "Given the level of performance required in this position, I would expect you to offer me between $45,000 and $50,000."

The employer may come back with another range, perhaps saying, "We're figuring on offering $43,000 to $46,000." Your next move involves convincing the employer that, with your skills and experience, you deserve to be paid the $46,000. Alternatively, the employer may offer a specific figure, such as, "I'm prepared to offer you $42,500." In this situation, silence is your most powerful negotiating tool. Take a minute or two to absorb the offer, to think about how it fits with your expectations and your needs. Maintain a poker face regardless of whether the offer is considerably more or a lot less than you expected. Employers have been known to spontaneously increase the offer to break the silence. If nothing happens, ask, "Is that the best you can do?"

The remainder of the negotiation involves coming to an agreement that all parties can comfortably live with. Fringe benefits will be discussed, and they are a significant part of the total compensation package. Items typically include life insurance, health and dental insurance, educational benefits, vacations and leaves, and retirement programs. Some positions provide stock options, a company car, memberships in organizations, profit sharing, and customer discounts. When specific talent is scarce, sign-on bonuses become an attractive incentive. See the discussion of benefits on page 105.

Still other positions involve commissions, especially on sales generated. Be sure that you are comfortable with the commission structure; it could be part salary and part commission or salary to start but eventually 100 percent commission. Are you willing to be paid based on the volume of business you generate? What if you are paid on the basis of the performance of your sales team?

It may also be appropriate to negotiate your first review. If an organization asks you to start working for them at a salary below your expectation, they may agree to review your performance and, if you are doing well, raise your salary in three or six months instead of waiting a year.

These suggestions are designed to help you feel comfortable in negotiating a salary that reflects both the market and your worth as a professional.

FOLLOW UP, FOLLOW UP, FOLLOW UP

After every job interview, write a thank-you letter restating your interest in the position. You can also add new information. You may have learned in the interview that they hope to hire someone with experience in an area you have but did not include on your resume. They may want an insurance adjuster who speaks Spanish or a software developer who knows the restaurant business. Thank-you letters provide an ideal format for including additional information about your qualifications.

Another use for thank-you letters is to clear up any confusion or to provide a more complete response to a question that caught you off-guard during the interview. "When discussing my skills for the position, I neglected to mention my . . ." or " When describing my experiences with teams, I got sidetracked with my basketball stories and never got to explain my experience working with a sales team . . ."

Thank-you letters add a nice personal touch, and they keep you at the front of the employer's mind. Should you be interviewed by several people in one long day at the company, one thank-you letter to the person overseeing the search is sufficient. Mention that you enjoyed meeting the others. Figures 11.3, 11.4, and 11.5 contain sample thank-you letters.

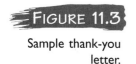

FIGURE 11.3

Sample thank-you letter.

1658 Sunny Slope Drive
Flushing, New York 11375
April 14, 1998

Jason L. Pelletier, Police Commissioner
Dade County Police Department
500 Main Street
Miami, Florida 33133

Dear Commissioner Pelletier:

It was a pleasure meeting with you yesterday to discuss the personnel needs of your department. The challenges you described to me confirmed my commitment to becoming an outstanding police officer. I, too, am a firm believer that maintaining a visible presence on city streets and interacting with members of the community deter crime. Your grant-funded project targeting youth at risk is of particular interest to me.

My experiences as a security officer and youth worker as well as my studies in criminal justice have prepared me well for this position. I look forward to working with you to reduce crime and make Dade County a safer place to live. Please give me a call when you are scheduling second-round interviews. I can be reached at 212-488-9321.

Sincerely,

Pamela Watson

Commonwealth Drive
Boston, MA 02230
September 12, 1999

FIGURE 11.4

Sample thank-you letter.

Ms. Linda Patterson
Business Manager
New England Cable News
Western Avenue
Newton, MA 02459

Dear Ms. Patterson:

I would like to take this opportunity to thank you for the interview on September 10. I left with an extremely favorable impression of your operation. At New England Cable News I would:

- Be part of a high-tech growing and changing environment.
- Be in a position to support industry growth and quality of service.
- Bring my full-range accounting and finance skills to the telecommunications industry.
- Work independently and simultaneously as a member of your team.

During our interview, you asked about what I've been doing since the reorganization at Phoenix that resulted in my being laid off. I mentioned my income-producing activities but failed to mention that my job search is my top priority. I am eager to return to permanent employment status with a growing company.

I am looking forward to a second in-depth interview, with the opportunity to meet other members of your staff.

Very truly,

Bruce Woodward

Telephone or e-mail follow-up can also be a wise strategic move, especially when you are a finalist for a position and the time frame for making a decision is short. Again, restate your strong desire to be offered the job. Ask if they have any concerns about your candidacy and if you can help them to make a decision in your favor. Your message should confirm your strong interest in the position.

ADDITIONAL JOB-SEARCH CORRESPONDENCE

A few additional situations may require business letters. They include letters withdrawing your candidacy, accepting a job offer, and turning down an offer of employment. These situations are sometimes handled in person or over the telephone, but in some situations it may be required or be more comfortable to resort to the written word.

After an interview, you may decide the job is not for you. You may want to withdraw your candidacy without waiting for the hiring manager to further

Sample thank-you letter.

78 Belleview Boulevard
Newport, RI 02840
401-848-1234
June 16, 1999

James D. Hanna
Executive Director
Providence Museum and Historical Society
Main Street
Providence, RI 02800

Dear Mr. Hanna:

Thank you for the opportunity to discuss the position of IT Manager on June 15. Your description of the needs and requirements of the position, both technical and political, has given me a clear picture of the challenges and the opportunities. My meetings with current technical staff and with board members have further informed me and excited my interest in the position.

First, let me review my technical skills and assure you that they match the position requirements:

Hardware: IBM PC, Mac, IBM 3081D, VAX 11-780
Software: MS Office 97, Excel, PowerPoint, Lotus 1-2-3, dBASE
Systems/Networks: Windows NT, Windows 95, Novell, Unix, Mac OS
Internet: HTML, CGI, Javascript, Adobe Photoshop

My experience overseeing the software conversion and database development at Rhode Island College prepared me for the analogous tasks of your project. Acquiring updated equipment and establishing a fully networked organization are realistic one-year goals, given your proposed budget and projected staff additions. Establishing a Web site and offering interactive educational programs online would fall into years two and three.

Second, you described a political situation that could potentially torpedo the project. Success will depend on gaining buy-in from competing factions. My ability to win people over and foster collaboration is legendary with my previous employers. I encourage you to speak with them personally.

The ultimate success of the upgrade, conversion, and expansion of your information technology depends on your finding an IT Manager whom you can fully trust and support. If you are confident in my abilities and comfortable with our developing working relationship, then let's meet again to work out the details. I would be delighted to bring your vision to fruition.

Most sincerely,

Arthur Norwood

---

evaluate your candidacy. It may be that you felt uncomfortable with people you met or that the job was not as originally described to you. Perhaps you learned in the interview that extensive overtime was required (more than your personal situation allows) or that the company is being threatened with a hostile take-over, leaving its future uncertain. Regardless of your reason for deciding to withdraw, you want to leave a positive impression with the organization. Figure 11.6 contains sample letters withdrawing from consideration for a position.

FIGURE 11.6

Sample letters
withdrawing job
candidacy.

Dear Ben,

Thank you for your call informing me that your search has been put on hold because of an unexpected change in staff. I can certainly understand how this would alter your timetable.

Unfortunately, I am unable to suspend my job search. I have had a number of interviews recently and anticipate an offer shortly. Given the circumstances, I think it best that I withdraw from further consideration by Hewlitt Packard.

It was a pleasure meeting you. I wish you success in rebuilding your team.

Best regards,

Deborah Sorento

....

Dear Ms. Foster:

It was a pleasure meeting with you last week. I have given careful consideration to the position of Installation Manager and have decided to withdraw my candidacy.

While I have the requisite technical skills and strong experience in customer relations and cost containment, I have decided that I prefer a banking or financial services environment to a medical setting. Our conversation helped me to clarify my best next move; I thank you for helping me to further focus my goals.

I wish you success in your search. Again, my thanks for your time and consideration.

Sincerely,

Niho Kozuru

Another letter that you may be required to send is a written confirmation of your acceptance of a job offer. This letter, incidentally, is a legal document and should not be sent casually to an organization. Some people think they can accept a job offer to "hold" their spot while they continue to look for a better opportunity. This kind of behavior is unethical and unwise.

A letter of acceptance states your acceptance of the position, restates the terms of the offer, and refers to the agreed-upon starting date. If you have questions about the terms, you may want to clarify them by telephone before writing the letter. Some organizations simply send you an offer letter and ask you to sign and return a copy of the letter as indication of your agreement. Figure 11.7 contains a sample acceptance letter.

A letter turning down an offer should always be positive and leave the door open for future connection. Be as honest as you can about your decision not to accept the offer, but be very tactful at the same time. If you raised concerns during the interview process, you might refer to those concerns again

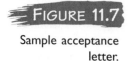

FIGURE 11.7

Sample acceptance letter.

Diane Amory
New York Life
New York, NY 10002

Dear Diane,

I am thrilled to accept your offer of employment as Manager of Customer Service, East Coast. I understand that the terms of the position are: salary of $63,400, reviewed annually; full medical and dental insurance coverage; and life insurance equal to twice the total compensation package (valued at $81,000). In addition, New York Life has agreed to fully reimburse my moving expenses as I relocate from North Carolina to New Jersey or Connecticut (to be determined in the next few weeks!).

I will be reporting to work on Monday, April 3, at 9:00 A.M. I've arranged to stay at the Sheridan in Rye while I hunt for a house. My search is well underway, thanks to the help of the relocation group; they've been informative and resourceful so far.

Should you need to reach me in the interim, you can call me at 1-888-593-7452 or e-mail thogan@aol.com I look forward to coming onboard and working with you.

Very truly,

Tom Hogan

---

when rejecting the offer. Perhaps your in-depth knowledge of their systems leads you to believe their timetable for change is unrealistic, or their budget for new equipment is inadequate, or maybe their compensation package is way below market value. There are many legitimate reasons to refuse a job offer. Figure 11.8 contains a sample letter turning down an offer.

DEALING WITH REJECTION

Being turned down for a position that you want can be agonizing. When you are rejected after sending in your resume, you may feel frustrated not to have been given a chance at the position; however, your emotional investment in the position was probably minimal. When you have interviewed one or more times for a position and discover that the job is exciting and the people are terrific, a rejection can be devastating. Acknowledge your disappointment. Your feelings are legitimate. Share them with other job hunters who truly understand your pain.

Dealing with the disappointment will help you to maintain a positive attitude about your search. Keeping your momentum is critical at this time. If you are getting interviews, and particularly if you are invited back for the second round, you are getting mighty close. Something will break for you soon. Continue to put yourself out there, applying for positions and networking.

When you are turned down for positions after interviewing, ask the employer for feedback. Try to determine if there is anything about your presentation that can be improved. In other words, transform the disappointing rejection into a learning opportunity. Calling the employer to ask for feedback

Robert Rizzo
Vice President of Information Services
University of Connecticut
Storrs, CT 06268

FIGURE 11.8

Sample letter turning down job offer.

Dear Vice President Rizzo:

Thank you for the offer to work under your direction as Manager of Academic Computing at the University of Connecticut. Wednesday was a most productive day, meeting with deans and directors of the institution and visiting the computer facilities. I was impressed with both the level of technology at UConn and your vision for the future of information services.

Unfortunately, I have decided not to accept your offer at this time. As you know, I have received several offers and have been in the position of having to choose. It has not been easy. Ultimately, I have decided to remain in Massachusetts where my family is happily ensconced.

Thank you for your full endorsement of my candidacy. It was a pleasure getting to know you and your operation. I hope we can stay in touch as we have many common interests and challenges. My best to you and your team.

Most sincerely,

Margaret Newhouse

---

is a courageous move that will leave a positive impression. You might also ask the employer if he or she knows of other opportunities and if you may stay in touch just in case the person selected doesn't work out. By pursuing the connection, you are inviting the person who has turned you down to become part of your professional network. This can become a fruitful relationship in the long run. It is not unusual to be turned down by an organization only to be hired within months for the original or a different position, providing the door has been left ajar.

BREATHING NEW LIFE INTO A WEARY SEARCH

Sometimes job searches drag on forever with only disappointing results. If you are committed to making a change, you may need to become more flexible. Reexamine your preliminary decisions about the scope of your search. At this point, does it make sense to expand your geographic preferences? Will you take less money or a different position in order to get in the door? Are there jobs you could do for a while that are related to your dream job? Could you do temporary or contract work in your field to get experience? Could you do volunteer work at least for a little while to expand your experience base?

If the strategies you've been relying on don't seem to be working, try a new approach. If you've run out of people to call, revisit the contacts you made a couple of months ago. You might even call people with whom you interviewed earlier in your search. Perhaps they have a lead. Reassess your marketing package; your resume or cover letter may need a new look. Try a different professional society to find new contacts. Persistence, resourcefulness, and patience are key ingredients throughout your search. When they run thin, crank up your sense of humor.

Eventually, you will succeed in landing a job. You will receive one or more offers and decide to accept one of them. When you do, be sure to share your good news with your network. This is just one more way to stay connected to people in your field.

Chapters Ten and Eleven have offered suggestions for conducting an effective job-search campaign. We have discussed job-search correspondence and professional networking, the art of interviewing, and the fine art of negotiating offers. When you have accepted a job offer, you will turn your attention to getting off to a good start in your next position. Chapter Twelve addresses the topic of fitting in and making a positive contribution in a new job.

WORK IN PROGRESS

Interview Practice

Purpose: This activity is intended to get you talking out loud about your candidacy for positions.

Directions: From the newspaper's Help Wanted advertisements, clip two job descriptions that match your qualifications. Bring your resume and the clippings to class to complete this activity.

In class, find a partner and take turns interviewing each other for the positions you selected. Make each interview 15 minutes long. Before you begin, spend five minutes preparing questions for your partner. When you have finished each interview, spend five minutes giving your partner constructive feedback. Use the following questions for your discussion:

- Did your partner convince you of his or her qualifications and suitability for the position? How? If not, how can your partner improve?
- Did your partner convey enthusiasm? What made you think your partner wanted the job? How can your partner show more interest?
- Did your partner display a grasp of the position requirements?
- Did your partner maintain eye contact and demonstrate good communication skills? How could your partner improve?

Reflections: In the full group, discuss how it felt to practice interviewing. How can this stressful ordeal be made more comfortable? Does practicing aloud help you organize your thoughts? What else do you need to do to feel more confident about your interviewing skills?

Practicing Solo

Purpose: This exercise will help you to practice your interviewing skills on your own. It was invented by the client whose case study appears on page 16.

Directions: You will need a tape recorder, the list of interview questions found in Figure 11.1, and behavioral interview questions suggested on p. 201. Turn on the tape recorder, ask yourself one of the interview questions, and then (after a pause) answer the question to the best of your ability. Go through five or six questions in this manner, and then play them back. Listen to each response to determine whether you have given the best possible answer.

Think about different ways of answering the same question. Which response communicates the most useful information about your skills and experience? This exercise can be done many times with different selections of questions.

Reflections: Can you see how interviewing provides you with an opportunity to shape how someone perceives you? In an interview, it is your responsibility to communicate your strengths to the interviewer. It is not the interviewer's responsibility to drag out information from you. With practice, is it becoming more comfortable to promote yourself and your experience?

Your Interview Agenda

Purpose: This exercise will help you focus on the specific information and impressions you wish to leave with interviewers.

Directions: First, state your current career goal.

....
....
....

Next, identify a job-interview situation for which you need to prepare.

....
....

Now, identify and list the information you want your interviewer to know about you by the end of your interview. Make your selections based on the position you identified above. Include both skills and experiences that relate to the position.

....
....
....
....
....

Next, list the impressions you want to leave with the interviewer about your attitude, character, and personality.

....
....
....
....
....

Finally, check the interview questions below that give you the best opportunity to communicate your agenda:

.... Tell me about yourself.
.... What can you offer this company/department/team?
.... Why should I hire you?
.... What can you do for us?
.... What are the strengths you bring to this position?

Reflections: How can you make job interviewing work for you? How can you help the interviewer make a decision in your favor?

ADDITIONAL TOOLS FOR YOUR CAREER

Krannich, R. L. *Interview for Success: A Practical Guide to Increasing Job Interviews, Offers, and Salaries,* 7th ed. Manassas Park, VA: Impact Publications, 1998.

Medley, H. A. *Sweaty Palms: The Neglected Art of Being Interviewed,* reprint rev. ed. Berkeley, CA: Ten Speed Press, 1992.

Yate, M. J. *Knock 'em Dead with Great Answers to Tough Interview Questions.* Holbrook, MA: Bob Adams, Inc., 1991.

Yate, M. J. *Knock 'em Dead.* Holbrook, MA: Adams Media Trade, 1998.

CHAPTER TWELVE

MAKING A CONTRIBUTION

All your efforts to examine yourself and the marketplace, to make decisions and set goals, and to look for a position will finally pay off when you start your new job. You will no doubt approach the day with feelings of excitement and joy, mixed liberally with fear and doubt. You will be making a major change! Have you made the right choice? Are you well suited to this new direction? Are you up to the challenges? *Have confidence in your transition process.* You have worked diligently to make the best possible choice for yourself. This chapter will provide sound advice on making a good start in your new organization. We will also examine the subject of career stages, which will provide structure for looking at both your new situation and your future career development.

Some of you will not be ready to make a transition when you read this chapter for the first time. You may be continuing your education first. The information contained here can also be applied to part-time work situations, internships, and noncareer jobs that pay the bills. Plan to reread the material when you are preparing to take a new position launching the next phase of your career.

SEIZE THE OPPORTUNITY

A new position offers you a chance to make a clean start in a new organization, with new people and new challenges. Develop a positive attitude about yourself, your job, your boss and colleagues, and the organization. Plan to give your very best effort. Open your mind to new ideas and new ways of doing things. Leave negative attitudes and beliefs behind; they can only pull you down. Affirmations and visualization techniques discussed in Chapter Nine may be helpful as you prepare to undertake your new responsibilities. A midcareer changer used this affirmation when he moved from marketing to sales: "I, Jason, am experiencing satisfaction and success in my new position. I am developing positive working relationships with customers and colleagues and exercising sound judgment in prioritizing and carrying out my responsibilities."

Practice Exceptional Professional Work Habits

Convey your competence and positive attitude

The workplace of today is a demanding arena. Whether the organization you have chosen is team-centered or more bureaucratic, a great deal will be expected of you right from the start. At least in the beginning, you may have to put a disproportionate amount of time and effort into your work.

A number of behaviors will convey your competence and positive attitude. On a daily basis, arrive early for work and stay late. Keep track of and deliver on all the agreements you make. Meet any imposed deadlines. Turn out accurate work products, and prove your technical competence. Prepare in advance for meetings, training sessions, and interviews with new associates and customers. Should you make a mistake, admit it. Honesty is the only way to build trust. Demonstrate your overall commitment and enthusiasm by delivering on the assurances you made during your interviews for the position.

Learn All About the Organization

You researched the organization and formed impressions during the interview and hiring process. It's time now to expand your knowledge. As an insider, you have access to additional literature, including the employee handbook, product promotional materials, in-house newsletters and memos, and business or program proposals that either flew or crashed. Absorb whatever information you can. Learn more about the leaders of the organization and their career journeys.

Study the organizational chart, analyze the culture, and learn about the informal power centers. Notice how customers are treated and how employees are grouped, both formally and informally. Pay close attention to clues that will increase your understanding of the internal politics. Meanwhile, stay completely neutral; do not get drawn into any turf battles. Accept the realities of the organization; every organization has strengths and weaknesses, warts and beauty marks.

Resist the temptation to change the organization before you have been around long enough to understand the mores. There are usually good reasons that things are done the way they're done and that the other players are in the positions they're in. Don't embarrass yourself by spouting ideas and suggestions until you know the history.

Get to Know Your Boss

Develop a solid working relationship with your boss from day one. Schedule time at his or her convenience for your orientation and a discussion of your first assignments. Especially at the beginning, involve your boss in decisions you make about prioritizing assignments. One mistake many people make in their zeal to make a good impression is functioning too independently. That pattern backfires when it comes to light that your efforts are going toward low-priority projects. Rather than devoting 50 hours a week for 3 months designing the wrong accounting solutions, check in with your boss about how you thought you'd spend your time. Listen carefully to the feedback.

Ask your boss about goals and objectives, preferred work style and communication preferences, and about any pressures he or she may be under and how you might help. Understand your own work style and how you may need to adapt to your boss's expectations. Always keep your boss informed, and be selective about using his or her time and resources (Gabarro & Kotter, 1980). The quality of projects assigned to you will be based on your boss's confidence in your competence. To get the more exciting, cutting-edge projects, excel in your first assignments.

In all encounters in the organization, support your boss. Even if he or she is rarely available or hypercritical of your work, speak with colleagues about the good qualities and positive experiences. As you begin to produce for the organization, give credit to your boss for the opportunity and the teaching you received. Remember, your future in the company is currently in the hands of this individual; right now, this is your most important professional relationship.

Always support your boss

Focus on Your Customers

Whether you work in a product or service industry, your customers are your bread and butter. Their satisfaction is priority number one. Find out how your position serves the customers; knowing this will help you to prioritize your responsibilities. Your boss will be able to help you identify your customers both inside and outside the organization. For example, if you are in the marketing department, your customers will include the product managers and sales managers in-house as well as the people who purchase the company's products.

Add Value to the Organization

Your survival in a position is tied directly to your ability to constantly add value to the organization. This is done by making money for the company or your clients or by saving them money. You can—and should—calculate this mathematically. In *Multipreneuring*, Tom Gorman (1996) presents the following formula:

Know how you add value

Value added = Your $ Contribution – $ You Are Paid

In reality, this can be complicated to compute because your work is often tied to others'. However, as a way of thinking about yourself in relation to your employer, it is a powerful perspective—one that your employer is viewing regularly. The better you are able to see and articulate your contribution to the bottom line, the stronger your staying power. The awareness will also be useful when you decide it's time to request a raise.

Build a Support System

In today's flattened, team-oriented organizations, it is often necessary to develop a network of contacts throughout the organization. One way to start is by making appointments with people you will be working with, either formally (asking for informational meetings where you can learn about their piece of the puzzle) or informally (making plans for lunch or coffee and casual, work-related conversation).

Ask questions about their department or team and their individual areas of expertise. Explore ways that you can support one another's efforts. Also, find out on whom they rely in the organization to get things done; get to know those people as well.

Be Discreet

As you meet colleagues across the organization, you may also get into discussions of personal matters. Move slowly in this area; don't be too quick to self-disclose. Be on the lookout for kindred spirits: another single mom or midlife career changer, a fellow African American or Asian American, another active member of Alcoholics Anonymous, or another gay professional. Over time, you will learn whom you can trust. In the interim, ask a lot of questions and listen up!

As you learn personal information about colleagues, avoid the temptation to demonstrate that you are an insider by disclosing your knowledge to others. *Do not gossip!* Consider your conversations confidential, especially when they relate to people's personal lives or relationships with coworkers. Conversations about the organization and your job do not have to be treated as confidential, but always use discretion in sharing information gathered from others.

Outside the company, never disclose proprietary information, that is, information about the organization's new products, secret recipes, customer or mailing lists, in-house systems and software, or other information that contributes to the organization's competitive advantage in the marketplace.

Work Collaboratively

In all professional situations, work cooperatively with other people. Share information and resources, and offer to help when others have deadline crunches. A collaborative spirit is highly valued in the better (and healthier) work settings.

There may also be an element of competition in the organization that keeps people on their toes. Keep the mission of the organization and the charge of your department in focus. Double-check with your boss before making major shifts in priorities. You need to balance the demands of cooperation and competition.

Anytime others pitch in and help you, or when people reporting to you deliver on projects and work products, be certain that you show your appreciation. You know how much you value positive feedback; it works both ways! Also, be aware of and regularly acknowledge the contributions of support staff. Their efforts are all too often made invisible, yet they can make or break your effectiveness and success. Work with support staff, include them in the information and decision-making loops, and help remove obstacles to their effectiveness.

Resolve Conflicts

When you sense tension or conflict at work, attempt to uncover and resolve differences before they become major impediments to your success in the organization. Try to communicate openly with others and display a win–win attitude. This often means taking risks with people, such as acknowledging uncomfortable feelings. Avoid accusing other people of any negative behaviors. Instead, use "I" statements such as, "I'm feeling some tension" or "I'm sensing that you don't agree with my decision concerning . . ." These statements give the other person a chance to open up and give you an opportunity to learn more about alternate viewpoints. Together, you can try to find common ground.

When introducing new ideas or changes in policies or procedures, go individually to colleagues to share your plans and seek their input. Develop support for your plans before announcing changes. In this way, you improve your ideas and build consensus for them.

While we have emphasized collaborative and cooperative work environments, some settings are overly competitive, back-stabbing, cutthroat, dysfunctional hotbeds. These are difficult environments in which to survive and thrive. You can try to create change, but it is almost impossible for one person to transform the culture of an organization. You will have to ask yourself how badly you want or need the job. No position is more important than your health and happiness.

Look for a Mentor

Most successful people attribute a part of their success to having had a mentor who guided their career. A mentor is usually a well-respected person further along the career path who provides informal training, shows you the informal systems, assigns you challenging work, and fosters your visibility in the organization. Watch for someone who may be able to offer you these inside advantages (Dalton & Thompson, 1993). You can also learn a great deal by observing and emulating the professional behaviors of people you highly respect both in your organization and in your outside network.

Maintain Your Network

Continue to stay in touch with the many professional colleagues you contacted during your career transition and job search. Share information and resources, and return the support you received. Stay connected to your professional organization and, when you've settled into your job, consider serving on a committee for that organization. This will help you become established in your profession and provide affiliation that is likely to stay constant through several job changes.

Build Skills and Knowledge

In every field of endeavor, change is a constant element. Embracing change will lead you to an awareness of emerging opportunities. Do your best to stay on top of changes in your field. Subscribe to and read journals and trade publications, affiliate with professional organizations, and nurture your network of professional contacts. Take advantage of training opportunities in-house and, where there are gaps, continue your education part-time during off-work hours. All of us must constantly be retooling for the future. Your boss or mentor may be able to suggest courses that would enhance your opportunities within the organization or field. However, make choices that are interesting and meaningful to you as well. Gain your employer's support for your continuing education efforts. In addition to financial support, you may be able to negotiate release time for studying.

As a career changer, you may have expertise that you are not currently using. Make sure to let others know about these strengths as they could be pivotal to your getting a promotion or being assigned to a special project. Your present career in biotechnology could get a boost because of your past experience in human resources.

Watch for Opportunities

Often, new employees work very hard to exceed their boss's expectations. In their hearts, they may be hoping for a promotion, yet they may never share that goal with those who have the power to make it happen. It is as though they are hoping to be discovered. Put the boss's hat on for a moment. If someone is doing a terrific job for you, would you want to rock the boat? Probably not. As an employee, you have to take responsibility for your career. Let your boss know that you aspire to a higher-level position or to broader responsibilities.

Keep in mind that in today's workplace, career ladders are disappearing. As you increase your knowledge and experience, you increase your contribution to the organization and expand your sphere of influence. This may be recognized through pay increases or opportunities to work on new projects. However, it may not always be reflected in a title change or promotion. Career growth is harder to define today. Rather than climb ladders, you may expand your contribution and your influence, becoming more and more valuable to the organization (Dalton & Thompson, 1993).

Always keep your eyes and ears open for new developments and opportunities. Never get too comfortable. Change will continually occur, and you will want to be part of it. You may even help to create it. If you do all of the other things we have recommended, you are likely to be well poised to take advantage of new opportunities as they materialize.

Maintain a Healthy Balance

There are times, especially during transitions, when it makes sense to devote most of your energy to your evolving career. However, when taking a holistic view of your life, a healthy balance is critically important. Maintain your physical and emotional health, nurture your family relationships and friendships, and don't forget to laugh and play!

If you have relocated for your new job, develop new friendships outside of work. Socializing exclusively with your new colleagues may leave you feeling smothered by the job.

UNDERSTAND THE STAGE OF YOUR PRESENT CAREER

As companies and organizations transform themselves, they appear flatter and leaner. Cross-functional teams have replaced hierarchical structures. In the process, traditional career ladders have disappeared, and job descriptions have become obsolete (Bridges, 1994). The workplace has become a confusing environment. To understand where you are in your career during this time of transition for you and transformation for organizations, it may be helpful to review the career stages outlined in Figure 12.1. Authors Gene W. Dalton and Paul H. Thompson have studied numerous work settings and career paths and have concluded that most employees fall into one of the following four stages in Figure 12.1.

CHARACTERISTICS OF CAREER STAGES

FIGURE 12.1

Four career stages.

Stage I (Apprentice)

- Works under supervision and direction of more senior professional in the field
- Is never entirely working on his or her own, but assignments are given that are a portion of larger project or activity being overseen by a senior professional
- Lacks experience and status in organization
- Is expected to willingly accept supervision and direction
- Is expected to do most of the detailed and routine work on a project
- Is expected to exercise "directed" creativity and initiative
- Learns to perform well under pressure and accomplish task within time budgeted

Stage II (Independent Contributor)

- Goes into depth in one problem or technical area
- Assumes responsibility for definable portion of project, process, or clients
- Works independently and produces significant results
- Develops credibility and reputation
- Relies less on supervisor or mentor for answers, develops more of own resources to solve problems
- Increases in confidence and ability

Stage III (Reciprocator)

- Is involved enough in own work to make significant technical contributions, but begins working in more than one area
- Demonstrates greater depth of technical skills and application of those skills
- Stimulates others through ideas and information
- Is involved in developing people in one or more of the following ways:
  a. Acts as idea leader for small group
  b. Serves as mentor to younger professionals
  c. Assumes formal supervisory position
- Deals with the outside to benefit others in organization (i.e., working out relationships with client organizations, developing new business)

Stage IV (Director)

- Provides direction for organization by:
  a. "Mapping" organization's environment to highlight opportunities and dangers
  b. Focusing activities in areas of "distinctive competence"
  c. Managing process by which decisions are made
- Exercises formal and informal power to:
  a. Initiate action and influence decisions
  b. Obtain resources and approvals
- Represents organization:
  a. To individuals and groups at different levels inside organization
  b. To individuals and institutions outside organization
- Sponsors promising individuals, to test and prepare them for key roles in organization

Source: Dalton, G. W., and P. H. Thompson. *Novations: Strategies for Career Management.* Provo, UT: Gene W. Dalton & Paul H. Thompson, 1993.

To further understand the career stages, we will look at the professional development of an ambitious and hardworking adult student named Patrick.

Patrick at Three Stages

Patrick has been a client of Career Services intermittently for the past eight years. The positions he has held during that time illustrate the first three stages of Dalton and Thompson's model.

Patrick the Apprentice: When Patrick first came to a job-search seminar, he was working for a mutual fund company as a customer service representative. He answered telephone inquiries from customers all day long, logging about 200 calls each day. When customers called to question telephone trades they had previously made, Patrick would have to go through batches of hand-written trade tickets that were organized by date and by company. When he found the trade in question, he would then play back the original taped telephone conversation to see if the verbal instructions matched the trade ticket. If the fund had made an error, Patrick corrected it. This was tedious work.

As Patrick became proficient at solving customer problems, he was given larger assignments, such as reconstructing customer accounts that had been lost because of computer glitches. However, all of his work was closely supervised on a daily basis. Patrick consulted his boss on all decisions that had to be made.

Patrick the Independent Contributor: Patrick lost his job in the mutual funds industry during a downsizing. He had completed his associate's degree in accounting by then (attending school part-time at night) and eventually landed a position with a large, reputable hospital, where he managed six receivable accounts. His duties included billing, collecting, troubleshooting, and chasing aged accounts. He computed trial balances, produced statistical summaries and written reports, and represented the department at meetings. For the most part, Patrick worked independently, reporting to his supervisor on a weekly basis.

Patrick stayed in this position until one year after he had completed his bachelor's degree. During his last year, he applied for three in-house accounting positions that would have meant an upgrade. In every instance, he came in second to a more senior employee. Discouraged, he started to network outside of the hospital.

Patrick the Reciprocator: A personal friend of Patrick's recommended him for an accounting position with the property management firm where he worked. The company owns and/or manages numerous commercial properties and apartment complexes all over the country. Patrick applied for the position and, after four rounds of interviews, was brought onboard. He now manages 16 apartment complexes, performing all of the accounting functions for their many accounts. He prepares and monitors annual budgets, reconciles bank statements, posts receivables, maintains ledgers, reviews bills and financial statements, calculates depreciation and amortization schedules, and processes security deposits.

In addition, Patrick supervises 16 site managers who oversee the day-to-day operations of the facilities. It is critical that he foster positive, cooperative relationships with the site managers since they are responsible for keeping their buildings fully rented and hiring contractors to maintain, renovate, and repair the facilities.

Patrick had a strong accounting background but no real estate industry experience when he began working for the property management firm, so he had to learn a great deal of information rapidly. Once he understood the industry, he helped the company upgrade its computer systems to greatly increase efficiency. With this contribution, Patrick demonstrated a full understanding of the company's complex business operations and added value to the bottom line.

As he grows in this position, Patrick may take on additional properties, more staff, and more challenging problems. These additional responsibilities would lead to salary increases. Although he sees plenty of opportunity for growth in his present career, Patrick does not see himself moving to stage IV of the model for many years.

While Patrick's careers in financial services, hospital accounting, and property management have brought him advancement through three stages of career development, career paths that others pursue may involve less climbing. For instance, you may choose to spend your entire career at the stage of individual contributor. There is nothing wrong with this choice. Many research scientists, engineers, and teachers function happily at stage II throughout their work lives. In addition, many people who, in the 1980s, held stage III positions as middle managers are now working in companies (either permanently or as contractors) as stage II independent contributors. They are using their industry expertise or technical knowledge rather than their managerial skills. How they are faring financially depends on the importance of their contribution. At what career stage is your present position? Do you want to work at a different stage later in your career? Why or why not?

In this chapter, we have discussed the skills needed to succeed in new positions. We have also presented a model for understanding the different stages of career development. The model delineates different levels of responsibility and shows how positions relate to the organization as a whole. In the next chapter, we will consider an alternative to finding and fitting into a position within an organization: starting your own business. This alternative appeals to millions of individuals who want to be their own bosses.

Celebrate Your Positive Change

Purpose: This activity is intended to remind you to reward yourself for your achievements.

Directions: You have succeeded in landing a new job. Bravo! You have earned the right to a special reward, one you give to yourself. What kind of activity would appropriately acknowledge your achievement? Perhaps you would like a special dinner at your favorite restaurant with your spouse or a friend. Maybe you want to get away for a weekend to a country inn or health spa. You may want to buy yourself a commemorative gift. Try to identify an activity or gift item that symbolizes for you the change you are making. Whatever feels meaningful, appropriate, and affordable, *do it*. In the space below, write down some ideas of possible rewards for your career change; next to each idea, indicate the meaning symbolized by the reward.

REWARD   MEANING

(sample) Buy a briefcase   Professional position

....

....

....

Reflections: Many people these days have such fast-paced lifestyles that they find little time to acknowledge milestones. They often skip their graduations, ignore birthdays and anniversaries, and just keep on running. This is a formula for burnout. So, make a great big deal out of your career transition . . . and all the other achievements you tick off along your journey!

12.2 Mapping Your New Start

Purpose: This activity is designed to get you thinking about your short-term goals for your new job.

Directions: Interview two people about their recollections of starting a new job. What helped them to get oriented? How did they find their way around, make friends, and learn the ropes? Then, using their insights, make a detailed list of *your* goals for starting your new job. As soon as you begin to work with your new manager, you will be setting additional priorities with him or her. These goals are for you, to help you get acclimated. Use a timer. Write for one minute on each section. When you are finished, review and edit as needed.

On the first day, I will:

....

....

....

Within the first week, I will:

....

....

....

Within the first month, I will:

....

....

....

Within three months, I will:

....

....

....

Reflections: Do you feel ready for your new undertaking? What do you need to do in order to feel more confident and prepared? How can you make that happen?

Using Career Stages

Purpose: This activity is intended to give you a chance to apply and test career stage theory.

Directions Reread the Characteristics of Career Stages in Figure 12.1 on page 223. Then review your experiences conducting informational interviews (see Work in Progress 6.2 at the end of Chapter Six). Select one of your subjects to evaluate, based on career stages. Decide at what career stage your interview subject was performing. Write a brief paragraph explaining your assessment.

....

....

....

....

Decide what stage fits your current or most recent position. Write a paragraph identifying your career stage and describing the aspects of your duties that made you choose that stage.

....

....

....

....

Reflections: Do the career stages described by Dalton and Thompson make sense to you? Do they help you to understand where you are in your career? How can you use this information to plan your future career development? What stage fits your current work? What stage fits the kind of work you would like to do in the future? Explain your choices.

....

....

....

....

Career Reflections Journal

Purpose: The intent of this activity is to establish a new work habit that can help you stay on top of your new career.

Directions: This assignment can be done either on a computer or in a journal notebook. Store your journal where others won't read it.

On a daily basis, record/enter your reflections on your work experiences, achievements, contacts, ideas, and frustrations as you become a contributor in your new career position. Keep track of observations, information, mixed messages, plans, priorities, conflicts, and so forth. This journal is not intended to replace your calendar where you record all deadlines, appointments, meetings, and so on. Use the journal for recording and sorting out your thoughts and feelings about the many changes you are experiencing. Plan to keep the journal for at least the first three months; if it proves useful, continue it indefinitely.

CHAPTER THIRTEEN

STARTING YOUR OWN BUSINESS

Starting your own business is often referred to as the American dream. We see that borne out in the hopes and ambitions of many adult students and alumni/ae exploring career alternatives. While there are huge risks in starting a business, the payoffs also can be great. You have an opportunity to create something that is uniquely yours, and to have your fortunes and failures rest solely on your efforts. You decide who will work for you or if you prefer to work alone. You determine the product or service you will provide, and you decide where to locate your business. You literally create your work life.

In this chapter, we will look at entrepreneurship as a vital career alternative and then view four different types of small businesses: working as an independent contractor, establishing a private practice, buying a franchise, and pursuing a portfolio career. There are many other kinds of small businesses that are beyond the scope of this book. Resources for further reading are listed at the end of the chapter; there is much to learn and consider before you take the leap of starting your own business.

Small businesses have been around for thousands of years. They were part of almost every ancient civilization. When we talk about small business today, we need to define the term; the wide range can include the single individual in private practice and the small company that employs hundreds of people. For example, the U. S. Department of Commerce classifies a business as small if it employs fewer than 500 people; yet close to 90 percent of the small businesses in this country employ 10 or fewer people. Collectively, however, small businesses employ half the workforce, so they represent a major contribution to the economy (Siropolis, 1996).

Do You Have What It Takes?

A certain mystique surrounds entrepreneurs. Unless you come from a family of small-business owners, the independent spirit and business savvy needed to survive may elude you. If you are drawn to the entrepreneurship option but are unsure of your ability, talk to businesspeople to learn about the realities of business ownership. Many small businesses start at kitchen tables and in home basements and garages, and many never go beyond those humble beginnings. Other businesses grow into thriving enterprises.

Entrepreneurs are "men and women who create a venture from the raw materials of their own ideas and hard work" (Siropolis, 1996, p. 39). Successful entrepreneurs seem to have an uncanny ability to spot opportunity; they know, for instance, how to buy low and sell high. When Art opened his sporting goods consignment store, he received a call from someone who had closed a ski touring center and offered him her entire collection of rental skis, boots, and poles in graduated sizes for kids and adults, all for $500! Art jumped on the opportunity and quickly quadrupled his investment. He also delighted his customers, who knew that their $50 ski packages were bargains. Art did two things well here: He recognized and capitalized on an opportunity, and he passed the good deal along to his customers. By pricing the packages below market value, he moved the products quickly and earned instant customer loyalty.

Ask yourself the following questions as you consider whether owning your own business is an appropriate and realistic option for you.

Do You Have a Great Idea?

Perfecting a creative idea can be the start of a new enterprise

A successful business starts with a good idea, a unique idea that sets the business apart from the competition. Your town may have several pizza shops, but the first one to offer free delivery no doubt grabbed a large share of the market. The business idea often starts with identifying something that is needed, something missing in our lives. In the 1970s, the Umbrola stroller, built in a garage, turned its creators into millionaires. Before their product came out, baby strollers were large and heavy; you couldn't easily fold them to carry on a bus or pop into a car. Umbrolas, which were lightweight and collapsed like umbrellas, literally transformed the way parents traveled with small children.

More recent headlines have been stolen by software developers and other high-tech geniuses who have started small companies, designed something badly needed in the industry, and been bought up by Microsoft or another industry lion for a huge sum of money.

Robert Hisrich and Michael Peters, in *Entrepreneurship*, suggest many sources for ideas for small businesses. The best ideas often come from consumers: Ask people what they want, what they need, and what's wrong with what they have. Other ideas come from existing companies: What products and services are out there in the market, and how good are they? What improvement can be offered? Distribution channels are another source of ideas for products and services. They include distributors, retailers, and wholesalers. They talk to customers and see the competing products that presently exist; they often know what is missing. The government can also be a source of ideas in two ways: examination of patent office files and research on new governmental regulations that may create markets. Research and development, whether informal or formal, is the last and potentially strongest source of new ideas for a new business. Whether you tinker in your basement or brainstorm with a group of inventive engineers, working with and perfecting a creative new idea is the seed of a successful new enterprise (Hisrich & Peters, 1997).

Are You Willing to Give Your All?

Successful entrepreneurs tend to be ambitious and hardworking; they *become their business, working day and night and all weekend. Even when they aren't working, the wheels are turning in their active minds.* Janice, a real estate investor from Colorado, was up every morning at 5:00. She claimed she did her best thinking in the shower; by 6:00 A.M., she was on the phone wheeling and dealing with clients on the East Coast, where it was 8:00 a.m. She negotiated deals and massaged numbers until midnight, ending her day with potential customers on the West Coast. The next day, she got up and did it all again!

Starting a business requires a tremendous commitment of time and energy. It is not for those who want to leave work behind at 5:00 P.M. Entrepreneurs often have a vision of a business that they want to create. The majority of the work, both physical and mental, will be done by the individual who conceives the idea.

Starting a business can be all-consuming

Do You Believe in Yourself?

When you decide to start your own business, you are essentially hiring your own boss. Are you the person you want to hire? Entrepreneurs are typically people with high self-confidence. They know and believe in their strengths and may have a tendency to minimize their weaknesses. Do you see yourself as the person to carry off the idea that you have? Honest assessment is critical here. What aspects of the business play to your strengths? What areas may require the genius of others?

Are You a Risk Taker?

In Chapter Eight, you did an assessment of your comfort level with risk taking. Starting your own business involves many risks. Some people mortgage their homes and borrow to the maximum on credit cards in an effort to get a business going. And they could lose every penny of that money if they are unsuccessful. How do you feel about taking financial risks? There are other risks involved as well, the huge unknowns that remain regardless of how much preparatory research you do: Will the phone ring? Will they buy? Will the concept fly? Can you live with the risk of uncertainty? Can you walk out to the end of the limb without knowing if it will hold you? Are you willing to put other people's money at risk by taking on investors?

The small-business owners described later in this chapter all began their businesses gradually and with minimal financial investments. They built their businesses incrementally. Their methods kept risk to a minimum.

Should You Start a Family Business?

Paul Karofsky at Northeastern University's Center for Family Business points out that when a business is a family affair, it is crucial that two things occur. First, the involved family members must define clear and separate roles for themselves as they design the business operations. Assign functions such as purchasing materials, managing finances, hiring and training staff, and super-

Family businesses have their own pitfalls

vising operations according to skills and interests. Over time, you may reallocate roles as circumstances change.

Second, establish boundaries between your business and your family life.
Set a few ground rules that allow you to maintain family relationships separate from your business. You could agree, for instance, to ban business talk at
the dinner table or after 8:00 P.M. These measures allow you to work more efficiently in your business endeavor and to maintain a healthy balance between
work and family life.

CHOOSING A FORM OF BUSINESS

There are three primary options when considering legal business formation.
The options are sole proprietorship, partnership, and corporation. We will
look at some of the pros and cons of each.

Sole Proprietorship

A sole proprietorship is the simplest, most common, and least costly form of
business to establish. Owners are the persons who start and operate the business. They make all the business decisions for their enterprise and report
earnings or losses on their personal income taxes. The only start-up cost for
initiating the business may be a fee for filing a business or trade name. A proprietor is liable for all aspects of the business. If the business incurs debts or
is sued for some reason, the owner is personally responsible. That means that
the owner's home or other assets could be taken in settlement.

On the other hand, sole proprietors have the right to sell their business
or transfer part of the assets. Owners needing to raise capital must borrow;
money borrowed from a bank will most likely need to be secured by col-
lateral. Failure to meet loan payments could result in liquidation of the
business.

Partnership

Partnerships have been likened to marriages in that they can be wonderful
and exciting, but they can also be tricky, especially when there is disagreement over business decisions. Partnerships are legally more complicated than
sole proprietorships so they cost more to establish. An attorney usually assists
in writing the partnership agreement, which spells out the rights, responsibilities, and duties of those involved. An important issue needing clarification
is the right of partners to transfer or sell their interest. Raising of capital will
also be complicated, often requiring a new partnership agreement. As with
proprietorships, the owners are personally liable for debts incurred by the
partnership.

Business decisions are made by the partners, so it is essential that they
have a positive working relationship. A typical basis for a partnership is one
person having a great idea or terrific contacts, and the other having the money to invest in a business. When there is disagreement between partners,
majority usually rules, unless the partnership agreement says otherwise. The
sharing of profits and losses in a partnership is proportional to the partners'
investments, but each partner is wholly responsible for the actions of the other partners. There are a number of variations on partnerships; research this
option thoroughly and then contact an attorney.

Corporation

A corporation is a legal business entity composed of owners, directors, officers, and employees operating within a defined structure. Ownership is conveyed through shares of stock. While an S corporation is limited to 35 shareholders, there is no limit to the number of shareholders in other corporations. The employees of the corporation can be stockholders and have a vested interest in the company's success.

The primary advantage of a corporation is the limited liability of owners. Since the corporation is an entity that is taxed and absorbs liability, the owners are liable only for the amount they have invested.

To form a corporation, the owners are usually required to register the name and articles of incorporation and to meet specific statutory requirements that vary from state to state. There are usually filing fees, organization taxes, and fees for doing business in each state. An attorney can assist in this process.

Transfer of ownership is easiest with corporations; there is no need for consent from other shareholders. There are also far more options for raising capital; stocks or bonds may be sold and loans may be negotiated in the name of the corporation, thus protecting owners from personal liability. Major stockholders influence long-range planning of a corporation, but day-to-day operations are in the hands of management, who may or may not be stockholders. A young, entrepreneurial corporation may have major stockholders involved in all phases of the business, but as it grows, the separation will become necessary.

Corporations distribute profits to their shareholders through dividend payments. They also use profits for capital investments and new business development.

As you have seen, there are advantages and disadvantages to each of the business forms discussed above. Be sure to research the options thoroughly and consult with an attorney, and perhaps an accountant, before finalizing your choice. Once you have determined the form you want your business to take, you are ready to turn your attention to developing your business plan. There are many aspects of your new business that need to be considered.

WRITING A BUSINESS PLAN

Although most small businesses are started without a written business plan, all the how-to books strongly suggest that you undertake the disciplined thinking and planning necessary to write a plan. If you intend to approach investors for financing, you will most likely be required to present a written proposal. The parts of a business plan include all of the following.

Executive Summary

Although this will probably be the last section you write, it is the first one read. It contains an overview of your plan, highlighting the main points of the other sections. It may be written in the form of a cover letter.

Nature of the Business

In this section, discuss your vision for the business, including a description of the product or service and a plan for the operation of the business. Explain your business's niche in the marketplace and how it will meet the needs of prospective customers.

Analysis of the Competition

Readers will be interested in the depth of your understanding and appreciation of the competition. Focus on what sets your product or service apart and makes your offering unique; avoid bad-mouthing other companies' products or strategies.

Organizational Plan

Decide whether to form a sole proprietorship, a partnership, or a corporation, and explain your choice. Develop an organizational chart that clarifies roles and responsibilities of the people involved. Elaborate management structures and fancy titles are not necessary and may work against you. Identifying the president, vice president, secretary, and treasurer is usually adequate.

Financial Projections

Project your sales revenues over a three-year period. In the first year, develop monthly projections, in the second year quarterly, and in the third year annual. While this numbers-crunching exercise is hypothetical, it forces you to analyze virtually every aspect of your business and the economy. Develop a cash-flow budget, showing how much money you will need to open your business and how much cash you anticipate will flow in and out. Identify initial capital expenses, such as fit-up costs, equipment purchases, furniture, signs, and computer installation. Project major monthly expenses, such as rent, utilities, insurance, and payroll. Indicate when you expect to start making a profit. Develop an accounting system that makes sense of all this information and that presents it in a way that is easy for you and your investors to understand.

DEVELOPING A MARKETING PLAN

An effective marketing plan is essential to business success

No matter how good your business plan is, the business could founder if it is not properly marketed. Failure to market effectively is a primary cause of small-business failure. In a time when everyone feels bombarded by television commercials, intrusive telemarketers, and junk mail, how can you launch and continuously promote your small business? The answer will be different for every business, depending on the target audience. If you plan to open a retail store in a heavily trafficked mall, you may not have to advertise at all. On the other hand, if you are selling specialized items that would appeal to a small segment of the population, you may want to explore purchasing a mailing list and designing a direct-mail marketing piece. The Internet is another option for bringing your product or service to market.

Start by identifying your customers. Who are they? Where are they? Why do they want or need your product or service? What are they using now? How do they get it? What would attract them to your product or service? If your product or service is something they may already have, why is yours better? How do your prices compare with the competition's? What is the best way to reach them? What marketing techniques are used by the competition? What works well? What does not work? What are your objectives for the first year? Beyond? You may want to experiment with one marketing technique and evaluate the results before formalizing your marketing plan. There are a number of resources available to help you with market research; some are listed at the end of the chapter.

ESTABLISHING A PRIVATE PRACTICE

Going into private practice lends itself well to many practitioners. Doctors, dentists, accountants, financial advisors, career and personal counselors, consultants in many technical and nontechnical areas, spiritual healers, and social workers are all examples of people who may establish a private practice. They can work out of their homes or rent or purchase office space. They can organize as a sole proprietor or in partnership, or they can incorporate. A private practice is usually a one-person operation, or possibly a small group.

Valerie Goes into Private Practice

Valerie is a physical therapist with a thriving private practice. She earned her bachelor's degree from McGill University and, after graduation, worked for a private rehabilitation hospital for four years, earning $14 an hour treating patients. Two things motivated Valerie to establish a private practice. First of all, she wanted to be in a position to make decisions about treatment programs for her patients. Secondly, she wanted to earn more money.

In the hospital setting, Valerie's work was managed by hospital administrators and regulated by insurance companies. She mentioned one patient in particular, a young mother who had suffered a stroke and was partially paralyzed. The insurance provider mandated that this patient receive only six weeks of treatment. Valerie was convinced that this woman could recover fully, but she needed many months of physical therapy. Valerie wanted the latitude to make treatment decisions with her patients.

Concerning the money issue, Valerie was aware that her services were billed by the hospital to the insurance company at $150 per hour; $136 of that money went to administration and overhead, and $14 went to Valerie. She wanted to earn what her services were worth.

Making a leap into private practice was intimidating, so Valerie chose to make the transition gradually. She began by cutting her hospital schedule back to four days per week. On day five of each week, she first researched starting her own business. She took a course in entrepreneurship at a local college and met with a representative of SCORE (Service Corps of Retired Executives, part of the Small Business Administration). She learned about tax laws and billing practices. She quickly found another practitioner with a young practice and rented space from her, first by the hour and eventually for a full day each week. The advantage of sharing office space was that the treatment table and other basic furnishings were there. Valerie's initial cash outlay went to business cards, advertising, and rent.

As her practice grew, Valerie cut back to three days a week at the hospital and rented an office. At this point, she borrowed $3,000 from a bank and purchased her own treatment table. She also raided her parents' attic for a desk and two chairs. She rented an ultrasound machine and a computer. Little by little, Valerie developed relationships with area doctors, who then referred patients to her for treatment. In less than a year, she paid back her bank loan. As her practice grew, she made the transition to a full-time private practice and purchased a used ultrasound machine. Since then, she has added one piece of capital equipment each year, including a computer and a photocopier.

Valerie is extremely happy in private practice and looking at the next steps in the growth of her business. She attributes her success to making her transition incrementally. By expanding her practice only when the demand was actually there and by making purchases only when she had the money for them, she never incurred large debts. She still does all her own billing, record keeping, and tax returns. She contracts with an accountant to audit her books annually.

As she looks to the future, Valerie is considering a number of options to increase profitability. Since her patients usually want morning or late afternoon appointments, she is thinking about renting her office to another practitioner during early afternoon hours. She may also increase her marketing efforts in order to expand her practice and then hire another physical therapist to work for her. The rehab hospital where Valerie used to work has asked her to return on a consultancy basis to develop treatment plans for patients; this work pays much more than her old job. Or, she may look for other practitioners, such as occupational therapists and nutritionists, to form a group practice offering holistic patient services. Valerie's canvas is still only partially filled.

BUYING A FRANCHISE

When you purchase a franchise, you are buying a business that has a proven track record in other geographic locations. You are also buying the right to establish the business within a specified area without competition from another member of the same franchise. A franchise usually provides you with a detailed business plan, a recognized name, a proven track record, and computerized systems for billing, ordering, and recording business activity. If the franchise is a retail store like The Gap, the business will likely come with instructions for fitting up the store and ordering merchandise. A restaurant franchise, such as McDonald's, comes with menus, recipes, food products, and a restaurant design. A franchised service operation, like Jiffy Lube, comes with business systems, mechanical systems, specified products and tools, uniforms, and training programs for all personnel.

Prices of franchises vary widely, depending on what is provided and its track record. A franchise could cost $10,000, $100,000, or more. If running your own business appeals to you but creating a business from scratch seems like too much work or too much uncertainty, buying a franchise might be for you. Keep in mind that, for most people, buying a franchise means going heavily into debt. Further research is in order.

Craig and Gretchen Buy a Franchise

Craig and Gretchen are married with two children. Four years ago, Craig was working as a college counselor, and Gretchen was a registered nurse. Both were tired of their jobs and eager to make a transition. Owning a business was intriguing to them, but the risks seemed enormous. One Sunday, they spontaneously decided to attend a business opportunities fair in a city two hours from their New Hampshire home. Hundreds of franchisers were represented at the fair.

A business called The Mug Factory caught their attention. It consisted of selling mugs imprinted with customers' personal photographs. Craig and Gretchen liked the mugs and thought they would make great gifts. They left the fair with tons of literature and new enthusiasm about their future.

At home, they studied the material from many companies but followed up with The Mug Factory. They decided they could run the business part-time and contacted their local mall about renting a cart during the upcoming Christmas season. Meanwhile, Gretchen traveled to North Carolina for training in operating the equipment that decorated the mugs. When she returned, they purchased the franchise. Next, they ordered the equipment and the plain white mugs; bought signs, gift boxes, and wrapping paper; and started practicing. They got photos from family and friends and transferred the images onto mugs for use in displays.

The mugs were a huge hit, so much so that Craig and Gretchen weren't sure they would survive their first Christmas season. Since they both still had full-time jobs, they had to hire and train four people to tend the cart and decorate the mugs. They dealt with a near catastrophe when they ran out of mugs and didn't receive another shipment for three full days right before Christmas. They took orders and when the mugs finally came in, they worked night and day transferring the photos.

For the next two years, Craig and Gretchen rented the mall cart intermittently before major holidays: Valentine's Day, Easter, Mother's Day, Father's Day, and the like. They paid off their business debts and saw profits within the second year. Meanwhile, they began to think about a larger retail business and looked into owning a candy store. After months of careful research and deliberation, including negotiating with the same local mall, they sold their mug franchise and opened a candy store. At that point, Craig left his job at the college to run the store full-time while Gretchen continued to practice nursing part-time.

WORKING AS AN INDEPENDENT CONTRACTOR

Working as an independent contractor—also known as a consultant, contingent worker, temporary worker, or freelancer—appeals to many people who have grown tired of being tied to an organization. They like the freedom and the flexibility of working for a limited time on a special project, completing the task, and moving on. Other professionals have landed in the temporary pool against their will, unable to secure a permanent, full-time job with an organization. For these workers, having to continuously market themselves for new assignments is unappealing.

Many new companies have sprung up to market and broker contingent workers. Meanwhile, older, established companies are growing rapidly. Manpower is the largest single employer in the United States today! Some temporary agencies are offering fringe benefits, such as medical insurance, to their employees. This area of the economy is growing rapidly.

Greg Becomes an Independent Contractor

Greg was a computer programmer who had worked for three companies in eight years. In each position, the pattern was the same: In the first year, the work was creative, exciting, and intense; in the second year, conversion projects were completed and functions became routine; in the third year, the company became shaky, and downsizing led to a layoff. In his third position, Greg decided to prepare well in advance for the layoffs. He decided to set up his own company as a sole proprietorship and market himself as an independent contractor.

Greg contacted an accountant, who helped him complete the necessary forms and calculate his quarterly income-tax estimates. He then obtained a directory of agencies that place independent contractors and identified those that specialized in high-tech and computer placements. He designed a mailing to these agencies and arranged to interview the most promising ones.

When the layoffs came for the third time, Greg was ready. He contacted the agency he preferred and was placed in his first temporary assignment at $60 an hour. While that may sound like a lot of money, remember that he must pay his own taxes and insurance, plan for vacation and retirement, and anticipate downtime when there may be no assignments available. Greg is optimistic that he will do at least as well financially as a contractor as he did as a full-time, in-house programmer. He is most excited about working exclusively in a creative mode; when the design phase of a project is completed, he will move on to another exciting challenge—no more maintenance work and no more waiting for the ax to fall.

CREATING A PORTFOLIO CAREER

A portfolio career is characterized by multiple income-producing activities, all generating income streams. Some people call this model *multipreneuring.* The activities involved may be related, but they don't have to be. For example, an artist may earn money by selling paintings, teaching art classes at a college, consulting to private high schools on art curriculum, contracting with a publisher to produce illustrations for children's books, and counseling artists who experience creativity blocks. The amount of time this artist spends on these activities will vary, depending on the season and the market.

This model can be adapted to suit anyone in any field or mix of fields. It requires planning to ensure that enough money is coming in to meet financial obligations and goals. In recent years, there have been increased opportunities for part-time employment. A part-time job, or two for that matter, can be combined with a fledgling small business. As the business grows, the part-time job(s) can be cut back or eliminated.

Deb Pursues a Portfolio Career

Deb has been in private practice in career counseling for 20 years. She maintains an office where she sees clients individually for parts of three days each week. Because her business has grown to where she can't accommodate everyone who wants to see her, Deb has brought in an employee to take over some of the counseling. She receives a portion of the revenue produced by the other counselor. In addition, Deb does personal and career coaching several hours each week. This work is done primarily by telephone. Clients contract with her for a designated number of sessions, establish specific goals, and pay for sessions in advance.

Deb's fourth income stream comes from career consultation work that she provides to a local corporation one day per week. This contractual arrangement is in its 10th year. Recently, Deb partnered with a friend to offer a series of weekend workshops for women, focused on spiritual development. This idea evolved out of her own spiritual practice. This new endeavor will also produce revenue. Finally, Deb has partnered with a colleague to write a career self-help book, under contract with a publisher. It may sound like Deb has little time when she is not working, but all of these activities have peaks and valleys. When one area is particularly demanding, she can cut back in another. By having multiple options, she maintains a steady and reliable flow of income.

In this chapter, you have explored the option of starting your own business. You have learned what it takes to start a small business, and you have been introduced to a couple and three individuals who are in business for themselves. If this option is attractive to you, a wise next step would be to take a course in entrepreneurship or attend workshops provided by SCORE (or other organizations) that specialize in small business. Continue to read (many publications are suggested at the end of the chapter) and talk with business owners. Use the decision-making model in Chapter Eight to help you organize this major decision. Starting a small business is a major undertaking. If the business is well conceived, well planned, and well timed, it could be successful! We wish you every success in your endeavor!

Idea File

Purpose: This activity is intended to help you start thinking about business ideas for possible future development.

Directions: This activity can be done alone or with a few trusted friends. Begin with a brainstorm. List any ideas you have for starting a business. Think of services needed in your community. Think about products that could make your life easier. Think about what is missing, what is needed. Write down all of your ideas. Try to think creatively.

After your initial brainstorm is complete, start to carry your list around with you. As new ideas occur to you, record them in the same notebook or file. Become an observer of your community. What new businesses are forming? What ideas are others trying? What else might take off? Visit other towns or cities. Are there businesses in these locations that might do well in your community? Visit the library. What new businesses are being featured in the business press? Do any of these businesses give you ideas?

Reflections: How is the idea of starting your own business feeling to you with the passage of time? Are you becoming more interested and enthusiastic? Are you losing interest? Are you building momentum with your project of searching for ideas? It is important to see if you are able to sustain the activity necessary to investigate this option thoroughly.

"Try On" the Chamber of Commerce

Purpose: This exercise is intended to put you in touch with local resources that can help you decide about starting a business.

Directions: Contact your local Chamber of Commerce. Find out when they are meeting next and ask if you can attend. Let them know you are considering starting your own business. At the meeting, speak with as many business owners as you can. Find out about their businesses: how they are doing, how they started, and what needs they see for new businesses in the area. Find out how the Chamber can be of assistance to you.

Reflections: How did it feel to be associating with other business owners? Do you see yourself as potentially being one of them? Did you get any useful new ideas? Are you excited about the prospect of starting a business? Why or why not?

ADDITIONAL TOOLS FOR YOUR CAREER

Hawken, Paul. *Growing a Business.* New York: Simon & Schuster, 1987.

This delightful book will make owning a small business come alive for you. Written by the founder of Erewhon Trading Co., and Smith and Hawken, the author offers "straight talk about what works and what doesn't, and why."

Popcorn, Faith, and Lys Marigold. *Clicking: 16 Trends to Future Fit Your Life, Your Work, and Your Business.* New York: HarperCollins, 1996.

The sequel to *The Popcorn Report,* this book analyzes social trends, including our evolving living and buying patterns, and identifies new-product needs for our complex, consumer-driven world. The authors consult for major corporations, seeking new products or repositioning old ones. The book is lively and eye-opening reading—must reading for anyone thinking of starting a business.

Hisrich, Robert D., and Michael P. Peters. *Entrepreneurship: Starting, Developing, and Managing a New Enterprise,* 3rd ed. Burr Ridge, IL: Irwin-McGraw-Hill, 1994.

This book and the one following are 600+-page textbooks used in college-level courses in small business. Both are loaded with detailed information and packed with case studies.

Siropolis, Nicholas C. *Small Business Management: A Guide to Entrepreneurship,* 6th ed. Boston: Houghton Mifflin, 1996.

Additional Resources for Entrepreneurship and Small Business

Bartsch, Charles, ed. *Guide to State and Federal Resources for Economic Development.* Washington, DC: Northeast-Midwest Institute, 1988.

Benson, B. *Your Family Business: A Success Guide for Growth and Survival.* Homewood, IL: BusinessOne Irwin, 1990.

Blum, Laurie. *Free Money for Small Businesses and Entrepreneurs,* 3rd ed. New York: John Wiley & Sons, 1992.

Bork, D. *Family Business, Risky Business.* Aspen: Bork Institute, 1993.

Burnett, Ed. *Complete Direct Mail List Handbook.* Englewood Cliffs, NJ: Prentice-Hall, 1988.

Connory, Thomas F., ed. *Markets of the U.S. for Business Planners,* 2nd ed. 2 vols. Detroit: Omnigraphics, 1995.

Consultants and Consulting Organizations Directory, 18th ed. 2 vols. and suppls. Triennial. Detroit: Gale Research, 1997.

D&B Consultant's Directory. Parsippany, NJ: Dun's Marketing Services. Annual.

Franchise Annual. St. Catherine's, Ontario, Canada: Info Press. Annual.

Godfrey, Joline. *Our Wildest Dreams: Women Entrepreneurs Having Fun, Making Money, Doing Good.* New York: Harper Business, 1992.

Gorder, Cheryl. *Home Business Resource Guide.* Tempe, AZ: Blue Bird Publishing, 1989.

Holland, Phil. *How to Start a Business Without Quitting Your Job.* Berkeley, CA: Ten Speed Press, 1992.

Horowitz, David, and Dana Shilling. *Business of Business: How 100 Businesses Really Work.* New York: HarperCollins, 1989.

Jaffe, D. T. *Working with the Ones You Love: Strategies for a Successful Family Business.* Berkeley, CA: Conari, 1991.

Jessup, Claudia, and Genie Chipps. *The Woman's Guide to Starting a Business,* 3rd ed. New York: Holt, 1995.

Maki, Kathleen E., ed. *Small Business Sourcebook.* 2 vols. Biennial. Detroit: Gale Research, 1996.

Pratt, Stanley E., and Jane K. Morris. *Pratt's Guide to Venture Capital Sources,* 21st ed. Annual. Boston: Venture Economic, 1997.

Ratliff, Susan. *How to Be a Weekend Entrepreneur: Making Money at Craft Fairs, Trade Shows and Swap Meets.* Phoenix, AZ: Marketing Methods Press, 1991.

Silver, A. David. *Up Front Financing: The Entrepreneur's Guide.* New York: John Wiley & Sons, 1988.

Small Business Start-up Index. Detroit: Gale Research, 1991.

Source Book of Franchise Opportunities. Annual. Homewood, IL: Dow Jones-Irvin, 1993.

Weinstein, Art. *Market Segmentation: Using Demographics, Psychographics, and Other Niche Marketing Techniques to Predict and Model Customer Behavior.* Chicago: Probus Publishing, 1994.

Winter, Barbara. *Making a Living Without a Job: Winning Ways for Creating Work That You Love.* New York: Bantam, 1993.

Journals

The following publications are available at your library or your local newsstand. When you have decided which you like the best, you may want to subscribe for a while.

Black Enterprise. Monthly. New York: Earl G. Graves Publishing, 212-242-8000.

Entrepreneur: The business opportunity magazine. Monthly. Santa Monica, CA: Chase Revel, 714-261-2325.

Family Business: The management guide for family-owned companies. Quarterly. Philadelphia: MCR Publishing, 215-790-7000.

Inc.: The magazine for growing companies. Monthly. Boston: United Marine Publications, 1-800-234-0999.

Specialty Retail Report. Norwell, MA, 781-659-7675.

Success: The magazine for today's entrepreneurial mind. Monthly. New York: Success Magazine.

Venture Capital Journal. Monthly. Wellesley, MA: Capital Publishing.

CHAPTER FOURTEEN

MANAGING YOUR CAREER

As we have seen, today's work environment is demanding, fast-paced, and ever changing. To succeed in that kind of atmosphere, we have to actively manage our careers at all times. This means that we are vigilant, aware of our thoughts and feelings and of what is going on around us. Picture a tennis player waiting for an opponent's serve: positioned at the back of the court, knees bent with weight balanced on both feet, body low and ready to spring, and racket poised for either a forehand or backhand swing. The player's mind is completely engaged in both internal and external scanning. That image of alert anticipation and readiness is a perfect metaphor for today's worker.

The Career Action Center describes career self reliance as a life-long commitment to actively managing your worklife and learning in a rapidly changing environment. Figure 14.1 shows the elements of career self reliance. Notice that you have engaged all of these behaviors as you have moved through this textbook. The trick, now, is to keep the process alive.

We have emphasized throughout this book that developing your career is a lifelong process. You will likely reinvent your career many times over the course of your work life. We hope that this book has provided a guide for you through what might otherwise seem like a maze. We have discussed the process of transition and readiness to make changes. We have walked through the steps for making career changes: self-assessment, career exploration, decision making, goal setting, job search, and career success. At each step, we provided information and activities to assist you in completing the step. You have done a great deal of work to arrive at this point, and we applaud your efforts.

Most of us are likely to reinvent our careers several times

Having been through the process once, and having completed the steps in a thorough manner, you are well equipped to repeat the process again and again as necessary throughout your work life. And repeat the process you will!

FIGURE 14.1

Career self reliance.

Career Self Reliance: A lifelong commitment to actively managing your worklife and learning in a rapidly changing environment.

Self-Aware

You know who you are and where and how you do your best work. You understand and can articulate the value you add.

Values-Driven

You have determined the values that give direction and meaning to your work.

Dedicated to Continuous Learning

You regularly benchmark your skills and create a personal and professional development plan to keep your skills current.

Future-Focused

You look ahead to assess customer needs and business trends. You consider the impact of those trends on your work and your development plan.

Connected

You maintain a network of contacts for learning and sharing ideas. You work collaboratively with others toward mutual goals.

Flexible

You anticipate change and are ready to adapt quickly.

Source: Career Action Center, Cupertino, CA.

(No groans, please.) As we have emphasized, everyone is likely to reinvent or redirect their careers several times. The pace of change continues to accelerate, causing continuous change in the global economy. Business and industry continue to transform, creating new products, services, and jobs and eliminating others. Social, political, and environmental conditions continue to evolve as well, creating new opportunities and challenges.

When you view your life within the context of the larger world, you see that change will indeed have an impact on your options and choices. While the external forces need to be taken into consideration, you must also maintain a clear vision of your own goals and aspirations, hopes, and dreams. By balancing the external realities with your own inner drives and needs, you have the chance to create and continuously re-create your life and your career. By doing so, your career can be a satisfying and meaningful facet of your life. The canvas and brushes remain in your hands.

As you move on, keep this book handy for future review. Should you find yourself feeling restless in your work, review the process on your own. Or if you find yourself the victim of a painful downsizing or an untenable reorganization, remember that you have options. Even when you feel like you have no control over your life or your work, you do. You can take your career into your own hands and make a change that is satisfying to you.

Give yourself a career tune-up on a regular basis, perhaps once a year. Ask yourself probing questions about your satisfaction with your career and with your immediate work situation. If you aren't altogether satisfied with the results, consider ways to change things for the better. Annual tune-ups may help you to avoid, or at least be prepared for, a major career crisis.

There are many ways to enrich your present position and continue to grow professionally. For example, if you are a permanent employee, there may be additional experiences you could gain by making a lateral move in your organization. Making a lateral move allows you to broaden your skills and experience, thus increasing your value to the organization. There may also be contacts you can make in the organization that could prove useful later on. Knowing people throughout the organization increases your visibility and your mobility.

Give yourself a career tune-up on a regular basis

You may also want to ask if additional training is available. If it's not, consider enrolling in a program on your own in order to keep abreast of changes in your field. Join a professional association, and meet people in your field working in different settings. This will keep you current in your field and broaden your perspective. You have to be *ready* to move, no matter how comfortable and safe you feel in your current situation.

If you are employed as a temporary or contract worker, find out if there are new, marketable skills you could acquire if assigned to certain projects. There may be particular companies, individuals, or products that would be advantageous for you to work with. There may also be associations you could join to become better known. Since all temp jobs eventually end, you will need to have new contracts lined up. Some contract workers manage their own marketing, while others work through temporary agencies or consulting firms. Either way, you need to remain on the cutting edge professionally. If your technical expertise becomes obsolete, you could become unemployable.

If you own your own business, you may want to consider offering new product lines, expanding your services, or adopting new marketing techniques. Find out what the competition is up to. Now may be a good time to borrow money and expand the business, perhaps by establishing a second site. Or perhaps it's time to develop a Web site. Even small-business owners must stay on their toes or risk losing market share.

Another option you may want to consider at some point is downshifting. After many years of intense work and life/work juggling, you may be ready to simplify your life. Many people are choosing to work less, which usually results in their earning less money. In order to manage on a reduced income, they cut back on expenses. Some people move to less expensive homes, eliminate social memberships, sell one or more cars, take modest vacations, and consume less in general. The simplification movement is gaining in popularity. Several books incorporating this theme have recently been published.

It may be time to simplify your life

You will continually face these issues as you sharpen and define and reevaluate your career choices. It will be up to you to determine what you need and what is best for you at any given time. More than ever, you must take full leadership responsibility for your career.

LISTEN TO CAREER CHANGERS WHO HAVE GONE BEFORE YOU

The final word belongs to students who have been through this process before you. About 200 of them were surveyed prior to the writing of this book. One of the questions asked was, "What is not written in career books that you most want other adult students to know about finding a job, about finding yourself, about working, or about life in general?" Here are some of their responses:

Joyce: "It's never too late to make a career change. I'm trying to convince my husband of this right now!" (Administrative assistant in a graphics company to systems trainer in a software company)

Laurie: "Research your company before you take a job. Ask more questions. Why did the person you are replacing leave? How financially secure is the company?" (Forecasting for a retail company to forecast analyst/inventory planner for a wholesale company)

Christopher: "I know the hardest thing for me was to come back to school. Once I did come back, everything sounded good. The problem was that I had little confidence and did not know which direction to go in. So choosing some sort of school goals should be very important!" (Stock clerk to call director for customer service department)

Patrick: "I'm trying to personally secure my future rather than rely on a company to do it." (Accounting clerk to property manager)

Ross: "I'm more aware of my own vulnerability to the downswings in the economy. Always look out for yourself because no one else will do it for you." (Hospital management to marketing/advertising for an energy research firm)

Charlotte: "If you cannot find an opening in the field that you are searching for, apply for jobs that closely resemble your experience. Once you are in the company and people see your performance, this could work into an area you want to pursue." (Sales to purchasing agent)

Michael: "Set reachable goals and accomplish them. Most people tend to wander. When set on a course, most people do very well." (Career advancement within hospital administration)

Ann: "The most helpful information I received from the class relates to goal setting. Something almost magical *does* happen when that goal is written down. I find some are accomplished almost effortlessly then. Before taking your class, I probably set goals, though not consciously or purposely. Now, I do them religiously! I *love* my goals! I have a much stronger sense of where I'm headed in life, and I'm confident that as long as I'm breaking down those goals into small, manageable steps, I will always know how to get there." (Self-employed)

Ken: "Be flexible!! Continue to learn new concepts; stay up with trends in your industry. Stay well-read about employment opportunities." (Configuration management/engineering; has so far survived in department that has been reduced by 60 percent)

Phyllis: "It's so important to have a balanced life—not all work-related. Leisure time is important!" (Secretary in property management company to property manager in another company)

Linette: "Even in the most adverse situations, people must take a positive outlook, make decisions, and move forward." (Executive assistant to human resources manager)

Colleen (with a quote from Alexander Graham Bell): "When one door closes, another opens; but we often look so long and so regretfully upon the closed door that we do not see the one which has opened for us." (Corporate trainer to computer systems administrator)

Darlene: "Acknowledge your strengths. Focus on what will leave you with a sense of accomplishment every day." (Sales representative to mom)

Lynda: "Be willing to take some chances. You can always lower the risk by saving up some money beforehand so you have something to fall back on. Many people I meet tell me how much they hate their jobs, but they aren't willing to take any chances or try anything new. You have to look at all your options and see what's right for you." (Collector/customer accounts to nurse)

Diane: "Be flexible—you cannot predict what your priorities will be in the future. We can plan, but due to changes in family structure, health needs (both mental and physical), life outlook at different ages, local and global concerns, etc., we can only move toward our goals and reevaluate from time to time." (Marketing support representative to day-care provider and mother of twins)

Thank you to all of my students for letting me be part of your career development process. The opportunity you gave me to work with you was truly a gift, one that I will always cherish. I wish you the best as you continue your journey.

Hats off to all of you who have dared to take another look, have risked the unknown, and have found new direction and new meaning in your career. Please share your stories with me. Your experiences and your thoughts on the transition process will help make the next edition of this book even more helpful. Write to:

Kit Hayes, Director of Adult Career Services
Northeastern University
Post Office Box 895
Boston, MA 02117
Or E-mail me at: k.hayes@nunet.neu.edu

Course Goals Revisited

WORK IN PROGRESS

Purpose: This activity is intended to bring closure on an activity begun in the first week of class.

Directions: (Instructors, please return the goals written by the students at the beginning of the course.) Students, when your goals are returned to you on the last day of class, open the envelopes and read the goals you wrote at the beginning of this course. Think about what your intentions were, and assess your level of achievement.

Reflections: How did you do? Did you achieve all or some of your goals? How does that make you feel? Of those goals that you did not complete, can you see why you didn't finish them? Are the goals you didn't complete still important to you? What is your next step in goal setting?

Next Steps

Purpose: This activity is designed to help you focus on some next steps as you are leaving this course.

Directions: Take a few minutes to identify some next steps for yourself as you are leaving this class. Remembering the goal-setting work you did in Chapter Nine, write down some goals for yourself, to be completed three months from now. Make the goals clear and specific, measurable, and realistic! What do you want to accomplish in the next three months? Think about home, school, career, and personal goals. What can you do in the next three months to keep your life moving forward?

(Instructors, you may want to have the students seal the goals and address the envelopes to themselves; you can drop them in the mail three months from now.)

Reflections: You have made some commitments to yourself for the next 12 weeks. How do you feel about your next steps? On a scale of 1 to 10, with 10 being totally committed, how committed are you to the goals you have set? When you leave your class, begin to work on your goals. Focus your energy, take bold steps forward, and trust in the magic of the universe to support you.

Kudos To The Class

Purpose: This activity is suggested as a way to end the course with all class members getting a final reminder of their value as unique human beings.

Materials: Felt-tip colored pens, tape, and a sheet of paper for each person, including the instructor.

Directions: Write your name on your piece of paper, decoratively if you wish, and then tape it on the wall at eye level and about two feet from the next person's paper. When all the papers are up, take 10 minutes to complete the following activity: Quickly go to each person's paper on the wall, and write a brief note telling the person something that you saw in him or her that was special. *Write only positive comments.* You can also use this as an opportunity to wish people well. Appropriate comments could be, "You were very supportive to me" or "Great sense of humor" or "You'll make a great accountant/ teacher/chemist." Move quickly so you can get to everyone's sheet before the time is up.

Reflections: When the time is up, collect your sheet and enjoy the comments of your classmates. If you like what they wrote, tape it to your refrigerator so you can be reminded of your many good qualities.

APPENDIX

In Chapter Two, you read about Dr. Barbara Okun's theory of adult development and the developmental tasks associated with the career component of adult life. Below are the developmental tasks for the individual and family components of adult life identified by Dr. Okun.*

INDIVIDUAL DEVELOPMENT

Early Adulthood

DEVELOPMENT OF INTIMACY

Clarify sex role.
Develop mutual sexuality.
Develop mutuality in relationships.
Balance individuation, family, and career demands.
Reassess relationships.
Withstand conflicts and disappointments within relationships.

Mid-30s Transition

CONSOLIDATION OF INTIMATE RELATIONSHIPS

End some relationships and begin others.
Finalize commitments to family and others.
Prepare for generativity.

Middle Adulthood

Midlife Transition

Reappraise identity.
Recognize mortality.
Change one's time perspective.
Reappraise relationships with and commitments to spouse, children, friends, family of origin, and career.

*Source: From *Working with Adults: Individual, Family, and Career Development* by B. F. Okun. Copyright ©1984 Brooks/Cole Publishing Company, a division of International Thomson Publishing, Inc., Pacific Grove, CA 93950. Adapted by permission of the publisher.

The 40s: Entering Middle Adulthood

Develop interiority.

Reassess and restructure interpersonal relationships.

Cope with the climacteric.

The 50s

Renegotiate relationships.

Learn new roles: in-laws; grandparents.

Make preretirement plans.

Take health-care measures.

Late Adulthood

Senior Citizens

Redefine identity: physiological, psychological, social, and economic changes.

Adjust socially: friends, family, and community.

Reallocate energy and resources.

Manage stress.

The Elderly

Redefine identity: ego integrity, ego transcendence, and body transcendence.

Separate emotionally.

Maintain body integrity.

Accept loss of personal autonomy and competencies: conserve strength and resources; accept dependencies.

Adjust socially to loss of peers and to transient, fluid relationships.

FAMILY DEVELOPMENT

Early Adulthood

The Beginning Family

Join as a couple.

Negotiate boundaries (between couple members).

Renegotiate boundaries with others and between self, spouse, and career.

The Infant Family

Expand intimacy boundaries to include infant.

Learn parent roles.

Renegotiate roles, rules, and boundaries of the couple system.

Renegotiate boundaries with significant others.

Renegotiate boundaries with career.

Ensure direct communication with spouse; separate couple and parent subsystems.

The Preschool Family

Differentiate couple-system and parent-system boundaries.

Learn appropriate preschool parenting roles.

Socialize children.

Replenish the marital relationship.

Balance self, family, and work roles and responsibilities.

Differentiate communication styles between couple and parent systems.

Renegotiate other relationships and commitments.

The School-Age Family

Renegotiate boundaries with the outside world.

Facilitate the child's entrance into school.

Renegotiate relationships with the school-age child.

Reevaluate couple roles and responsibilities.

Renegotiate parental roles and responsibilities.

Balance the couple and parent subsystems.

Balance the self, family, and work.

The Adolescent Family

Differentiate.

Negotiate boundaries: adolescent/parents; adolescent/siblings; siblings/parents; family/outside world; family/work/self.

Clarify communications.

The Launching Stage

Let go.

Renegotiate boundaries: couple system; parents/launched offspring; couple/friends; elderly parents; community; parents/remaining siblings; launched offspring/siblings.

Restructure communications: power; rules.

The Postparental Stage

Create new roles: with elderly parents; with grandchildren.

Renegotiate boundaries: in-laws; grandchildren; adult offspring; elderly parents; friends and community.

Restructure multigenerational communications.

Late Adulthood

The Postparental Stage

Renegotiate boundaries: parents/adult offspring; parents/in-laws; parents/grandchildren; spouse; couple/outside world; couple/friends.

Differentiate communications: couple system; adult offspring; grandchildren.

Cope with survivorship.

The Elderly Family

Renegotiate boundaries: spouse bonding and letting go; parents/adult offspring; grandparents/grandchildren; parents/great-grandchildren; couple/ friends; couple/outside world.

Cope with survivorship: mourning process; renegotiation of relationships with family; renegotiation of relationships as survivor with friends and outside world.

Readjust communication patterns.

REFERENCES

Boyett, J. H., and H. P. Conn. *Workplace 2000: The Revolution Reshaping American Business.* New York: Dutton, 1991.

Bridges, W. *Transitions: Making Sense of Life's Changes.* Reading, MA: Addison-Wesley, 1980.

Bridges, W. *JobShift: How to Prosper in a Workplace Without Jobs.* Reading, MA: Addison-Wesley, 1994.

Brown, D., L. Brooks, and associates. *Career Choice and Development: Applying Contemporary Theories.* San Francisco: Jossey-Bass, 1990.

Chitayat, D., and G. Berens. *Motivation Advance Process.* New York: Institute for Research and Development in Occupational Education, CUNY, n.d.

Colvin, Geoffrey. "M & A and You: Career Power." *Fortune,* June 22, 1998, p. 173.

Dalton, G. W., and P. H. Thompson. *Novations: Strategies for Career Management.* Provo, UT: Gene W. Dalton & Paul H. Thompson, 1993.

Economic Report of the President and The Annual Report of the Council of Economic Advisors. Washington, DC, February 1998.

Figler, H. E. *A Career Workbook for Liberal Arts Students.* Cranston, RI: Carroll Press, 1975.

Gabarro, J. J., and J. P. Kotter. "Managing Your Boss." *Harvard Business Review,* January–February 1980.

Gorman, Tom. *Multipreneuring.* New York: FIRESIDE, Simon & Schuster, 1996.

Gottfredson, Gary D., John L. Holland, and Deborah Kimiko Ogawa. *Dictionary of Holland Occupational Codes,* 3rd ed. Palo Alto, CA: Consulting Psychologists Press, 1996.

Grier, Peter. "The Big Switch." *World Monitor,* January 1993, pp. 23–27.

Hakim, C. *We Are All Self-Employed: The New Social Contract for Working in a Changed World.* San Francisco: Berrett-Koehler, 1994.

Hammer, Michael, and James Champy. *Reengineering the Corporation: A Manifesto for Business Revolution.* New York: Harper Business, 1993.

Handy, C. *The Age of Unreason.* Cambridge: Harvard Business School Press, 1990.

Hawken, P. *Growing a Business.* New York: Simon & Schuster, 1987.

Hay, Louise L. *You Can Heal Your Life.* Santa Monica, CA: Hay House, 1994.

Heilbroner, R., and L. Thurow. *Economics Explained: Everything You Need to Know About How the Economy Works and Where It's Going.* New York: Simon & Schuster, 1994.

Henderson, David R. "The Case against Antitrust." *Fortune,* April 27, 1998, pp. 40–44.

Hisrich, Robert D., and Michael P. Peters. *Entrepreneurship: Starting, Developing, and Managing a New Enterprise,* 4th ed. Burr Ridge, IL: Irwin, 1997.

Holland, J. L. *Making Vocational Choices: A Theory of Vocational Personalities and Work Environments,* 3rd ed. Englewood Cliffs, NJ: Prentice-Hall, 1997.

Kennedy, J. L., and T. J. Morrow. *Electronic Job Search Revolution*, 2nd ed. New York: John Wiley & Sons, 1995.

Kirkpatrick, David. "Microsoft: Is Your Company Its Next Meal?" *Fortune*, April 27, 1998, pp. 92–102.

Kiser, Jane. "Behind the Scenes at a Family Friendly Workplace." *Dollars & Sense*, January–February 1998, pp. 21–24.

Krannich, R. *Careering and Re-Careering for the 1990's*. Woodbridge, Impact, 1991.

Lakein, Alan. *How to Get Control of Your Time and Your Life*. New York: Phyden, 1973.

Lapid-Bogda, G. "Office Politics and the Pursuit of Power": Managing Your Career. The *Wall Street Journal*, Spring 1994, Princeton, NJ.

Lewis, Diane. "Bath Shipyard Accord Reflects Fight to Remain Competitive." *The Boston Globe*, September 5, 1994, pp. 1, 7.

Markusen, A., and J. Yudken. *Dismantling the Cold War Economy*. New York: Basic Books, 1993.

McConnell, C. R., and S. L. Brue. *Economics: Principles, Problems, and Policies*, 14th ed. New York: McGraw-Hill, 1998.

"Mergers: Why This Historic Boom Will Keep Making Noise." *Fortune*, April 27, 1998, pp. 148–156.

"Mergers & Acquisitions." *Economist*, August 15–21, 1998, p. 5.

Myers, I. B. *Gifts Differing*. Palo Alto, CA: Consulting Psychologists Press, 1986.

Nash, K. *Get the Best of Yourself*. New York: Grosset & Dunlap, 1976.

Okun, B. F. *Working with Adults: Individual, Family, and Career Development*. Monterey, CA: Brooks/Cole Publishing, 1984.

Oldfield, K., with N. Ayers. "Pay the New Job Dues, Avoid the New Job Blues." *Personnel Journal*, August 1986.

Popcorn, Faith, and Lys Marigold. *Clicking: 16 Trends to Future Fit Your Life, Your Work, and Your Business*. New York: HarperCollins, 1996.

Reich, R. *The Work of Nations*. New York: Vintage, 1991.

Siegel, Bernie S. *Love, Medicine & Miracles*. New York: HarperCollins, 1990.

Simon, Sidney B. *Meeting Yourself Halfway*. Sunderland, MA: Values Press, 1991.

Singer, June. *Boundaries of the Soul: The Practice of Jung's Psychology*. New York: Doubleday, 1994.

Siropolis, Nicholas C. *Small Business Management: A Guide to Entrepreneurship*, 6th ed. Boston: Houghton Mifflin, 1996.

Smolak, L. *Adult Development*. Englewood Cliffs, NJ: Prentice-Hall, 1993.

Sonnenfeld, J. A., and J. P. Kotter. "The Maturation of Career Theory." *Human Relations*, Volume 35, Number 1, 1982, pp. 19–46.

Strong, Susan C. "The Business of Peace." *Boston Review*, XIX, Number 2, April/May 1994.

Taylor III, Alex. "GM's $11,000,000,000 Turnaround." *Fortune*, October 17, 1994, pp. 54–74.

Thurow, L. *Head to Head: The Coming Economic Battle Among Japan, Europe, and America*. New York: Morrow, 1992.

"Today's Jobs." *Occupational Outlook Handbook* 1998–99, pp. 1–6.

U.S. Department of Labor. *Occupational Outlook Handbook*. Washington DC, 1998.

U.S. Department of Labor and U.S. Department of Commerce. *Fact Finding Report: Commission on the Future of Worker–Management Relations*. Washington, DC, May 1994.

Weinrach, Stephen G., and David J. Srebalus. "Holland's Theory of Careers," in *Career Choice and Development*. San Francisco: Jossey-Bass, 1990, pp. 37–67.

INDEX